LU JUL 2012

RU Oct '13

Socrates in the City

SOCRATES
IN THE CITY

———

Conversations on "Life, God,
and Other Small Topics"

———

ERIC METAXAS
Editor

 DUTTON

DUTTON
Published by Penguin Group (USA) Inc.
375 Hudson Street, New York, New York 10014, U.S.A.
Penguin Group (Canada), 90 Eglinton Avenue East, Suite 700, Toronto, Ontario M4P 2Y3, Canada (a division of Pearson Penguin Canada Inc.); Penguin Books Ltd, 80 Strand, London WC2R 0RL, England; Penguin Ireland, 25 St Stephen's Green, Dublin 2, Ireland (a division of Penguin Books Ltd); Penguin Group (Australia), 250 Camberwell Road, Camberwell, Victoria 3124, Australia (a division of Pearson Australia Group Pty Ltd); Penguin Books India Pvt Ltd, 11 Community Centre, Panchsheel Park, New Delhi—110 017, India; Penguin Group (NZ), 67 Apollo Drive, Rosedale, Auckland 0632, New Zealand (a division of Pearson New Zealand Ltd); Penguin Books (South Africa) (Pty) Ltd, 24 Sturdee Avenue, Rosebank, Johannesburg 2196, South Africa

Penguin Books Ltd, Registered Offices: 80 Strand, London WC2R 0RL, England

Published by Dutton, a member of Penguin Group (USA) Inc.
First printing, October 2011
10 9 8 7 6 5 4 3 2 1

REGISTERED TRADEMARK—MARCA REGISTRADA

LIBRARY OF CONGRESS CATALOGING-IN-PUBLICATION DATA

Socrates in the City : conversations on "Life, God, and other small topics" / Eric Metaxas, general editor.
p.   cm.
ISBN 978-0-525-95255-8
1. Socrates. I. Metaxas, Eric.
B317.S635 2011
210—dc23   2011032708

Printed in the United States of America
Designed by Daniel Lagin

Contents

SOCRATES IN THE CITY

AN INTRODUCTION

Can you imagine how happy I am that this book has come out? If not, let me tell you how happy—very, very. It's a tremendous joy for me to look at the evidence of something we've been doing for ten years now and to realize that these talks are just as fresh on the page as they were the actual evenings of the events. That is saying a lot, because most of these events were magical. Just ask the people who have attended over the years.

In reading the talks in this book, I've come to the conclusion that they are treasures, nothing less, and to think that they are available to the readers of this book—that they are not lost to the ether but are right here for you to enjoy, just as we enjoyed them on the evenings of our events—absolutely thrills me.

But before I say more, perhaps you don't really know what Socrates in the City is. Let me explain: We are a UFO cult. There, I've said it. Of course, that's not for public consumption. To the public we present ourselves as an elegant and upscale Manhattan speakers' series. So, I'll have to stick with that description going forward in this essay, but you and I will know that I am really talking about a UFO cult and that underneath our terribly sophisticated street clothes, we wear cult-issue silver unitards with a nifty lightning-bolt-and-leaping-leprechaun logo. It's quite a logo. But we won't mention this again.

But seriously, it's hard to believe it's been more than ten years since I started Socrates in the City with the simple idea that the philosopher Socrates was quite right when he famously said that the "unexamined life is not worth living." It struck me that in New York City, where I live, people weren't being much encouraged to think deeply about the big questions—or should I say, the Big Questions. It seemed that there was something about our culture which worked against examining the Big Questions. I wanted to remedy that a bit.

Also, I realized that I have had the privilege of being acquainted with a number of brilliant writers and speakers who had thought rather a lot about the Big Questions and who had some pretty terrific answers to those questions. Why not bring them to New York? And why not invite my friends to hear them? And why not serve wine and hors d'oeuvres? And so, Socrates in the City was born.

As it happened, eight of our first ten speakers were named Os Guinness. That's not a weird coincidence, but it is evidence of the generosity of a dear friend, to whom we here gratefully doff our caps.

I remember that our second event—Os was not the speaker—took place the day after the hotly contested 2000 election between Al Gore and George W. Bush. Everyone had stayed up till three or four A.M. the night before, hoping to find out who had won. Little did they know the issue would drag on for many weeks.

So, the next night a handful of our audience members had some difficulty keeping their eyes open during David Aikman's terrific talk on Solzhenitsyn, Nelson Mandela, and Elie Wiesel. *Quel dommage!* In all these years that has never happened again, but should it ever happen to you at a Socrates event, you should probably consider getting a good night's sleep the night before and cutting back on the pre-talk libations. The act of open-mouthed snoring while Bishop N. T. Wright or Sir John Polkinghorne—or any other ecclesiastical worthy—is holding forth is still considered déclassé in most respectable New York social circles.

Almost all of our events have been held in the ornately gorgeous rooms of the most exclusive private clubs of Manhattan. The Union League Club, the University Club, the Union Club, and the Metropolitan Club have been a few of our favorites. The art in some of them is reason enough to attend Socrates in the City events. Besides, listening to a talk on how a good God can allow suffering is always somehow improved if your gaze can wander to a 1903 bas-relief of Hercules slaying the Erymanthian boar. We don't know how this works, but it does.

We always begin our events with a reception where wine and hors d'oeuvres are served. Because of a lawsuit, we've had to cut back on the unlimited sangria and shrimp, but please keep praying; perhaps the judge will see things our way. After the reception, we begin our program with my introduction of the speaker.

My introductions have always been calculatedly dopey—or dippy—because we firmly believe that's the surest way of letting the audience and the speaker know up front that we expect to have fun and that this will not be a ponderous intellectual exercise. We will not abide pretentiousness, but we *will* sometimes countenance a freewheeling Marx Brothers approach to the search for truth. To this point, my opening comments and introductions have often taken their cues from the speeches of Foster Brooks and Charlie Callas at Dean Martin's celebrity roasts. This is intentional.

After all, who said that the exploration of the Big Questions and fun can't go together? It was probably La Rochefoucauld, but who cares what he thinks? Seriously, I think that the fun we have is vital to what we do. We know that no matter how serious the subject (suffering and evil and death, for example), we will enjoy ourselves. We hope we've captured something of that juxtaposition between the covers of this book.

My philosophy is that answering the Big Questions about "life, God, and other small topics" can be fun if you know in advance that there are actually good and hopeful answers to those questions. Somehow, we actually do know that. Don't ask me how. But it does follow logically that if you know there are good and hopeful answers to these Big Questions, then asking them becomes far less frightening. It is our firm belief that one shouldn't fear asking such questions, and so, we do not. On the contrary, "let us beard the lion in his own den!" Or something like that.

So, yes, over the last ten years we have asked some of the biggest, baddest questions imaginable, and I think it's safe thus to say that we have had some of the most wonderful evenings imaginable. It has always bothered me that more people couldn't be there to experience them—which is one reason we've put this book together.

Our goal in this book was to somehow capture the ineffable—dare we say *tingly*?—feeling of what it is like to be at an actual Socrates event. Of course, there are limits. For example, our publisher balked at providing assorted nuts, cheeses, and two glasses of wine with every copy of the book. They suggested that this might be more cost-effective when the book comes out in paperback; so, keep your fingers crossed. But we really have tried hard to approximate the feeling of being there, of hearing my introductions and the speakers' fabulous talks and the terrific question-and-answer section at the end of each talk.

In order to retain the freshness of these evenings, we have only lightly edited the raw transcriptions. To make the reading process a little bit smoother, we have, of course, removed any *um*s, *ahem*s, and *achoo*s from the originals. If you find an *achoo* in your copy, please keep in mind that it may have gotten there after the book was printed; so, you might want to ask your friends and family if they are responsible. And if you find that there is an errant *um* or an *ahem*, by all means feel free to contact the publisher or your local bookseller about it. But to save time, we always recommend first dipping a clean rag in some club soda and dabbing at the unnecessary word with short, vigorous strokes. If that fails, you might try some benzene and cotton or wool. Sometimes a fresh India rubber will also do the trick.

I should say that this book contains some heavy thinking, and thus it is not meant to be read in one sitting. It is meant to be savored and read slowly. Some of these essays are intense and will require periods of serious concentration. Please do not attempt to read them while driving a rickety panel van or operating dangerous machinery. The point of reading Peter Kreeft's talk on suffering is not to get points on your license or lose a limb! Please read responsibly. As Socrates once said: "Know thyself"—and thy limits.

Incidentally, no Socrates in the City event would be complete without a celebrity sighting! Was that Abe Vigoda in the men's room just now? Is that Godzilla slap-fighting Mothra in the coat-check line? Very sadly, we could not coax any celebrities into making appearances in this book. Jackie Mason made an appearance in some early proofs, but regretted that he could not stay for the initial printing.

But seriously, we have had a number of notable persons show up at our events over the years, many actors among them. Tina Louise (*Gilligan's Island*), Tony Roberts (*Annie Hall*), Patricia Heaton (*Everybody Loves Raymond*), and

Armand Assante (*Kojak, Belizaire the Cajun*) have all visited us. The vegan pop star and musician Moby has attended, as has the carnivorous Ann Coulter. The incomparable Dick Cavett has come to a number of our events—and finally, this year we persuaded him to be our special guest speaker on the subject of "celebrity, fame, and other genuinely small topics." Were you there? Incidentally, that was no piñata; that was the celebrity exercise guru Richard Simmons!

Usually, we simply have a speaker, but sometimes we've tried other formats, with great success. In September 2010, we hosted a terrific debate between King's College president, Dinesh D'Souza, and Princeton's Peter Singer entitled "Is God the Source of Morality?" Though the heavy rain that evening scared off a few of the wimpier New Yorkers among us, more than six hundred people attended nonetheless.

And in 2006, we had our first Socrates on Broadway film premiere. Norman Stone, who is the director of *Shadowlands*, the BBC film on C. S. Lewis, had just finished another Lewis film titled *Beyond Narnia*. So, that April, we premiered the film and then had a killer panel discussion featuring C. S. Lewis scholar Thomas Howard,* Bel Kaufman (the ninety-four-year-old friend of Lewis and his wife, Joy Gresham), Anton Rodgers (the actor who played Lewis in the film), and Mr. Stone himself.

But for the most part, our events are just like what you see in this book—an introduction and a talk and some questions and answers. Our goal in these evenings is not to answer these questions definitively and finally but to whet the audience's appetite for further exploration. So, we hope that anyone who comes to our events—and who reads this book (that would be you, specifically)—will want to dig further and read the books written by our speakers. We hope you will want to continue the conversation, as it were. Yo, *what it is*. *[Exit, pursued by a bear.]*

You might wonder how with so many terrific talks to choose from we chose the eleven in this book. Basically, we were looking for the most typical

---

* Dr. Howard has also been a Socrates in the City speaker, giving a spectacular 2003 talk on his must-read book *Chance or the Dance?* That talk would be in this book, but we somehow lost the recording of it. Rest assured we are still lashing ourselves with wet noodles over this, by way of penance. We do very highly recommend that staggeringly wonderful book to you, dear reader. It's published by Ignatius Press.

and representative talks over the last ten years. All of the more than sixty talks we've had in the last decade are wonderful in their own way, with the embarrassing exception of the last talk in this book, which was shoehorned in by the board of Socrates in the City over the angry objections of the speaker, who is currently lawyering up like crazy for a battle royale that will likely fill the pages of the *New York Post* for months. Just you wait.

Let me close by saying that we would love for you to come to an actual event in New York City. Even though we've done a handful of events in other parts of the country—Chicago and Dallas and San Francisco—Socrates in the City is very much a Manhattan-based phenomenon. By the way, I almost forgot to mention that we have even had invitations to hold SITC events in London and Berlin.

Where were we? Oh, yes, we would love for you to visit us and experience our events for yourself. That's a fact, and we look forward to meeting you in person. But until you can join us at one of our events, we are genuinely thrilled to be able to bring the spirit and substance of Socrates in the City to you in this handy book form. It is our sincere privilege and pleasure to be able to do so. *Soli Deo gloria.*

Eric Metaxas
Founder, president, and host, Socrates in the City
May 2011

Socrates in the City

Belief in God in an Age of Science

SIR JOHN POLKINGHORNE, FRS, KBE

October 29, 2003

Introduction

Good evening, and welcome to Socrates in the City. My name is Eric Metaxas, and I will be your server for the evening. Anytime you like, you can make your way over to the salad bar, and in a few moments I will be back to tell you about our specials. Thank you.

I'm amazed by the crowd tonight. I'm curious: How many people are here at a Socrates event for the very first time? Would you raise your hands? Amazing.

Now be honest. . . . How many people are here tonight for the *last* time?

Before I get into anything profound, I want to say that we are anxious to stay in touch with you. We've been having administrative problems, because I am the administrator.

I hide behind the idea that I am a right-brain person; so this isn't easy for me. They were on your seats a moment ago, blue or salmon-colored index cards. Blue or salmon. Salmon is kind of a pink, for those of you who don't know that.

If you would do this, while I'm talking—certainly not while Dr. Polkinghorne is talking—but if you would, before the evening is over, put down your name and address, even if you have done this before, because we're starting a new database, and I know that we've lost a few of you. Put down your name and address, SAT scores. . . .

Socrates in the City, for those of you who are new to these events, is designed to help busy New Yorkers take a moment out of our busy lives to stop and think a bit more deeply about what life is all about—to answer the big questions or to try, at least, to begin to answer them. Socrates famously said, "The unexamined life is not worth living." I think many of us could probably do with a bit more self-examination. I know I could, and having speakers like Dr. Polkinghorne is meant to make that process a bit easier for us.

Of course, these events are only the tip of the iceberg. We would like to think that these events, these evenings, would kick off the Socratic process in each of us and that in between these events, you might read one or more of these books that are available on the book table. I recommend them very highly to you. We're selling them at no profit to us. They're wonderful books, and they're wonderful to give away to your particularly unthoughtful friends. Of course, Dr. Polkinghorne will happily autograph his books, and I will autograph any of the other books that you would like to have autographed.

By the way, I should say that tonight's event is generously being sponsored by the New Canaan Society, a group I had a very small hand in founding almost nine years ago. The New Canaan Society is a men's fellowship that has, as its modest goal, the idea of helping its members be better husbands and fathers. We have dinner events in New York about once a month, among other things, and if you would like more information, we've got some literature on our front table.

We proudly count David Bloom, the NBC correspondent who recently died in Iraq, as one of our members, and he certainly was a dear friend.

So, to tonight's subject: belief in God in an age of science. In the last one hundred years or so, many people have come to think that somehow "modern man" ought to be beyond believing in God. This idea has continued to enjoy a kind of strangely unchallenged popularity and has rather dramatically affected our culture, often negatively, as is the case with many unchallenged assumptions. I thought it behooved us to apply a bit more rigor to our examination of this matter than we have generally applied, and tonight is meant as a small initial application of that selfsame rigor. And I can repeat that sentence.

It has come to my attention that for some of the very brightest minds on our planet, there is, in fact, no disparity between the truth as promulgated in the biblical faiths and the truth promulgated by scientific discovery. But, as I say, we don't often hear from those bright minds, and I'm very happy to remedy that tonight, with, if I may say so, one of the brightest. I think no matter where you come out on this issue, it will do us all kinds of good to hear from our guest speaker tonight, Sir John Polkinghorne.

I first came to hear Dr. Polkinghorne in Cambridge, England, just over a year ago at a C. S. Lewis conference that was held at Oxford and Cambridge universities. As luck would have it, Oxford and Cambridge universities are located in Oxford and Cambridge, England, respectively. It is all a little too neat, isn't it?

In any case, I was very taken with Dr. Polkinghorne, and I asked him to come to New York City and speak at Socrates. And, of course, here he is.

Now, I have to say that we have never had a Knight of the British Empire at Socrates in the City, at least not that I know of. I'm not quite sure what the protocol is exactly. I assumed that the fact that Dr. Polkinghorne was a knight didn't mean he would necessarily be wearing armor. Just to be on the safe side, I asked him not to wear any armor. It seems that he has complied with my request, unless he's hiding a Kevlar vest under there, which we will never know.

But I said to him that if he *did* feel compelled to wear armor, he might at least wear his beaver up, like Banquo's ghost in *Hamlet*, so that we might better hear what he had to say.

Thank you to all the Banquo fans out there for laughing at that.

A bit of a word on our format. Dr. Polkinghorne will speak for about thirty-five to forty minutes, and then we will have plenty of time for questions and answers. If you have a question, I implore you, please, to step to the microphone here. I implore you to be brief and to speak clearly—and to end your question with a proper punctuation mark. I think you know what I mean.

Nothing like a punctuation-mark joke to get the crowd warmed up.

Now, to introduce the Reverend Dr. John Polkinghorne, KBE, FRS, DDS, Notorious B.I.G. That's a typo. That's a hip-hop joke. I don't expect you to get it, Dr. Polkinghorne.

In any case, the Reverend Dr. John Polkinghorne comes to us from Cambridge University, England. He is a fellow of the Royal Society; a fellow and former president of Queens College, Cambridge; and Canon Theologian of Liverpool Cathedral.

Dr. Polkinghorne is married to Ruth Polkinghorne. They have three children: Peter, Isabelle, and Michael. Dr. Polkinghorne's distinguished career as a physicist began at Trinity College, Cambridge, where he studied under Dirac and others. He became a professor at Cambridge in 1968. In 1974, he was elected fellow of the Royal Society. During that time he published many papers on theoretical, elementary particle physics in learned journals. If it sounds as if I know what I am talking about, I just want to say I got a 1 on my AP physics exam. That is not a good score.

In 1979, Dr. Polkinghorne resigned his professorship to train for the Anglican priesthood. He served as curate in Cambridge and Bristol, and was vicar of Blean from 1984 through 1986.

In 1986, he was appointed fellow, dean, and chaplain at Trinity Hall, Cambridge. In 1989, he was appointed president of Queens College, Cambridge. His own words in reaction to this honor from his official bio: "You could have knocked me over with a feather." That is actually in the bio. You can go online and look that up.

I have to say that I'm surprised that particularly as a top physicist, Dr. Polkinghorne would have been so naive as to believe that someone might have actually knocked him over with a feather—even a very, very, very large feather. One from an emu or ostrich, perhaps, would hardly be able to knock over an average-sized adult male, even if he were temporarily stunned by his appointment to the presidency of a Cambridge college. As I say, even I, as a nonphysicist, who got a 1 on his AP exam, know that, and I am embarrassed to report that Dr. Polkinghorne, with all his fancy degrees and honors, somehow did not know that.

Given Dr. Polkinghorne's weight and any reasonable μ ["mu"] friction coefficient, I think the idea of his being knocked over by a feather is patently and demonstrably absurd. But I'm sure that by now, he has repented of the statement.

In any case, Dr. Polkinghorne retired as president of Queens College in 1996. He is a member of the General Synod of the Church of England and of the Medical Ethics Committee of the British Medical Association.

He was appointed KBE—Knight Commander of the Order of the British Empire—in 1997. Now, a word to the wise: I am told that like many knights, Sir John is handy with a broadax, and if you aren't in full agreement with his talk tonight, he might very well be forced to smite you or *cleave* you, as the case may be.

As most of us know, Dr. Polkinghorne has published a series of remarkable books on the compatibility of religion and science. These began with *The Way the World Is.* He said, "It was what I would have liked to have said to my scientific colleagues who couldn't understand why I was being ordained." *The Way the World Is* is available on our book table. It's a fabulous book.

Just last year, Dr. Polkinghorne won the prestigious—very prestigious—Templeton Prize for progress in religion. The award has previously been awarded to such figures as Mother Teresa and Alexander Solzhenitsyn. Contrary to popular belief, it has never been awarded to Sir Elton John or to Sting. Glad to clear that up for some of you.

So, let me say then what a pleasure it is now to welcome to this podium at Socrates in the City—Sir John Polkinghorne.

Talk

O h, dear, what an act to follow. Let me say, I'm very pleased to be
here to try to stumble along in Eric's wake.

You gather that I am someone who wants to take science abso-
lutely seriously, and I think that we are right to do so in this age of science. I
am also someone who wants to take religion, particularly my own religion,
Christianity, absolutely seriously as well. I believe that I can do that, not, of
course, without puzzles occasionally, but without intellectual dishonesty and,
indeed, with some degree of mutual enhancement, because it seems to me that
science and religion have one extremely important thing in common—they
both are concerned with the search for truth.

The question of truth is as important to religion as it is to science. Religion can do all sorts of things for you. It can comfort you in life and in death,
but it cannot do any of those things unless it is actually true. Of course, science and religion are looking for different aspects of the truth.

Science has purchased its very great success by the modesty of its ambi-
tion. Science does not seek to ask and answer every sort of question. It restricts
itself essentially to asking questions of process, which are "how questions" of
how things come to be. It also restricts the kind of experience that it takes into
account in framing and finding its answers to those questions. Science treats
the world as an object, as an *it*, as something that you can put to the experi-

mental test, that you can pull apart to see what it is made of, and we have learned all sorts of very significant things by doing that.

We also all know that there is a whole realm of human experience—personal experience—and, I would wish to add, the chance personal experience of encounter with the sacred reality of God, a realm of experience in which testing has to give way to trusting. If I'm always setting little traps to see if you are my friend, I would destroy the possibility of friendship between us. Religion is asking a different set of questions, deeper questions, and, in my view, more interesting questions, even than those of science—questions of meaning and purpose: "Is there something going on in what is happening in the world?"

So, there are lots of questions, it seems to me, that are necessary to ask and meaningful to ask, but which are just not scientific questions in their character and, therefore, are questions which science by itself is unable to answer. Interestingly enough, some of those questions arise from our experience of doing science but take us beyond science's self-limited power of inquiry. You might call them *meta-questions*—questions that take us beyond.

I want to start by considering briefly with you two of those meta-questions, and the first one is this. It's a very simple question, so simple, in fact, that most of the time, we don't even stop to think about it, but I think it's worth thinking about. It is simply this: Why is science possible at all? In other words, why can we understand the physical world in which we live?

Why is science possible at all? In other words, why can we understand the physical world in which we live?

"Well," you might say, "that's pretty obvious. We've got to survive in the world. If we don't understand the world, we'll soon come a cropper [British term meaning 'run into trouble']."

Of course, that's true up to a point. It is true of everyday knowledge and everyday experience. If we couldn't figure out that it's a bad idea to step off the top of a high cliff, then we would not stay around for very long. We would stay around a bit longer in my part of the world, which is extremely flat. Nevertheless, we would obviously come to grief.

But it does not follow from that everyday practicality that somebody like Isaac Newton can come along and, in a quite astonishing, imaginative leap, see that the same force that makes the high cliff dangerous is also the force that holds the moon in its orbit around the Earth and the Earth in its orbit around the sun and discover the mathematically beautiful law of universal inverse square or gravity, and in terms of that can explain the behavior of the whole solar system. Of course, back two hundred years after Newton, Einstein comes along and discovers general relativity, which is the modern theory of gravity; then, in terms of that, he is able to explain not just our little local solar system but to frame the first genuinely scientific cosmology account of the whole universe. Incidentally, he got it wrong, but that is another story.

So, why do we have this amazing power? I worked in quantum physics, in small-particle physics, the smallest bits of matter, and the quantum world is totally different from the everyday world. In the quantum world, if you know where something is, you don't know what it's doing. If you know what it's doing, you don't know where it is. That's the high-and-low of Heisenberg's uncertainty principle in a nutshell. That world is totally different from the everyday world, and if we are to understand it, we have to think differently about it. But we have learned how to do that. We have powers to understand the world that greatly exceed anything that could be considered as just a survival necessity, just a mundane necessity, or, indeed, be considered as some happy additional spin-off from necessities of that kind.

I don't know whether you are a Sherlock Holmes fan, but I hope you might be, and if you are, you will remember that when Holmes and Watson first meet each other, they're having breakfast in a London hotel, and right from the start, Holmes is pulling Watson's leg. He says to Watson, "I don't know, I don't know. Does the earth go around the sun? Or does the sun go around the earth?" The good doctor is horrified at this deplorable scientific ignorance, and Holmes just says, "Well, what does it matter for my daily work as a detective?" It doesn't matter at all, but we all know many, many things. Science has told us many, many things that are actually intellectually satisfying to know and that are certainly not connected with the certainties of everyday life.

So, why is science possible? Why can we understand the world so thoroughly and so profoundly? In fact, the mystery is greater than that even, because it turns out that mathematics is the key to unlocking the secrets of the physical universe. It's an actual technique in fundamental physics to look for theories whose mathematical expression is in terms of beautiful equations.

Some of you will know about mathematical beauty, possibly not all of you. It's a rather austere form of aesthetic pleasure but something that those of us who speak the language of mathematics can recognize and agree upon. This is the experience of three hundred years of doing theoretical physics in which the theories that fundamentally describe the world always turn out to be framed in terms of beautiful equations. It's an actual technique of discovery to look for equations of that sort.

The greatest theoretical physicist I've known personally was Paul Dirac, one of the founding figures of quantum theory and a professor in Cambridge for many years. He was not a religious man, nor a man of many words. He once said, "It is more important to have beauty in your equations than to have a fit experiment."

Of course, by that, he didn't mean it didn't matter, or [that] empirical adequacy is a dispensable thing in science. No scientist could possibly mean that, but if you had a theory and it didn't look as though, at first sight, your equations were going to fit the experiment, there were just possibly some ways out of it. Almost certainly you would have had to solve the equations in some sort of approximation. Maybe you made the wrong approximation or you hadn't gotten the right solution or maybe the experiments were wrong. We've learned that more than once, I have to say, in the history of science. But if your equations were *ugly*, there was no hope for you. They could not possibly be right.

Dirac was, undoubtedly, the greatest British theoretical physicist of the twentieth century. He made those discoveries due to a relentless and highly successful lifelong pursuit of beautiful equations.

Now, something funny is happening there. We're using mathematics, which, after all, is a very abstract form of human activity, to find out about the structure of the world around us. In other words, there seems to be some deep-seated connection between the reason within—the mathematical thoughts in our minds, in this case—and the reason without, which is the path and order of the physical world.

Dirac's brother-in-law, Dr. Eugene Wigner, who also won a Nobel Prize in physics, once asked, "Why is mathematics so unreasonably effective?"

Why does the "reason within" apparently perfectly match the "reason without," that is, the wonderful order of the world in which we live? That's a deep question, a meta-question, and those sorts of questions do not have simple knocked-out answers. They are too, too profound for that, but for me, a highly intellectually satisfying answer is the following: The reason within and the reason without fit together because, in fact, they have a common origin in the rational mind of the Creator, whose will is the ground both of our mental experience and the physical world of which we are a part.

You could summarize what I have been trying to say so far by saying that as physicists study the world, they study a world of wonderful order, a world shot through, as you might say, with signs of mind. If that's so, then it seems to me it's, at least, a hypothesis worth considering, because, in fact, the capital-*M* Mind of the Creator lies behind that wonderful order. I, in fact, believe that science is possible, that the world is deeply intelligible, precisely because it is a creation. To use ancient and powerful language, we human beings are creatures made in the image of our Creator. The power to do theoretical physics is a small part—a small part, no doubt—of the *imago Dei* [image of God].

So, that is one sort of meta-question, and it illustrates the way our religious belief and understanding does not tell science what to think in its own domain. We have every reason to believe that scientifically presentable questions will receive scientifically articulated answers, even though some of those answers may prove very difficult to find. But the meta-questions take us beyond science, and it seems to me that religion can provide intellectually satisfying and coherent responses, enabling science to be set within a wider and more profound setting of intellectual intelligibility.

I would like to ask a second meta-question: Why is the universe so special? Scientists do not like things to be special. Our instinct is to like things to be general, and our natural assumption would be that the universe is just a common-variety garden specimen of what our universe might be like— nothing very special about it. But as we've studied and understood the history of the universe, we've come to realize we live in a very remarkable universe, indeed, and if it was not as remarkable as, in fact, it is, we would not be here to be struck at the wonder of it.

The universe started extremely simply; 13.7 billion years ago is the rather accurate figure that cosmologists say. It started as almost a uniform expanding ball of energy, which is about the simplest possible physical system you could ever think about. One of the reasons why cosmologists talk with a certain justified boldness about the fairly early universe is because it is a fairly easy thing to think about. But our world is not so simple; it has become rich and complex, and after almost fourteen billion years, it has become the home of saints and mathematicians. We've come to realize, as we understood the steps by which that has happened, that though it took a long time—as far as we know, ten billion years for any form of life to appear and fourteen billion years for self-conscious life of our complexity to appear—nevertheless, the universe, in a very real sense, was pregnant with life from the very beginning. It is, in this sense, that the physical fabric of the world—that is, the given laws of nature that science uses as the basis of its exploration of what is going on, but whose origin science itself is unable to explain, which are the unexplained given, in terms of which science frames all its subsequent explanations—had to take a very precise, very finely tuned form, if the evolution of *any* form of carbon-based life, like ourselves, was to be a possibility in cosmic history.

Unless the physical fabric of the world was finely tuned for the possibility of carbon-based life, the universe could have evolved away forever, and nothing interesting would have happened.

Of course, the evolution of life, the evolution of the universe, was an ongoing process, but evolution by itself has to have the right material to act upon. Unless the physical fabric of the world was finely tuned for the possibility of carbon-based life, the universe could have evolved away forever, and nothing interesting would have happened. This history would have been boring and sterile in the extreme. So, we live in a very special world.

Let me just give you a couple of illustrations of why we think that is so. There are many, many arguments that point in that direction. I could spend all evening trying to list them, but I won't do that. I'll just give you a couple of examples. The first example is this: The very early universe is very simple, and so, it does only very simple things. For the first three minutes of the universe's life, the whole universe is immensely hot, immensely energetic. It is a sort of cosmic hydrogen bomb with nuclear reactions going on all the time.

As the universe expanded, it cooled. After just about three minutes, the universe was so sufficiently cooled that nuclear reactions on a universe-wide scale, on a cosmic scale, ceased, and the gross nuclear structure of the world was frozen out as, in fact, what we see it to be today, which is three-quarters hydrogen and a quarter helium. The early universe was very simple and made only very simple things. It made only the two simplest chemical elements, hydrogen and helium, and those two elements have a very boring chemistry. There is nothing very much that you can do with them.

The chemistry of life actually requires about thirty elements, of which possibly the most important is carbon. We call ourselves, when we think about it, *carbon-based life*. The reason for that is that carbon is the basis of those very long-chain molecules, and the chemical properties of carbon seem to be necessary for living entities. But the early universe has no carbon at all. So, where did carbon come from?

As the universe began to get a bit clumpy and lumpy as gravity began to condense things, stars and galaxies began to form. Then, as the stars formed, the matter inside the stars began to heat up, and nuclear reactions began again, no longer on a cosmic scale, no longer universe-wide, but in the interior nuclear furnaces of the stars. It is here in the interior nuclear furnaces of the stars that all heavy elements—there are ninety of them altogether and about thirty of them necessary for life—were made beyond hydrogen and helium.

One of the great triumphs of the second half of the twentieth century in astrophysics was working out how those elements were made by the nuclear reactions inside the stars. One of the persons who played an absolutely leading role in that was a senior colleague of mine in Cambridge called Fred Hoyle. Fred was with Willy Fowler from Caltech—they were thinking together about how these things might happen, and they were absolutely stuck at the start.

The first element they really wanted to make was carbon, and they could not for the life of them see how to make it. They had helium nuclei—we call them *alpha particles*—around. To make carbon, you have to take three alpha particles and make them stick together. That turns helium-4 into carbon-12, and that is a very, very difficult thing to do. The only way to do it is to get two of them and make them stick together. First of all, that makes beryllium, and then you hope that beryllium stays around for a bit. A third alpha particle comes wandering along and eventually sticks on and makes carbon-12. Unfortunately, it does not work in a straightforward way, because beryllium is unstable and does not oblige you by staying around to acquire that extra alpha particle.

So, Fred and Willy really could not figure out how to do it. On the other hand, there they were, carbon-based life, thinking about these things: *It must be possible to make carbon.* And then Fred had a very good idea. He realized it would be possible to make some carbon out of even this very transient beryllium if there was an enhancement—what, in the trade, we call a *resonance*—present in carbon that would produce an enhanced effect. That is, it would make things go much, much more quickly than you would expect. However, you not only had to have a resonance but also had to have it at the right place; it had to be at the right energy for this process to be possible. If it were anywhere else, it would not affect the rate at which things happen.

So, Fred is convinced that there must be a resonance in carbon at precisely this energy and writes down what the energy is. The next thing, he goes to the nuclear data tables to see if carbon had such resonance, and it is not in the nuclear data tables. Fred is so sure it must be there that he rings up his friends the Laurences, who are very clever experimentalists at Caltech, and says to them, "You look. You missed the resonancy in carbon-12, and I'll tell you exactly where to look for it. Look at this energy, and you'll find it." And they did—a very staggering scientific achievement. It was a very, very great thing, but the point is this: That resonance would not be there at that absolutely unique and vital energy if the laws of nuclear physics were in the smallest degree different from what they actually are in our universe.

When Fred saw that and realized that—Fred has always been powerfully inclined toward atheism—he said, in a Yorkshire accent, which, I am afraid, is beyond my powers to imitate, "The universe is a put-up job." In other words, this cannot be just a haphazard accident. There must be something lying behind this. And, of course, Fred does not like the word *God*; he said there must be some capital-*I* Intelligence behind what is going on in the world. So, there we are; we are all creatures of stardust. Every atom of our bodies was once inside a star, and that is possible because the laws of nuclear physics are what they are and not anything else.

Let me give you just one more example of fine-tuning. This is the most exacting example of all. It is possible to think of there being a sort of energy present in the universe, which is associated simply with space itself, and that energy these days is usually called *dark energy*. It used to be called the *cosmological constant*, but it has come to be called *dark energy*, because just recently astronomers believe they have measured the presence of this dark energy. In fact, it is driving the expansion of the universe.

What is striking about that expansion is that this energy is very, very small, compared to what you would expect its natural value to be. You can figure out—now, I won't go into the details—what you would expect the natural value of this energy to be. If you're in the trade, it is due to vacuum effects and things of that nature, but it turns out that the *observed* dark energy—if the observations are correct—is ten to the minus-120 times the natural expected value (10^{-120}); that's one over one followed by 120 zeroes.

Even if you're not a mathematician, I am sure that you can see that is a very small number indeed. If that number were not actually as small as it is, we would not be here to be astonished at it, because anything bigger than that would have blown the universe apart so quickly that no interesting things could have happened. You would have become too diluted for anything as interesting as life to be possible.

So, there are all these sorts of fine-tunings present in the world. All scientists would agree about those facts. Where the disagreements come, of course, is in answering the meta-question: What do we make of that? What do we think about the remarkable character of the world, the specific character of the world? Was Fred right to think that the universe is, indeed, a put-up job and that there is some sort of Intelligence behind it all?

I am sure you all know that these considerations about the fine-tuning of the universe are called the *anthropic principle*—not meaning that the world is tuned to produce literally Homo sapiens, but *anthropoi*, meaning beings of our self-conscious complexity. I have a friend who thinks about these things and has written, I think, the best book about the anthropic principle, *Universes*. His name is John Leslie. He's an interesting chap because he does his philosophy by telling stories, which is very nice. He's a parabolic philosopher. That is very nice for chaps like me who are not trained in philosophy, because everybody can appreciate a story, and he tells the following story:

You're about to be executed. You are tied to the stake, your eyes are bandaged, and the rifles of ten highly trained marksmen are leveled at your chest. The officer gives the order to fire, the shots ring out, and you find that you have survived. So, what do you do? Do you just walk away and say, "Gee, that was a close one"? I don't think so. So remarkable an occurrence demands some sort of explanation, and Leslie suggests that there are really only two rational explanations for your good fortune.

One is this: Maybe there are many, many, many executions taking place today. Even the best of marksmen occasionally miss, and you happen to be in the one where they all miss. There have to be an awful lot of executions taking place today for that to be a workable explanation, but if there are enough, then it is a rational possibility. There is, of course, another possible explanation: Maybe there is only one execution scheduled for today, namely yours, but more was going on in that event than you are aware of. The marksmen are on your side, and they missed by design.

You see how that charming story translates into thinking about the anthropic fine-tuning—the special character of the universe in which we live. First of all, we should look for an explanation of it. Now, of course, obviously, if the universe was not finely tuned for carbon-based life, we, carbon-based life, would not be here to think about it. But the coincidence is that the fine-tunings required are so specific and so remarkable that it is no more sensible for us to say, "We're here because we're here, and there's nothing more to talk about it," than it would be for that chap who missed being executed to say, "Gee, that was a close one." So, we should look for an explanation.

Basically, there are two possible explanations. One is that maybe there are just many, many, many different universes—all with different laws of nature, different kinds of forces, different strengths of forces, and so on. If there are enough of those universes—and there would have to be a lot of them, an enormous number of them—but if there are enough of them, then, of course, by chance, one of them will be suitable for carbon-based life. It will be the winning ticket in the cosmic lottery, as you might say, and that, of course, is the one in which we live, because we are carbon-based life. That would be a many-universes explanation.

Of course, there is another possibility. Maybe there is only one universe that is the way it is, because it is not just any old world but is a creation that is being endowed by its Creator with precisely the finely tuned laws and circumstances that will allow it to have a fruitful history.

So, many, many, many universes *or* design, a created design. Which shall we choose? Leslie says we don't know which one to choose. It is six of one and half a dozen of the other. I think in relation to what I have just been talking about—these anthropic fine-tunings—that Leslie is right about that. Both sug-gestions are what you might call *metaphysical*. Sometimes, people try to dress the many universes all up in scientific vestment, but essentially I think it is a metaphysical guess. We do not have direct experience of those many, many, many universes. That is a sort of metaphysical guess, just as the existence of a Creator God is a sort of metaphysical guess. So, what should we choose?

If that is the only thing we are thinking about, we can choose one or the other with equal plausibility, but if we widen the argument, then I think we shall see that the assumption that there are many, many, many universes does only one piece of explanatory work. The only thing it explains is to explain away the particularity of our observed and experienced universe. The piece of work is to diffuse the threat of theism, but the theistic explanation—it does seem to me—does a number of other pieces of work.

I have already suggested that a theistic view of the world explains the deep intelligibility of the world that science experiences and exploits, and I also believe, of course, that there is a whole swath of religious experience of the human-testified encounter with the reality of the sacred, which is also explained by the belief in the existence of God. So, it seems to me, there is a cumulative case for theism in which the anthropic argument can play one part, but only one part. It will not, of course, surprise you, given what you know about me, that it is that latter explanation which I myself embrace.

There we are. That is one aspect of the relationship between science and religion. The intelligibility of the world and the particular fruitfulness of the universe are striking things that science draws to our attention but does not itself explain. It seems to me that religion can offer science the gift of a more extensive, more profound understanding to set the remarkable results of sci-ence within a more profound matrix of understanding.

Science also, it seems to me, gives gifts to religion. The gifts that science principally gives to religion are to tell religion what the history and the nature of the world are like and have been, and religious people should take that absolutely seriously. Those seeking to serve the God of truth should welcome truth from whatever source it comes, not that all truth comes from science, of course, by any means. But real truth does come from science, and we should welcome that. The truth of science, in my view, is able to help religion with its most difficult problem.

What is the most difficult problem for religion? What holds people back from religious belief more than any other? What troubles those of us who are religious believers more than any other? I am sure we are likely to agree that it is the problem of the suffering that is present in the world—the disease and disaster that seems to be present in what is claimed to be the creation of a good and perfect and powerful God. I do not need to explain what that problem is. It is only too clear.

Interestingly enough, the insights that science offers—the world is an evolving world, and evolutionary thinking is fundamental to all scientific thinking about the history of the universe, not just the evolution of life here on Earth—is, of course, part of the story. But the evolving part of the universe itself—the processes by which the galaxies and the stars formed and so on—all of these are evolutionary processes.

It is interesting that when Darwin publishes his great work *On the Origin of Species* in 1859, there is a sort of popular, absolutely, totally, historically ignorant view that that was the moment of the fantastic head-on collision between science and religion, with all the scientists shouting, "Yes, yes, yes!" and all the religious people, the clergy particularly, shouting, "No, no, no!" That's absolutely, historically untrue!

There was a good deal of argument and confusion on both sides of the question. Quite a lot of scientists had lots of difficulties with Darwin. It was only when Mendel's discovery of genetics was rediscovered and the neo-Darwinian synthesis came along that people really began to see and feel on surer ground in relation to it.

Equally, there were religious people who from the start welcomed the insights of evolutionary thinking into the nature of God's creation. I am happy to say that two of those people who welcomed that were Anglican clergymen in England. One was Charles Kingsley, and the other was Frederick Temple, and they both coined the phrase that, I think, perfectly encapsulates the theological way to think about an evolving world. They said, "No doubt, God could have snapped the divine fingers and brought into being a ready-made world, but God had chosen to do something cleverer than that. For in bringing into being an evolving world, God had made a creation in which creatures could make themselves."

In other words, from a theological point of view, evolving process is the way in which creatures explore and bring to birth the deep fruitfulness of potentiality with which the Creator has endowed creation. That gift of being themselves, making themselves, is, I think, what you would expect the God of love to give to that God's creation. The God of love will not be the puppet master of the universe, pulling every string.

The God of love will not be the puppet master of the universe, pulling every string.

So, I think that a creation making itself, an evolving world which is a creation making itself, is a greater good than a ready-made world would be. However, it is a good that has a necessary cost, because that process of shuffling exploration of potentiality will necessarily involve ragged edges and blind alleys. The engine that has driven, for example, the evolution of life here on Earth has been genetic mutation in germ cells that have produced new forms of life, but the same biochemical processes that enabled germ cells to mutate and to produce new forms of life will necessarily allow somatic cells, body cells, also to mutate and become malignant. You cannot have one without the other.

So, the fact that there is cancer in the world, which is, undoubtedly, an anguishing aspect of the world and a source of grief and anger to us, is, at least, not gratuitous. It is not something that a God who was a little more compassionate or a little more competent could easily have removed. It is the shadow side of the creativity of the world. It is the necessary cost of a creation allowed to make itself. Now, you could argue whether it is a cost worth paying. I am not suggesting for a minute that this consideration I have been laying out in the last couple of minutes solves all the problems of evil and suffering, but it does at least help us. I say that it seems to indicate these problems are not gratuitous.

We all tend to think that if we had been in charge of creation, we would have done it better. We would have kept all the nice things (the sunsets, the flowers) and thrown away all the nasty things (the disease and disaster), but the more scientifically we actually understand the processes of the world, the more we see how inextricably interlinked all these things are and that there is a dark side as well as a light side to what is going on. That is a small hope, a small help, in relation to what is going on.

I always finish what I have to say, and the conversation will be the most interesting part of the evening. If you are totally convinced by everything I have said this evening, it would have led you no more than to a picture of God as the great mathematician or the cosmic architect. It has been a limited form of inquiry, and there is still much more that one might ask about the nature of God and much more that one might seek to learn about the nature of God; that will have to be found in other forms of human experience. A very important aspect of belief in God is that not only is there a Being who is the Creator of the world, but also this Being is worthy of worship, and I just indicate with a tiniest sketch how I would approach that issue.

I am deeply impressed by the existence of value in the world—something that science directly does not take into account. But our physical world, of which we are a part, is shot through with value, with beauty. For example, music is very interesting. Suppose you ask a scientist as a scientist to tell you all he or she can about music. They will say, "It is neuro-response—neurons firing away to the impact of vibrations in the air hitting the eardrum," and, of course, that is true and, of course, in its way, it is worth knowing. However, it hardly tells you all you might want to know about the deep mystery of music. Science trolls experience with a very coarse-grained net, and the fact that these vibrations in the air somehow are able to speak to us—and, I believe, speak truly to us of a timeless beauty—is a very striking thing about the world.

Similarly, I think we have moral knowledge of a surer kind than any that we possess. I do not, for a minute, believe that our conviction that torturing children is wrong is either some kind of curious, disguised genetic strategy or just a convention of our society. Our tribe just happens to choose not to torture children. It is a fact about the world that torturing children is wrong. We have moral laws. Where do these value-laden things come from? I think they come from God, actually. Just as I think that the wonderful order of the world and the fruitfulness of cosmic history are reflections of the mind and purpose of the Creator, so I think that our ethical intuitions, our intimations of God's good and perfect will, and our aesthetic experiences are a sharing in the Creator's joy in creation.

For me, theistic belief ties together all these things in a way that is deeply satisfying and intellectually coherent, and then there would be many other questions still remaining. Even if there is such a God worthy of worship, does that God care for you and me? That is a question I could not answer without looking into taking the risk both of commitment and ambiguity and looking into personal experience. For me, that would mean looking into my Christian encounter with the person and reality of Christ. That is a subject for another discussion.

Here I am. I stand before you as somebody who is both a physicist and a priest. I am grateful for both of those things, and I want to be two-eyed. I want to look with the eye of science on the world, and I want to look with the eye of my Christianity on the world. The binocular vision those give me enables me to see and understand more than I would be able to with either of them on their own.

But it would be nice to know what you think about these things, and I think the time has come to let you have a go. So, over to you.

I want to look with the eye of science on the world, and I want to look with the eye of my Christianity on the world. The binocular vision those give me enables me to see and understand more than I would be able to with either of them on their own.

Q & A

Well, thank you, Dr. Polkinghorne. I am sure there are people here who have questions. I am sure I know some of them personally. If anyone has a question or comments, as long as they end in a question mark and are very brief, get in line. So, go ahead.

Q: You started your speech stating that a common denominator of science and religion is the search for truth. When I was in school, I learned that the basis of science is the search for proof, not truth. So, I was waiting in your speech for some kind of sentence to the question about how you can prove that there is God. You know that this is the core question, and I am kind of missing that.

A: I think that is a very interesting comment to make. I think that we have learned that all forms of rational inquiry are a little bit more subtle than concluding with knockdown proof, knockdown argument. Even in mathematics, Kurt Gödel taught us that any mathematical system of sufficient complexity to include arithmetic, which means the whole numbers, will contain statements that can be made which can neither be proved nor disproved within that system. So, there is all openness, even in mathematics. In fact, a little act of faith is involved in committing myself to the consistency of a mathematical system. It cannot be demonstrated.

Not many people lie awake at night worrying about the consistency of arithmetic, but nevertheless, that is the case. So, I think we have learned that the proof in the knockdown rationale of the clear and certain ideas of the Enlightenment program which Descartes put on the agenda is a glorious, magnificent program, but it is a failure. No form of human life has that kind [of proof]. Science, though it certainly produces convincing theories, does not, I think, produce proof.

In my view, the greatest philosopher of science was Michael Polanyi, who was a very distinguished physical chemist before he became a philosopher and knew science really from the inside. In the preface to his famous book called *Personal Knowledge*, he says, "I am writing this book"—and he is writing about science, remember—"to show how I may commit myself to what I believe to be true, knowing that it might be false." I think that is, actually, the human situation.

What I think we are looking for—and what I am looking for in my scientific searches and in my religious searches—is motivated belief. I believe that the success of science and also the illuminating power of religion encourage the idea that motivated belief is sufficiently close to truth for us to commit ourselves to it. But, I think, proof is actually not the category that we might think it is.

Q: I had the fortune to meet Stephen Hawking at Caltech, and I had a question for him about the coded information that is in the biological world (and he wouldn't answer): did he believe in God? I was wondering, with your having been at Cambridge, what your thoughts were about his thoughts on that.

A: Stephen and I were colleagues in the same department for many years. It's not easy to have a conversation with Stephen, because it is so laborious for Stephen to produce things. When he does give an answer, he tends to say, "Yes," or "No." While the rest of us say, "We think of it this way, or maybe that way," he just can't do that with the handicap he has fought against so remarkably.

It is a very interesting question of why God keeps on popping up in the text of *A Brief History of Time*. God is not in the index. God is certainly there in the text, and it is a book about quantum cosmology, which does not require one to mention God from the start to finish for its prime purpose. I wouldn't try to presume to say what Stephen thinks.

A lot of people, a lot of my friends in the scientific world, are both wistful and wary about religion. They are wistful because they can see that science doesn't tell you everything. They wished there to be a mystique—a broader, deeper story of science that they can tell—but they are wary of religion because they know that religion is based upon faith and they think that faith is shutting your eyes, gritting your teeth, and believing six impossible things before breakfast, because some unquestionable authority tells you that is what you've got to do. They don't want to do that, and I don't want to do that. I guess that you don't want to do that.

What I am always trying to explain to my friends, and to you if I can, in a way, is that I have motivations for my religious beliefs. They are not just here in the Nicene Creed: "So, don't ask me questions, sayonara." I have *motivations* for my religious beliefs, just as I have motivations for my scientific beliefs. Of course, those two sets of motivations are somewhat different, because the types of truth dimensions of reality that are being investigated are somewhat different, but they have that in common. That is all that I mean by the search for truth.

Eric Metaxas: Can everyone in this area hear?

Polkinghorne: I am sorry. What should I do?

Eric Metaxas: You should berate one of the sound people.

Polkinghorne: That is cathartic but not very useful. I will try to stand closer to this [microphone]. I am sorry; forgive me. Look, nothing is more irritating on an occasion like this than for somebody to come up to you afterward and say, "I couldn't hear a word." If you can't hear what I'm saying, just wave, and I will do what I can.

Q: I believe you just missed the idea of many different universes operating with separate laws of engagement, instead of thinking of a universe that is finely tuned. I have read several studies, *New York Times* articles, and friends have told me about the possibility of alternative dimensions, more intriguing dimensions—four, five, six, seven. So, I am wondering how that idea, that reality, would coincide with what you were saying about the existence of many universes or one.

A: Many theories in modern physics have become very speculative. Take string theory. There was a program I saw on television about that the other night; it was a very interesting exploration of possible ideas, trying to guess what the world is like at sixteen orders of magnitude. That means sixteen powers of ten based on what we know from direct empirical or observational encounter. The lessons of history are against even the cleverest people being able to do that. So, I would be cautious about that.

Even if you did that, string theory is based upon a certain way of putting these things together. The existence of quantum mechanics, the existence of general relativity, of gravitational theory—where do they come from? They are indispensable items in a fruitful world. You need gravity to make stars and everything to produce structures. You need quantum mechanics because it is both orderly and open. It fixes some things; it doesn't fix everything, and you need a certain flexibility for the development of complex systems.

The universe would still have very remarkable properties to it, which would still demand some sort of explanation and would not be explained just by saying, "It is just our luck." So, I think there is something left to think about. I could have done a more nuanced discussion about that, but I didn't have time.

Technology takes knowledge and turns it into power, and not everything that you can do, you should do. So, you need to add to knowledge and power; you need to add wisdom, which is the ability to choose the good and refuse the bad.

Q: In your presentation of the anthropic principle and theistic evolution, you presented us with a God who was clever enough to allow us to be involved in the creation. With the current state of genetic research and potential manipulation, what are the limits, if any, of our involvement in that creation?

A: That is a very important question and obviously a pressing question. I just finished all of this now, but for about ten years I was involved with various United Kingdom government advisory committees connected with genetic advances.

What happens is that science gives you knowledge, and I think that knowledge is always a good thing. It is a better basis for decision than ignorance, but technology takes knowledge and turns it into power, and not everything that you can do, you should do. So, you need to add to knowledge and power; you need to add wisdom, which is the ability to choose the good and refuse the bad. There are obviously quite difficult things to decide there.

First of all, things have to be looked at on a case-by-case basis. There is no simple rule that says, "If you take five boxes out of seven, it is okay." You have to look at these things case by case, and you can't leave the judgments simply to the experts, because research is very exciting and you can get carried away by the technological imperative: "We have done this, we have done that; come on, let's do the next thing." The next thing may be the thing that you shouldn't do. So, you can't leave it to the experts. That is why society has a role to play.

Of course, you cannot do without the experts, because the experts might tell you what might be on the agenda. So, we need a debate, and it much grieves me that in my own country—and I rather suspect in this country too—so much of moral debate is the clash of single-issue pressure groups, one side shouting, "X is wonderful," and the other side shouting, "X is terrible"— whatever X is. It is very unlikely to be either of those things. X could be good for some purposes and bad for others. We need a more careful, temperate, and nuanced ethical discussion.

Q: My question is aimed more at the artistic side of the search. I now am a playwright and a designer, and one of the things that I come across more than anything is the search for truth, both in my clients and in myself. I am a Christian, and I feel very strongly. In one of your books, you had said that art is between, I think, theology and physics or theology and science. You also had said in that book something about how Earth is the theater where all this plays out. So, could you possibly elaborate on that a little bit?

A: It is a big subject, and I did refer to it very briefly. At the end, I was talking about God being worthy of worship and the role of value. One of the things I am always trying to encourage in myself and others is to take a rich and generous view of the world we live in, the multilevel reality within which we live; for example, to believe—as I do, indeed, believe—that the personal is as important, indeed more important, than the impersonal; that the unique and unrepeatable is as significant as the repeatable. Science is concerned largely with the impersonal and the repeatable.

In my talking to my friends, it's hard to get from science to God in one step; that is far too big a leap. So, I ask them what they think about music—and I broached that subject very briefly this evening. I ask them what they think about music, and it encourages them, I think, to take seriously a more generalist metaphysic. That is a very important thing.

If you think science told you everything that is worth knowing, it would be a very cold, impersonal world that we so described. We wouldn't find ourselves in that world. So, I think the arts are very, very significant in that respect, if we reflect on human nature. For example, what is it to be a human being? One of the prime windows into human nature is through literature. Great literature is always concerned with the individual and the personal. The subject of great literature is not every man or every woman, but Hamlet or King Lear or whatever it is. We have to take those things seriously.

Q: I first have a comment. I observe that the unfortunate relationship between religion and science is that religion is often a science-stopper. That is, for example, in the creationist-*versus*-evolution debate, there were problems in science about what the creationists called *irreducible complexity*. The answer to this problem was God—the God of the gaps. I think there are biochemical processes we understand where a lot of these problems of irreducible complexity have been addressed.

I have two questions. Basically, I think, you have presented two arguments for, at least, an Intelligent Designer. One is the conformity between the reason within and the reason without, and you say that this is a metaphysical question beyond the realm of science. I am wondering if we can pose this as actually a scientific question. How is it that human beings are able to reason about deep, abstract mathematical truths?

I would guess that one answer is that the very same cognitive processes of generalization and inductive reasoning which allow a person to look at one cliff that has one shape and another cliff that has one shape and generalize that when you go over both of them, you die—these are the very same cognitive processes that allow us to think deeply and abstractly about mathematical problems.

The second question is with the anthropic argument. I am wondering if you would agree that there are two premises behind the anthropic argument that are unproven, one that it is possible for the universe to have other cosmological constants or other natural laws. I think it is an unproven premise of the argument. The second premise is like ten marksmen aiming at a person—that it was highly improbable that the constants are what they are. Again, I think that is a premise that has not been proven. I am wondering if you would agree with those statements.

A: The first question is about everyday reasoning leading us to unreasonable effectiveness in mathematics. I tried to deal with that, and I think the answer is "No, it won't." The quantum world requires a type of thinking about it—indeed, it requires a type of logic that is different from the Aristotelian logic of the everyday world. So, we certainly didn't get that out of just somehow generalizing our everyday experience. I think my answer would be *no*.

Let me try to answer the last part. Some people suggest that maybe the true constants of nature are absolutely fixed by consistency of the theory. I think that is only even remotely credible if you already suppose the theory has to contain quantum theory and gravity, because that is the only thing that would sharpen it up. But supposing that would, I am still very doubtful there will not be scale parameters in any successful combination of those two theories. Secondly, suppose it was the case that the only logically consistent theory happened also to be a theory that produced beings of our complexity. I would think that [to be] the most astonishing anthropic coincidence of all, in actual fact.

Q: Regarding what you said about mutations being both beneficial and harmful as part of your model of a created-by-design universe, as a layman, I have observed and heard constant news reports about genetic defects and so on, and that obviously points to harmful mutations. Do we have actual evidence—observable and empirically so, in the laboratory or in just everyday life—of bona fide beneficial mutations, as opposed to something by inference that we assume from billions of years ago?

A: We certainly have in things like bacteria, which have very rapid reproduction rates. It is beneficial to bacteria, but it is not beneficial to us. They mutate and produce strains that resist antibiotics, and then those strains, of course, become dominant. So, at the bacterial level, certainly we see that, and maybe a bit higher up, too. I think we do have that; that does happen.

Q: If natural laws reflect the mind of the Lawgiver and if natural laws contemplate cancer as a necessary component of evolution, what do you say to the skeptic who rejects the idea of God based on God's culpability for the content of his laws?

A: That is a very fair point, and I did say that I didn't think that observation removed, by any means, all the difficulties. They are considerable. We live in a world that is remarkably fruitful and beautiful, remarkably chilling and frightening and destructive. It is a very ambiguous sort of picture, and somehow or other, the bad things are the necessary cost of the good things. That is not an argument you can utter without a quiver in your voice. The world is too complex and too strange for that.

I have to say one specifically Christian thing this evening: For me, the possibility of religious belief really centers on my Christian belief. A Christian understanding of God's relationship to suffering is not that God is simply a compassionate spectator looking down on the strange and bitter world that God holds in being. As a Christian, I believe that God is participating in the suffering of the world, that God is truly a fellow sufferer. The Christian God is the crucified God. That is a very deep and mysterious, though, I believe, true, insight. That is the deep level at which the problem of suffering has to be met, and the possibility for religious belief really, for me, rests at that level.

Q: This sort of involves both Eric and you, Sir John. In Eric's joke about you being able to be knocked over by a feather, could you maybe use your applied physics to determine when the joke reached terminal velocity? Or retrograde? I had to say that.

There are several people here who are artists, writers, and people from California with questions. Here you described a theorem or a mathematical equation, when it is right, being beautiful. There is order and structure, maybe even scientific structure, and that is involved in beauty. You also mentioned obviously in physics and life, there is a story, a history involved in science.

There are a myriad of books out there about the *right* structure to art or the *right* structure to storytelling. In reading Joseph Campbell and things as a writer, I've had lights go on in terms of there being true structures. I am wondering as a priest, as someone involved in the clergy and also in the Bible, whether you see structure to God's stories and to art in that there is something that you can determine empirically to be true.

A: I do believe that God discloses the divine nature through the unfolding of history and particularly, in particular people and particular events. There are particular occasions and particular persons through whom the divine nature is more visible than is normally the case. In my view, the authority of the Bible stems from the fact that it is an account of the history of Israel and then of the life, death, and resurrection of Jesus Christ, which, to me, are the prime events through which God has acted to make God's nature and purposes known.

Yes, there is an unfolding there. We have to read the story and accept the story on its own terms, so to speak, it seems to me. The story is not determined by our judgment beforehand. We have to respond to that. Authors tell me that about writing novels and that sort of thing, and I am inclined to understand that may be so. So, there is a sort of authenticity that is involved in story, whether it is a scientific story or not. I am sorry that is a very stuffy answer to a question that leaves me a little bit at sea, as you may perceive.

Q: I had a conversation today with my mom, and I just have a very basic question. John, verse something [3:16]: "God so loved the world that he gave his only" whatever. If you don't believe in him, you shall perish. Are we so right in our conviction that we are the ones that will be right? If you don't believe in him, you shall perish. I think that has far-reaching implications to Muslims, Buddhists, Shintos, and there are more of them than us.

A: I believe that God is merciful and loving, and I believe that God's offer of mercy and love is not a limited offer for this life only. After death, a curtain comes down, and if you are caught on the wrong side, God says, "Too bad, you had your chance; you missed it." That doesn't seem to be the God and Father of our Lord Jesus Christ. Equally, I believe that whatever decisions and actions we take in this life, the beliefs to which we commit ourselves are very important. Those who wittingly and willfully turn from God in this life will find it, to say the least, more painful and more difficult to accept God's mercy. I think more know Christ than know Christ by name.

I also believe that all will come to the Father through Christ ultimately, because believing, as I do, that Jesus is both human and divine, he is the unique bridge between the life of God and the life of created humanity, and that is the way. Our ultimate destiny is to share in the life and energy of God, I believe. The way into that is, indeed, the way through Christ. Again, I believe there are people who are on that way without knowing the name of the way in which they are coming.

Eric Metaxas: We have time for one question, and it can't be about evolution.

Q: You mentioned that evolution was absolutely fundamental to an understanding of science. As you know, in the biological world especially, the coded information passed on in DNA is extremely complicated—just the running of a body, the building of a body, and on and on. A. E. Wilder-Smith has made comments that in evolutionary theory, the missing fact is information. Could you comment on if the coded information that is in the biological world comes by chance through evolution, as you have talked about it?

A: Yes, that is a very interesting question. I think that the concept of information is going to be an extremely important concept in twenty-first-century science, and I venture to think that by the end of the twenty-first century, information in some sense—meaning the structure and the specification of dynamical pattern—will be as important a concept as energy has been in the last 150 years. We are just beginning scientifically to study the detailed behavior of complex systems—nothing as complicated as a single living cell, let alone a human being, but mostly models that are logical models that are run on computers.

Those already show us that complex systems in their totalities display astonishing properties that you would never guess from thinking about the properties of the constituent bits and pieces. Many of those properties relate to the spontaneous generation of extraordinarily high patterns of order, in other words, the spontaneous generation of something like information-bearing behavior.

Let me give you an example, chosen from Stuart Kauffman's book *At Home in the Universe*. Kauffman is a chap who works on so-called *complexity theory* and has an interest particularly in its application to biology. Consider a system consisting of electric lightbulbs. This will be a picture of it:

The bulbs are either on or off. The system develops in steps. Each bulb is correlated with two other bulbs somewhere else in the array. What those two bulbs are doing now—either on or off—determines what this bulb does at the next step in the array, and there are very simple rules that specify this.

You start the array off in a random configuration of illumination. Some bulbs are on; some bulbs are off. Then you let it just play away on your computer and see what happens.

I would guess nothing really interesting would happen. It would just twinkle away haphazardly as long as you would let it, but that is not true. The system soon settles down to a self-generated, extraordinarily ordered behavior cycling through a very limited number of patterns of illumination.

If there are ten thousand lightbulbs in the array, there are two to the ten thousand [$2^{10,000}$] or ten to the three thousand [$10^{3,000}$] different states of illumination, in principle possible. That is a one followed by three thousand zeros. In actual fact, you will find that the system will soon cycle through one hundred different patterns of illumination. One with three thousand zeros possibility has somehow spontaneously gotten focused down into a hundred possibilities. That is quite an astonishing generation of order. I can see that as the generation of information. In fact, I think, if I remember correctly, he calls that chapter "Information for Free."

So, there are still lots of things to discover. I don't say there aren't problems. Of course there are, and they certainly are not solved yet. I do think we should be wary of generalizing too quickly.

Making Sense out of Suffering

―――

PETER KREEFT

―――

January 23, 2003

Introduction

Good evening and welcome to Socrates in the City. I am Eric Metaxas. Socrates in the City takes its name from Socrates, who, of course, famously said, "The unexamined life is not worth living." Then he drank the hemlock and died.

Do I have that out of order? Oh, right. He said, "The unexamined life is not worth living," at some point earlier in his career, and he said it in a very positive way, meaning that we are to examine our lives. Of course, I think he was quite right.

We are, indeed, to examine our lives. It makes life much more worth living. So, a bunch of folks, most of them friends of mine, and I were thinking that most New Yorkers are so busy that we don't really take out the time in our lives to examine our lives with any particular rigor. We thought that putting on these events called Socrates in the City and inviting speakers like Dr. Kreeft to address some of the big issues of life would be advisable.

It actually turns out that we were dead wrong. These have been a disaster, and I think this will be the last one we do. I'm glad you're laughing.

These have been really extraordinary. I have to say I am humbled by the turnout tonight. The turnout has been consistently good, the speakers have been wonderful, and these things have been as successful as I have hoped. In any case, we call these events *Socrates in the City: Conversations on the Examined Life*, and they are meant to be conversations, not only in the question-and-answer that follows the talk but also after these events, when we leave from here. We hope that we have begun a conversation in your mind and that you will be thinking about these things beyond this evening.

In any case, you can't go wrong following Socrates's advice on the matter of examining your life. Of course, Socrates didn't have to pay New York rent and could spend all his time thinking about his life. But you get the idea—and it is a good idea—and we are thrilled you can be here tonight to do it with us.

Tonight, we are privileged to have the estimable Dr. Peter Kreeft with us. Dr. Kreeft is a philosophy professor at Boston College, which, I am told, is located in Boston—is that right?

He is also a very, very much sought-after speaker. Believe me, it was very difficult to get him; we are lucky to have him. He has written many books—over forty—and many bestsellers among them. Most notably for tonight, he has written an absolutely fabulous book titled, appropriately enough, *Making Sense out of Suffering*, and of course, that will be his subject.

The goal of Socrates in the City is to attack the big questions—the biggest questions of all: about the existence of God, what it means to be human, about evil and suffering, and about where we come from and where we are going. We shouldn't be scared by those questions.

Living in New York, you sometimes get the idea that the biggest questions we deal with are along the lines of "Do I take the cab or the subway?" Or, if I am on the second floor, "Do I take the elevator or do I walk down?" That is a big one for me.

For Boston, where Dr. Kreeft is from, I think one of the big questions that have really been in the minds of Bostonians and the people in Massachusetts for a long time now is "Why did Dukakis wear that absurd helmet?" I don't think there is an answer. It is almost a rhetorical question, isn't it? I don't think there is an answer.

Another question Bostonians have, of course, is "Why can't the Boston Red Sox* get it together and win the World Series?" I am sorry; that is probably below the belt. Dr. Kreeft, please don't leave. You have to keep in mind

---

* At the time of Dr. Kreeft's lecture, the Red Sox had not won a World Series since 1918; of course, this run of hard luck changed in 2004, when they beat the St. Louis Cardinals, breaking the eighty-six-year-old "curse of the Bambino."

that I am a Mets fan; I was born in Queens. So, we are brothers in our disdain for the Yankees. It is a bond that we share as a Mets fan and a Red Sox fan. Let's just pretend that the Bill Buckner thing never happened, and we will just be friends.

Anyway, tonight we are here to ask a big philosophical question. Woody Allen, in his writings, always had a knack for putting the huge philosophical questions right up alongside the picayune, practical problems of life. There are a couple of things that he wrote along these lines that I love, and I wanted to share them with you this evening. For example, he wrote, "Can we actually know the universe? My goodness, it is hard enough finding your way around in Chinatown." That's such a typical Woody Allen line that it's almost not funny, right?

He also said, "The universe is merely a fleeting idea in God's mind—a pretty uncomfortable thought, particularly if you just made a down payment on a house." And this is my favorite; it's more apocalyptic than it is philosophical. He wrote, "The lion and the lamb will lie down together, but the lamb won't get much sleep."

You'll never be able to stop thinking of that. I wish I had written it. Anyway, perhaps one big question many of us have here tonight is whether the speaker's name is pronounced "Kreeft" or "Krayft." At least it was for me. In dealing with Dr. "Krayft" over the phone, I have come to hear him say "Krayft" a number of times, and I just sort of assumed he would know. So, whether he is right or wrong, we will just follow his lead and drop that question going forward.

Seriously, folks, I have been privileged to read a number of Dr. Kreeft's books over the years, and I have to say that they are delightfully readable and lucid. I think that accounts for his extraordinary popularity as an author and as a speaker. I first heard Dr. Kreeft at Oxford University in England at the hundredth anniversary celebration of C. S. Lewis's birth.

Indeed, many people have said that Dr. Kreeft's writings remind them of C. S. Lewis's. I would agree. Like Lewis, Dr. Kreeft attempts and succeeds wonderfully at making the complicated simple, at explaining some very big things to little people like me. For that I am very grateful, because I have to admit that even though I am of Greek descent, I have had some difficulty with philosophy.

I remember in my freshman year in college, I took a survey course in ancient philosophy and got stuck at Thales. Two people laughed. Thank you. I never really got past Thales, and I can guess that most of you in the room probably never did either. I am sort of under the impression that probably most of you never got *to* Thales.

Anyway, for those of you who didn't know it, Thales was a pre-Socratic. Don't feel bad if you didn't know that he was a pre-Socratic, because Thales didn't know it either. Yeah, keep thinking about that.

Enough silliness. Our subject tonight is for me and for most people the ultimate big question. This is a biggie, maybe the biggest. Tonight's subject, of course, is how do we make sense out of suffering? I don't know how many times I have heard someone say, "How can you believe in a loving God with all the suffering that there is in this world?"

I think that is a very valid question. I do believe in a loving God, but that is a very valid and difficult question. It is a brilliant question. I think it is the question of questions and, therefore, could not be more appropriate for this forum and for Dr. Kreeft's attentions this evening. So, I hugely look forward to hearing Dr. Kreeft's thoughts on it. Please join me in welcoming Dr. Peter Kreeft.

Talk

———

Usually an introduction is just an introduction. How can I follow that?

What a wonderful idea—Socrates in the City! And what a wonderful place! I am also humbled. This is the meaning of one of the beatitudes: "Blessed are the poor in spirit." It doesn't mean blessed are the *cheap* in spirit; it means blessed are those who have the opportunity to be in a J. P. Morgan room so they can be humbled in spirit.*

Socrates in the City! Of course, New York deserves "the City," but I don't deserve "Socrates." However, I am here because I am from Boston. Boston has more philosophers than any other city in the world, per capita. This is because philosophy is the love of wisdom. Wisdom comes through suffering. We have the Red Sox.

As for Billy Buckner, the morning after, I asked twelve close Red Sox fans how they felt when they saw that ball roll through his legs, and they all said one of two things. Number one: "Ashamed. How foolish I was. I hoped, I thought it was possible. What an idiot. I forgot the curse." Or number two: "Happy. Suppose we had won? We'd be just like everybody else. We're special. We're the chosen people."

———

* The event was held in an opulent room of the Metropolitan Club on Fifth Avenue and Sixtieth Street, built by the wealthy industrialist J. P. Morgan.

I spent many years, months, hours in this great city. I was born in that place Woody Allen talks about in *Love and Death*—northern New Jersey. There's a great dialogue between him and Diane Keaton. After she says, "Do you believe in God?" he says, "Well, on a good day like this, I could believe in a universal, divine Providence pervading all areas of the known universe, except, of course, certain parts of northern New Jersey."

As to the problem of suffering, I love the line he speaks—I forget the title of the movie—he's a Jewish father, his boy has become an atheist, and his wife blames him. So, she says to him, "Tell our son."

"What's the problem?"

"Well, he wants to know why there's evil."

"What do you mean 'why there's evil'?"

"Well, why there are Nazis. Tell him why there are Nazis."

"I should tell him why there's Nazis? I don't even know how the can opener works," which is quite profound, and I can't do much better than that.

But let me play Socrates and do things logically: first, state the question; second, decide how important it is; third, explore the logic of the problem; and fourth, try to solve it.

I titled my book *Making Sense out of Suffering*. What is *sense*? *Sense* means an explanation. Unlike the animals, we don't simply accept things as they are, unless we're pop psychologists. We ask, we question, we wonder. We ask especially the question "Why?" When we're adults, we usually ask it only once. That's why adults are not philosophers.

Little children ask it infinitely, and that's why they're philosophers: "Mommy, why?" "Because . . ." "Because *why*?" They keep going.

Aristotle, the master of those who know, the most commonsensical philosopher in the history of Western philosophy, gave us one of the ideas that no one should be allowed to die without mastering—one of the ideas that is a requisite for a civilization—the so-called *theory of the four causes*. All possible answers to the question "Why?"—all possible *becauses*—fit into four categories.

I assume that you are all civilized, and therefore, I will insult you, but I have the privilege of insulting you for thirty-five minutes and making you sit through a purgatory of listening to a lecture, which is always dull. This way, you can get to the heaven of a longer question-and-answer session, which is always much more interesting, at least in my experience. Poor Socrates! The only time they made him make a speech, it cost him his life.

Number one, we can ask, "What is this thing?" Define it. What is its form, essence, nature, species? That's *the formal cause.* Second, we can ask, "What is it made of, what's in it, or what's the content of it?" That's what Socrates called *the material cause.* Third, we can ask, "Where did it come from? Who made it?" That's what he calls *the efficient cause.* The fourth and most important and most difficult question we can ask is "What is it for? Why is it there? What purpose does it serve?" That's what he called *the final cause.*

When we talk about suffering, there is not too much difficulty about the formal cause. We know what it is. The material cause is made of different things for different people. It's made of the Yankees for Red Sox fans, or it's made of the Red Sox for Yankees fans. But the efficient and the final causes are the mysteries—where did it come from, and what good is it, if any? These are absolutely central questions and can be seen by comparing a couple of thinkers.

Let's start with Viktor Frankl's wonderful book *Man's Search for Meaning,* one of the half dozen books I would make everyone in the world read at gunpoint, if I possibly could, for the survival of sanity and civilization. Frankl is a Viennese psychiatrist who survived Auschwitz but didn't just survive it. He played Socrates at Auschwitz. He asked questions, for example, "What makes people survive?" And his answer is: Freud is wrong. It's not pleasure. Adler is wrong. It's not power. Even Jung is wrong. It's not integration or understanding the archetypes or anything like that. It's *meaning.* Those who found some meaning in their suffering survived, even though all the other indicators predicted that they wouldn't. And those who didn't—didn't.

He writes, "To live is to suffer. Therefore, if life has meaning, suffering has meaning, too." That seems to me to be utterly logical. The corollary is that if suffering does not have meaning, then life does not have meaning, because to live is to suffer.

He observed that different people had different answers to the question "Why are we suffering this absurd and agonizing thing?" But all the answers had one thing in common: They all turned a corner from asking the question "Life, what is your meaning?" to realizing that life was questioning them by name, "What is *your* meaning?" They could answer the question only by action, not just by thought, and those who believed in a God behind life asked the same question of God: "God, why me? What are you doing, and why?" Those that turned the corner realized that God was questioning *them*, which is exactly what happened to Job. When God showed up, he didn't give answers; he gave questions. How Socratic God is!

A second thinker who takes suffering very, very seriously is Buddha, one of the greatest psychologists of all time. He based an entire—well, we can't quite call it *religion*; we can't quite call it *philosophy* (Buddhists don't quite find familiarity or comfort in those two terms)—but he based his entire religion-philosophy system upon four noble truths, the first of which is that *to live is to suffer*—the trauma of birth, the trauma of disappointment, the trauma of pain, the trauma of death. Life is trauma.

His whole religion—if you want to call it that—is geared toward salvation from suffering, and his startlingly simple diagnosis is that to end suffering, you must end its cause. Its cause is egotism, or selfish desire, but in his psychology, the ego or ego-consciousness and egotism are inseparable, and therefore, you must see through the ego as an illusion and transform consciousness.

Let's contrast Buddha to Christ, who also takes suffering very seriously and claims that he comes to address this problem. But his solution, like that of Frankl, is more a deed than a thought like Buddha's, and contrasting to Buddha, his way is a way into suffering, not out of it. Christ also claims to be a way of salvation, but the problem for him is not so much suffering but sin. It's a different sort of thing. That vaguely has something or other—philosophers like to be vague at first, before they hone in on exact definitions—to do with the whole moral order, and that brings us back to Socrates, who famously taught in the *Gorgias* that it is better to suffer evil than to do it.

In other words, suffering isn't so bad. Sin is worse. It is much worse to do evil than to suffer it. That sounds hopelessly idealistic. If you had the choice between doing something a little wicked—let's say, cheating the IRS on your income tax or being tortured and roasted over a barbecue spit for thirteen hours straight—unless you're very unusual, I can predict what you would choose. What in the world could he possibly have meant by saying, "It is better to suffer evil than to do it"?

Well, Socrates had this notion that at the essence of a person was this thing called *the soul* or *the self*, rather than just the body. He taught, almost with his last words, that no evil can ever happen to a good man, whether in this life or in the next—a very strange thing to say, because clearly he is a good man and he has just been unfairly condemned, misunderstood, sentenced to death, put into prison, and his life is taken from him. That's as bad a thing as we can do to people. So, what could he mean by "no evil could happen to a good man"? He's in the middle of evil happening to a good man, and he says, "It doesn't really happen."

To the question "Why do bad things happen to good people?" Socrates's answer is "They never do." What in the world could he mean by that? It sounds absurd—a person is the soul, and evil never happens to the soul. It happens to the body.

You know that two-word bumper sticker that summarizes all of human history with such eloquence: *It happens.* By the way, do you know where that came from? There's a real story behind that. Sometime in the sixties, there was a farmer walking across a cornfield in Kansas, minding his own business. It was a nice June day; somewhere out of the sky came something that crashed into his head, blew his brains out, and killed him. It was a two-foot square of frozen detritus, which had worked its way loose from a rusty airliner toilet. I can just imagine that family tradition: "Mommy, how did Grandpa die?" "Well, you know, kid, it happens."

But that only happens to the body. It doesn't happen to the soul. "I am the master of my fate; I am the captain of my soul." Oh, great evil can be done to the soul, indeed, but I am the agent of it. *I* am the agent and responsible for folly and vice, *not you.*

Once Socrates realized that, he could die with a smile. Jesus said something a bit similar, although, as a Jew, Jesus takes the body much more seriously, because it's part of the image of God and God created it and Jesus doesn't have this dualism that the Greeks had between body and soul. But Jesus too said—what seems, to me, the single most practical sentence uttered in the history of the world—"What does it profit a man if he gain the whole world but lose his own self?"

None of the aforementioned remarks are meant to be a solution to the problem of suffering. They are meant to hone in on its centrality. There are two parts, or forms, to the problem of suffering—one is practical, and one is theoretical.

The practical one is what can we do about it, and we have come up with a number of answers, all of which are inadequate. For example, in *Civilization and Its Discontents*, Sigmund Freud raises the wonderful question "Why, now that we have become gods, aren't we happy?" He says we don't need gods or God anymore, because we've got technology. Technology has attained the wishful thinking that produced religion. We would like to be above the thunder and lightning, knowing it and controlling it like Zeus. Instead, we cower in superstitious fear in caves, thinking that the thunderstorm is the wrath of an angry God. We've become God; so, we need not fear. We are Mercury sending messages through space at will. Since we've become gods, since these natural human desires have been attained, we certainly should be happier, because happiness is the fundamental desire, but we're not. The more civilized we are, the more happy we are? Oh, no, *not at all*.

Freud even toys for a while with Rousseau's notion that the more civilized we are, the more unhappy we are, and that we would be happier to go back to being a noble savage, which, of course, is impossible. It's a great question, and Freud confesses honestly, as a good scientist, that he doesn't know the answer to it.

So, practically speaking, we have not come up with an answer to the problem of suffering. The only thing we can do about suffering is to live through it. To live is to suffer.

So, let's look at the theoretical problem, the logic of the problem: Why must we suffer? Explain it. Maybe you can't solve it, but at least let's explain it. It makes a difference whether God is thrown into the equation. Suppose you're a Marxist. What's the cause of suffering? Inadequate social structures, class conflict. What can be done about it? They can be modified. Something like a heaven on earth can be attained by a bloody revolution, but you still have to die and you still have pain nerves all over your body.

Theoretically, the problem comes in much greater if you believe in God. If suffering just happens, then it just happens; but if the whole of our selves and our lives and our universe is a design—a deliberate design, not an accident—a novel written by God, then why does he write such a lousy novel? Thus, Job, the classic sufferer, the classic philosopher in suffering, would not have nearly the passion, including the intellectual passion, if he didn't have

God to get angry at. Perhaps one of the things God wants us to do is to get angry with him, because that makes us similar to Socrates. It makes us ask questions. I don't think God likes pop psychologists that tell you, "Accept yourself as you are"; in other words, "Be a vegetable."

Perhaps one of the things God wants us to do is to get angry with him, because that makes us similar to Socrates. It makes us ask questions.

I have never found an atheist who can state the problem of evil with the logical cogency and force and personal passion of a theist. The most sympathetic case for atheism in the history of the world, it seems to me, has been made by one of the great theistic writers, Fyodor Dostoevsky. Ivan Karamazov is the most persuasive atheist in the world's literature. I tell my students, "If your faith is weak and you're afraid to lose it, don't read *The Brothers Karamazov*."

I often teach philosophy of religion, and I play Socrates. I try to get the class to dialogue. I divide them into two groups—believers and unbelievers, or believers and skeptics, or strong believers and weak believers. Once I get the two groups, I say, "Now, we're going to dialogue about whether there's a God, but those of you who classify yourselves as believers, you're going to have to argue for atheism. And you who classify yourselves as unbelievers, you're going to have to argue for theism." They say, "That's ridiculous," and I say, "No, it isn't. If you don't understand the other position, you can't really argue against it."

I've done this three or four times. It's always turned out exactly the same way. There's no discernible difference in the intelligence level between the atheists and the theists, but the atheists always make a ridiculously weak case for theism and the theists always make a knock-'em-down, drag-'em-out case for atheism. And it's always based on the problem of evil—by far, the strongest argument for atheism.

So, after that happens, and the students are kind of surprised, I ask, "Why did that happen?" And then the real argument begins. The atheists, who were pretending to be theists, said, "Well, you had us argue for Santa Claus; it was a ridiculous position that you gave us." The theists, who are pretending to be atheists, said, "No, we see both sides; you don't. We see your best arguments; you saw our weakest ones," and then they argue about that.

Let me give you the strongest argument for atheism that I know, based on the problem of suffering. Emotionally, it's something like Ivan Karamazov, but intellectually—since being almost a New Yorker, I am impatient, and I like philosophers who can say much in few words—I love Thomas Aquinas, who in a single paragraph can write as much as modern theologians would take a lifetime to write.

Here is his incredibly succinct formulation of the problem of evil: "If one or two contraries is infinite, the other is completely destroyed, but *God* means infinite goodness. Therefore, if God existed, there would be no evil discoverable anywhere, but there is evil. Therefore, God does not exist." It's a very powerful argument. How do you answer it?

Atheists and agnostics also want an answer to suffering, although God is not in their equation. So, the question of suffering is universal, but it's worse for a theist.

I will try to give you six answers, none of which is original. Three of them come from natural reason—philosophical reasoning without any reliance on religion or divine revelation—and three of them do come from religion or divine revelation. The first answer, which is basically the answer of ancient Stoicism, is that we are finite creatures. We have desires that are not going to be satisfied; so, we have a choice of either adding to our inevitable frustration or not.

Here you are in the dentist's chair and the Novocain hasn't taken effect and the dentist says, "We're doing root canal work; so, you have to tell me where the pain is. There's no alternative." What choice do you have? You have a choice between enduring the physical pain and rebelling against it. If you rebel against it, you add psychological pain and terror and fear and make the pain worse. So, why not be a Stoic and just accept it? Red Sox fans understand that. So, one possible explanation for suffering is "We're animals; we are finite creatures."

A second answer that comes from an older source, namely all the myths, just about all the myths of all the cultures of the world, is that something happened way back when before history. Things aren't supposed to be like this. Once upon a time, Adam and Eve ate an apple. Once upon a time, Pandora opened a box. Once upon a time, the magic bird that was supposed to drop the magic berry of heavenly happiness into the mouth of primal man fell in love with himself and swallowed the berry.

There are various versions of the story, but it is astonishing how almost every culture has some myth of paradise lost. Now, that doesn't mean it's true, but it does mean that it's in the collective unconscious, and to say that there's no truth in it at all is to be a snob. This is my fundamental argument against atheism, by the way. If atheism is true, then the incredibly small minority of human beings—most of which are concentrated in our uprooted society—are the only ones who are wise, and everyone else is living their lives with a fundamental illusion at the center, exactly like Jimmy Stewart in *Harvey*. He believes in this thirteen-foot-high, invisible rabbit, even though he's in his forties. That's a pretty grim view of humanity. It doesn't prove anything, but at least it ought to give you a bit of pause.

This universal myth that our present situation is unnatural seems to correspond to our present psychological data, that is, we all have a lover's quarrel with the world. We can't obey the advice of our pop psychologists to accept ourselves as we are and to accept the world as it is. We just can't do it, if we're human. Animals can. There is a perfect ecological relationship between the animals' instinctive desires and their environment. What they want they can get, but there is one thing we want that nobody in the world has ever gotten: complete happiness. It's our glory that we can rise to the dignity of despair. Thus, a nihilistic existentialist like Nietzsche is nobler than a nice pop psychologist. He rises to this dignity of despair.

A third and very traditional answer to why we suffer comes from the Greeks and Red Sox fans: Suffering makes us wise. To quote Rabbi Abraham Joshua Heschel: "The man who has not suffered, what could he possibly know, anyway?" Or to quote Aeschylus, "He who learns must suffer. And even in our sleep, pain that cannot forget falls drop by drop upon the heart and in our own despair, against our will, comes wisdom to us by the awful grace of the gods." If wisdom is more important than pleasure, then it's a good deal. If we're so foolish that we wouldn't voluntarily make that deal, then how wise of the gods—whoever they are—to force us to that deal. While you're suffering, you don't want to make the deal. After you're finished, you're glad.

Think of the hardest thing you ever did or the biggest pain you ever had.

> **To quote Rabbi Abraham Joshua Heschel: "The man who has not suffered, what could he possibly know, anyway?"**

Are you glad now that you have gone through that? Oh, yes! To quote Nietzsche again, "That which does not kill me makes me stronger." But, of course, while you're there, you don't think that.

Suppose you throw God into the package. What's God's answer to the problem of suffering, when he finally appears and gives Job, the archetypal sufferer, his answer? Job asks all sorts of great questions, and God doesn't answer a single one of them. He says basically—if I may summarize his great rhetoric in a few much less great words: "Hush, child, you couldn't possibly understand. Who do you think you are, anyway? I'm the Author; you're the character."

After the first shock, we realize that makes immense sense. If, in fact, we are characters in a story written by a transcendent Author, then for us to understand each syllable of this mysterious play would refute the hypothesis that there is a transcendent Author. He would no longer be transcendent. He would be us; he would be a projection of us. In other words, it's utterly rational that life be irrational.

Or to use another argument, probably the most difficult verse in the whole Bible to believe, the most astonishing claim, the one that, like Socrates's almost last words, seems ridiculously wrong, is Romans 8:28: "All things work together for good for those who love God, for those who are called according to his purpose." Come on. You've got to be kidding.

Well, wait a minute; let's deduce that from three premises—and almost anyone except an atheist will accept these three premises. Number one, God is omnipotent. If God is weak, there is no God. Number two, God is omniscient. He knows everything. If he's stupid, there's no God. Number three, God is all good. If he's wicked and cruel, he's not God. Well, if he's omniscient, he knows exactly what we need. If he's omnipotent, he can supply it, and if he's all good, he does.

Therefore, as a logical deduction from those three premises, we must need everything that we get. It certainly doesn't seem that way. Once in a while, we see with Greek wisdom how suffering produces wisdom in us, and we can look back at our lives and say, "I'm glad I went through that." But much of the time we can't say that, which is exactly what we would expect of the hypothesis that there is such a God. Far from refuting the existence of God, suffering that seems irrational and cannot be explained fits that hypothesis.

It also fits the hypothesis of atheism. Thus, you are left free to choose.

You are left to do something like Pascal's wager,* since the theoretical arguments are inconclusive. Or if you think the theoretical arguments are inconclusive, then we can use a practical argument: What can you gain, what can you lose? You can gain nothing by atheism. Maybe you're right, but once you're dead, you're dead; there is no reward. What can you gain by theism? Well, maybe you'll gain nothing, no life after death, no rewards, and no punishment. But if it's true, you gain everything and lose nothing. That's not a very high and holy argument, but it's an utterly *rational* one, as anyone knows who has ever played poker.

But let me offer three more specifically religious arguments that depend upon faith in the supernatural and in a divine revelation—one coming from faith, one from hope, and one from love.

One answer to why we suffer is basically God's answer to Job: "Trust me." It's an invitation to trust—what parents give to children: "You're a child; you can't understand, but you can love, you can trust. You don't have to, but you can. Try it; you'll like it." That's basically Jesus's first version of the Gospel— the old Alka-Seltzer commercial: "Try it; you'll like it. If not, there's Alka-Seltzer." Look at Jesus's first words in John's gospel: "Come and see." What an open-ended invitation!

Secondly, there is hope, which is faith directed toward the future. Suppose the entire universe is a very small thing, a womb. When you were in the womb, you probably thought that was the whole universe; it was enormous. Is there life after birth? Maybe so, maybe not. You found out that there was. Well, maybe that'll happen again when you die, in which case you couldn't possibly understand the meaning of suffering here. This is only the womb. When you were a little fetus, you probably said, "Why do I have feet? Why am I kicking? There are no sidewalks." But now, you know. Probably 99 percent of what we do here is preparation for the next life, which we can understand about as well as our cats and dogs can understand our life.

It's possible to believe the astonishing claim of Saint Teresa of Avila, who suffered a lot and asked God about it and got some answers. She said, "The

---

* Simply put, Pascal's wager states that if you believe God exists and he doesn't, you have nothing to lose; however, if you do not believe God exists and he does, then you have everything to lose. So, why not believe?

most horrible life on earth filled with the most atrocious sufferings will be seen from the viewpoint of heaven to be no more serious than one night in an inconvenient hotel." If that's not true, then heaven is not heaven.

Finally, the deepest answer of all—love—which is, on a human level, solidarity with the sufferers. If you really love somebody, what's the fundamental thing you want? What's the aim of love, true, complete, deep human love? Unity, intimacy, closeness. Philanthropy, which is a genuine form of love, but not the most intimate form, wants to aid and benefit the other person, including giving him or her more happiness and less unhappiness, less suffering. But if you're more than a philanthropist, if you're a lover, then if your beloved is suffering, you want to be with him or her in the suffering, because you want to be with him or her everywhere.

According to Christianity, God acted that way. When he came to earth to solve the problem of suffering, he didn't give us a technique for getting out of it; he didn't give us a philosophical or mystical explanation of it. He invited us to participate in it, because he participated in ours. I think the most moving divine answer to the problem of suffering is the shortest verse in the Bible. When Jesus's close friend Lazarus died, he went to the tomb, and the words are "Jesus wept." In the next verse, everybody says, "See how he loved him." That shows us what God thinks of our suffering.

For some strange reason, we tend to think of God as an absentee landlord, cold and indifferent, with some philosophical or mystical answer to the problem of suffering, and from afar, he says that you must go through this, but according to the Old Testament, it's not like that at all. God is intimately present in the worst sufferings.

Where was God in the Holocaust? He was in the gas chambers. He is in every little baby who suffers. He is in the victim; he identifies with the victimized and never the victimizer. That doesn't solve the philosophical problem, but it certainly solves the emotional problem. I don't see how it's possible to love a God who doesn't identify totally with human suffering, because that's not a lover.

Suppose your car is stalled in the middle of the night in bad weather and you don't know how to fix it and there's no tow truck. What you would like, above all, is to have a cell phone with you to get a taxi or to get a tow truck. You can't. Let's say the only person you can reach is your brother-in-law, who lives nearby, and he comes and he doesn't know how to fix cars either and he doesn't have a cell phone or a tow truck. So, what does he do? He stays in the car with you all night, and then in the morning you're freed.

Aren't you much more grateful to him than even to a tow truck? So, even when God doesn't immediately tow us out of our suffering, the fact that he's with us in it is at least the most impressive and satisfying answer to the problem of suffering that I know. And therefore, God doesn't give us a lot of words to answer the problem of suffering. According to Christianity, he gives us a single word, and his name is Jesus.

Even when God doesn't immediately tow us out of our suffering, the fact that he's with us in it is at least the most impressive and satisfying answer to the problem of suffering that I know.

Q & A

———

Thank you so much, Dr. Kreeft. We're now going to take some questions. We don't have any time for monologues. So, please put the question in the form of a *question*. Ahem. Anybody willing to step up to the microphone?

Q: Romans 8:28 promises that God will work "all things together" for the good. It would seem that he is saying that for believers, for those who love him and "are called according to his purpose." How should we regard suffering in the lives of people who are ostensibly good people by the world's standards but who are not believers?

A: I don't know, because we don't know who are the chosen and who are not. I don't think we can make that judgment. We don't have the faintest idea. Relatively, when the disciples ask Jesus, "Are many saved?" he says, "Strive to enter in. Mind your own business." So, we're told about our path. We're not told about anyone else's. When the travel agent tells you how to get to Florida, she doesn't tell you how to avoid the swamps in Georgia; she tells you how to go to the beaches.

Q: I don't mean to imply that we necessarily know who are saved or who are not, but we do know that there are some who are not saved. How should we regard suffering in their lives?

A: I don't think we have any data about that. I don't have an answer. We haven't been told, as far as I know. We have been told the astonishing thing that for those who love God, all things work together for good. Now, that is hard to believe. I love Thornton Wilder's novel *The Bridge of San Luis Rey* about a Franciscan priest, Brother Juniper, who is losing his faith. He is a scientist, and he asks God for some clues, just some clues. "Life is a mysterious tapestry," he says. "I don't expect to see the front side where God is weaving it, but some loose threads on the back side, they should make at least some sense."

One day he reads in a paper that a rope bridge over this gorge has parted and five young people have fallen to their untimely deaths, and he is scandalized. He says this makes no sense at all; so, he makes a scientific investigation of their lives. He interviews family members and reads diaries and collects clues, and the result of the investigation is, he thinks, he gets just enough clues to believe; so, he concludes with a memorable sentence: "Some say that to the gods we are like flies swatted idly by boys on a summer's day; others say that not a single hair ever falls from the head to the ground without the will of the heavenly father." Both are possible choices.

Q: Is it possible to be happy without having ever suffered? Or are happiness and suffering mutually exclusive?

A: How can you be really happy if you've never suffered? You are a spoiled kid; you appreciate nothing. We appreciate things only by contrast. I just came from Hawaii. There was an international conference on arts and humanity. I thought it was a real conference; there were 1,687 people who went to that conference. They all delivered papers to about two or three people, and universities paid their way. It was just a scam to get to Hawaii. I'm a surfer; Hawaii is Mecca to me. But I didn't really deep down enjoy myself. Why not?

I guess because I am a New England, puritanical, Calvinistic Red Sox fan; there is no suffering out there. Things are so perfect. I couldn't live there. I would not appreciate the summer without the winter. You have to live through this kind of winter to appreciate the summer. And if we never died, we wouldn't appreciate life.

There's a fascinating book written about twenty years ago called *The*

Immortality Factor by a Swedish journalist Osborn Segerberg Jr. He first interviewed geneticists about whether artificial immortality was theoretically possible, and most of them said, "Yes," and that it will come in two hundred to three hundred years. Most scientific predictions, by the way, are much too long. It will probably come much earlier than that. That's another story. Then he looked at the old myths about immortality and the science fiction stories. Both the old myths and the modern science fiction stories—such as the myth of Thesonius the Greek or the Wandering Jew or the Flying Dutchman or the book *Tuck Everlasting* or *Childhood's End* by Arthur C. Clarke—almost all said this would be horrible, the worst thing conceivable. Without death, life becomes meaningless.

Then, Segerberg went to the psychologists and asked what would happen. Most of them said, "Oh, this would be wonderful—the end of suffering, the end of fear. We would have utopia on earth." He concluded that the myths were perhaps wiser than the psychologists. So, I guess we need suffering, because we're very stupid, and if you're very stupid, you have to have your nose rubbed in something, since you will appreciate something only by its contrast. I'm continually impressed by how stupid I am.

One of the most unpopular doctrines of Christianity is the doctrine of Original Sin. I have no difficulty at all believing that, because I know from my own experience that whenever I sin, I suffer, but I keep sinning. I wake up in the morning, and I get assaulted by a thousand little soldiers sticking pins into my brain and saying, "Think about this, think about this; worry about this, worry about this." If I kill them ruthlessly and give God a little bit of time in the morning, I'm happy, and everything happens well in the day. And if I don't, it doesn't. If I don't do it, I'm insane! We all are. So, we need to be slapped around a bit, I guess.

Q: I would love to hear your thoughts on reconciliation and the idea of suffering in the mind of somebody who believes he or she is unforgiven as the cause of suffering.

A: You would have to address their problem, which is the belief that there is something that is unforgiven. If God is totally good, he is not Scrooge. He does not forgive some things; he forgives all things. The only possible sin that cannot be forgiven is not accepting forgiveness, which is why in traditional Christian theology, pride is the worst of sins: "I am too good to be forgiven; there is nothing to forgive."

Q: Follow-up question: I mean unforgiven by another person, who has caused suffering.

A: Oh, that is a very serious problem. Yes, I suppose the only refuge there would be is the belief that since God forgives them, they have to forgive themselves. In other words, it can't be just a horizontal thing, because that is blocked very often. But if both the horizontal members are connected vertically, then in a way that I don't think we usually understand, there can be a reconciliation that we don't usually see. That is rather mystical, I guess. I think that works even in time. Since God is eternal, he can change the past. But we can't see that, because we are in time.

Q: You mentioned Aquinas, and, as I recall, he was a very practical Aristotelian type of thinker. How would you compare his views that you gave tonight with Augustine, who always appeared to be more Socratic? How would you compare their two views on faith, hope, and love, and, in particular, on suffering?

A: In his encyclical *Fides et Ratio* (*Faith and Reason*), Pope John Paul II speaks of faith and reason as the two wings of the dove—the human soul. I would say that within the intellect, Augustine and Aquinas are the two wings. Augustine is a wonderfully passionate thinker. There is nothing like *The Confessions*—a heart and a mind working at fever pitch together. I love the medieval statuary of Augustine. It always shows him with an open book in one hand and a burning heart in the other.

Aquinas, on the other hand, is a perfectly clear light, a perfect scientist. Augustine, you might say, is a mole burrowing through the deep mysteries, whereas Aquinas is the eagle soaring over it all, making a map. Together, they give you a great picture. Aquinas's answer to that problem that he formulates, by the way, is wonderfully Augustinian in the sense that it is dramatic. It is not just an abstract philosophical concept. The problem is, how can there be

God if there is evil? If one of two contraries is infinite, the other is destroyed. God is infinite goodness; if there were God, there would be no evil. There is evil; so, therefore, there is no God.

His answer—and he gets it from Augustine, who says that God would not allow any evil; God doesn't do it, but he allows it through human free will. God would not allow any evil, unless his wisdom and power were such as to bring out of it an even greater good. The fairy-tale answer. We are not yet in the happily-ever-after; we are struggling toward it.

Q: I think that one of the most difficult problems that many of us have in dealing with the problems of suffering is not how we deal with them individually, but how other people deal with suffering, as we perceive it. At the end of the movie that is now certainly drawing an awful lot of comment, *The Hours*, one of the lead characters describes her choice that has to do with leaving her children with a very familiar phrase. Of course, in the movie you never really understand that she's having a problem with this child; it's revealed only at the end. The movie is about suicide, if you haven't seen it. That is not the ending, which is much more dramatic; this is just a piece of it.

She says, "I chose to leave because I chose life." Now, that is not ordinarily the application of that phrase—that a mother would leave her children in order to choose life. There really is a whole lot more to the film, if you haven't seen it. I was just absolutely struck by the application of that phrase to what, to me, on the surface of it would be someone struggling to overcome evil as a very bad choice.

A: I think it's a fake. I haven't seen the movie, but her mistake is that she is thinking only about her own life. Life is like a tree, and it has many branches, many leaves, many roots. It is one. The idea of human solidarity, both in sin and in suffering, is rather hard for us uprooted, overly self-conscious individualists to understand, but almost any ancient people understood it better than we do. You can't really be happy and fulfilled and alive without those to whom you are deeply connected being the same.

Q: I see you wrote a book on Socrates and Jesus. In First Corinthians, the Apostle Paul says, "We preach Christ crucified . . . foolishness to the Gentiles." Apparently, Paul had some experience of talking to the Greeks, and as he talked to them, they said, "You are a fool." Now, what is it about Greek thinking that makes Paul a fool in their eyes?

A: Most people are fools. The percentage of non-fools is very small everywhere. I believe Paul wrote that epistle to the Corinthians after he had visited Athens. In Acts 17, he goes to Mars Hill, where Socrates actually philosophized, and addressed the philosophers. They said, "What is this strange saying?" Now he has the opportunity to talk to philosophers. Athens and Jerusalem are coming together.

I have never been to Athens, but I have been told that Mars Hill is at the top of a long road called "the Way of the Gods." There were statues to all of the gods, not just Greek gods, but gods of many other cultures, because people would come to Athens from many places and make sacrifices to their many gods. Paul refers to them in the first part of his sermon to the Athenians, when he says that, as he was walking up this road, he noticed that they are "very religious." That is sarcastic, because before that, he said that his heart burned within him, because of the idolatry. You would expect he is going to say something similar to what he had said to the Corinthians: "What fools you are." Astonishingly, instead, he says, "But one of these inscriptions I noticed was dedicated to an unknown God."

Socrates was, in fact, a stonecutter, and there were two kinds of stonemasons in ancient Greece. One just cut altars and letters, which was easy. Then there were the sculptors who had to do rounded human figures, and not too many people could do that. If you could do that, you got rich, but Socrates was very poor. So, Socrates cut things like altarpieces and inscriptions. As you know, if you read any of Socrates, you know that he worshipped the unknown God. He would not name this God, and he lost his life, because he couldn't name him Zeus or Apollo or any of the gods of the state. So, it may be that Socrates literally cut this very altarpiece that Paul refers to: *To the unknown God.*

What does Paul say about it? "The God that you are already worshipping ignorantly, I will now declare to you." I think that's the other side of the foolishness. Yes, there is Greek foolishness. Socrates is not a fool, because he knows that he is a fool. He will not name the God he knows he doesn't know. He is searching—and according to rather high authority, those who seek find. I would be very surprised not to find Socrates in heaven.

Q: I think that the apostle Paul ends First Corinthians, chapter 1, by saying, "of him we are in Christ Jesus," that is, it is God's choice who goes to heaven.

A: And it is also ours; it is not exclusive.

Q: That is true.

A: That is a paradox of predestination and free will, both of which are very clearly taught. That is the paradox of every great novel. Show me one novel without predestination by the author; show me one novel without free will by the characters.

Q: Well, I don't understand. It seems to me that you are involved in a self-contradiction. On the one hand, you are saying that Socrates is in heaven. On the other hand, the apostle Paul says that the debaters of this age did not know God. Now, are you saying that people who do not know God are going to heaven?

A: No, but I don't think Socrates is one of those people. I don't think he was a mere debater. He was a seeker.

Q: Paul does say the Greeks have called him a fool.

A: *The Greeks* is a vague term, like *the Jews*. To stereotype a whole people or a whole race is silly.

Q: I guess to make it a long story short, I would think you would have to introduce the question of regeneration.

A: Yes, but my very conservative and traditional belief that Jesus is not just a human being but the *Logos*, the eternal second person of the Trinity, justifies my rather liberal expectation that a lot of non-Christians will be in heaven. That is because John says in his gospel, chapter 1, verse 9, the *Logos* enlightens everyone who comes into the world. So, even though Jesus is the universal savior, you don't have to know him in his thirty-three-year-old, six-foot-high,

Jewish-carpenter body. There are other ways to know him, and maybe Socrates did.

Q: I wish I could agree with you, but I don't.

A: All right, some other day.

The Scripture said, "Jacob I loved, and Esau I hated." How do you defend to someone how a good and loving God can hate?

Q: My question has to do with the nature of God. The Scripture said, "Jacob I loved, and Esau I hated." How do you defend to someone how a good and loving God can hate?

A: I don't know Hebrew, but I would bet on the fact that the word *hate* there means the same thing that the Greek word for *hate* means in one of Jesus's strange sayings: "Unless you hate your father and your mother, you cannot be my disciple." *Hate* means "turn your back on, when necessary"—put second, rather than first.

So, it's not that God was burning with hatred for Esau, because Esau didn't exist yet. This is talking about predestination. Before they were even born, God said, "Esau is going to be the villain; Jacob is going to be the hero," like a novelist. That doesn't mean they don't have free will. The novelist gives them the free will to choose heroism or villainy, but he knows what they're going to choose.

Q: First of all, thank you for sharing your wisdom with us. Once, in a philosophy class, I heard the statement that evil is not part of creation but is the absence of good or goodness. I was wondering, first of all, if you could expand on that, and secondly, could you give me some background on where it originated, stated in that concrete manner?

A: That is probably referring to a great discovery Augustine made. He talks about it in *The Confessions*. He couldn't solve the problem of evil, so he became a Manichean for eleven years. The Manicheans believed that evil; is explained by the fact that there is an evil God and a good God and that they are equal and fighting and nobody is winning forever. The evil God made matter, and the good God wants to liberate you from matter into spirituality.

Augustine never felt right about Manicheism. He was always looking for a better answer, and he finally got one—the realization that since God is totally good and that since everything that exists and is made of matter is a creature of God, therefore, all matter is good—*Ens est bonum*, "Being as such is good."

Then, what is evil? Evil is not a thing; it is not stuff. It is neither God nor creature. It is not a being in that sense; it is nonbeing, but that doesn't mean it doesn't exist. It doesn't mean that it is not real. Blindness is not a third eye, and blindness is not a cataract that causes it. Blindness is the absence of a good thing—sight. Not just absence but privation. This microphone doesn't have sight, but that is not evil for it; it's not supposed to. But a person's eye is supposed to have it. So, the privation of good being in something that it is supposed to have is the answer to "What kind of stuff does evil have?" and "What is the metaphysics of evil—the being of evil?" That is the answer to an abstract question. It is not the answer to a concrete question, such as "Is evil real for me?" And "How does it appear in my life?" is a different question entirely. So, it is very important to keep those two unconfused. Otherwise, Augustine sounds like a cockeyed optimist: "Oh, evil isn't real; don't worry about it." He was *deeply* sensitive to it.

Q: My question is in two parts. The first one is this. James said, "[C]ount it all joy when you [fall into] divers temptation, knowing [this], that the trying of your faith worketh patience" [James 1:2–3, King James Version]. How do we look at and rationalize every attempt by man to eliminate human suffering, knowing that suffering is part of what life is all about? The second part of the question is this: Since we know that suffering is not something that man actually created in himself, should we believe that, instead of helplessness, the Lord is trying to alleviate these problems?

A: The practical answer to that question is very clear. Certainly, if you're a Christian, you believe that Jesus healed people from diseases and sufferings. He had great compassion and pity on suffering. He was completely human and showed us not just who God was but who the ideal man was. So, the Stoic attitude of indifference to suffering or the withdrawn attitude or even the Buddhist attitude of rising above it by being insensitive to it by transforming your consciousness, that is definitely not the Christian answer to suffering.

But your first question is a deep paradox. On the one hand, suffering is blessed. Count it as a joy when you go through manifold tribulations. On the other hand, we are supposed to relieve it—like poverty. Blessed are the poor— and yet the relief of poverty is one of the commandments of Christianity. Death, which is the fishnet that catches all the fish of poverty and every other suffering in itself, is the worst thing. It is the last enemy. Jesus comes to conquer it through resurrection.

On the other hand, death is glorious. There is an old oratorio that has this hauntingly beautiful line: *"Thou hast made death glorious and triumphant, for through its portals we enter into the presence of the living God."* Somehow or other, in this strange drama, the worst things are used as the best things. Even morally, the worst sin ever committed, the most horrible atrocity ever perpetrated in the history of the world, was the murder of God's Son, and Christians celebrate this as *Good* Friday and the cause of their salvation. It is very strange—like life.

Q: I have two questions that maybe you can expound on a little bit. The first is, isn't there a difference between suffering and evil? And the second is, wouldn't it be the case that evil is either the opinion of an infinite, perfect God or just every individual's random opinion in that without God evil can't really exist, and if somebody speaks of evil, it has to be in the context of an almighty and perfect God?

A: On the first question, you are clearer than I was. I accept your correction. On the second question, I am clearer than you were, and I hope you accept my correction. First of all, I have been talking so much about suffering that I virtually identified it with evil, and that is a mistake. There is the evil that you do, and there is the evil that you suffer. The evil that you do is much worse.

The evil that you do is, broadly speaking, sin. That is evil to your self, your character, your soul. Suffering is just evil to your body; that is the distinction Socrates played on when he said, "No evil can happen to a good man." But on the other question, evil is not an opinion. Evil is not a point of view;

evil is not psychological perspective. Evil is real; it is not a thing, but it is real. We can make mistakes about it. We argue about it. The fact that everybody argues about good and evil—"That's good." "No, it is evil"—means that we act as if we believe that evil is objectively real and not just a matter of opinion. We don't argue about mere opinions. We can, but not really. I love the Red Sox; you love the Yankees. We don't argue about that. We argue about facts. Will the Red Sox ever win a single World Series until the end of the world? We who are wise know the answer is "No, they're under a curse." Those who are not wise might say, "Yes."

So, what is true and false has to have reference to an objective truth. But a mere opinion or point of view is not just true and false. Evil is not just a point of view; evil is not subjective. If you believe that evil is a subjective point of view, well, I don't think most New Yorkers believe that anymore after 9/11. In the babble of voices that we heard after that horrendous event, one voice was conspicuously silent: *psychobabble*.

Q: I want to come at you from a ruthlessly pragmatic angle, being a New Yorker.

A: Wonderful.

Q: Pascal's bet works for me, except—and this is something Pascal addressed—he said that living by faith will not damage your life; you will live a better life. You will practice the virtues, and in the end you will have a happier life. Therefore, it is not really such a risk. But what about Ignatius and his three degrees of humility? The first degree is the willingness to renounce mortal sin for the sake of salvation. The second one is an indifference toward suffering and having a happy life or sad life, long life or short life, so long as you are doing the will of God. I am getting queasy here. The third level of humility is to actively prefer a short, unhappy life because it is more similar to Jesus's life on earth. Now, it seems to me that if your faith actually entails the third degree of humility, Pascal's bet ceases to make sense. This is something that has been vexing me for years so I would really appreciate your response.

A: I think Pascal would say that the bet still works in the long run, even if you are up to this third level. That means that in the long run, that is, in heaven, you will have more joy. You have hollowed out your soul by these ascetic exercises so much that you can see, appreciate, and enjoy more of God than others can. So, it is worth it, even in the long run.

Q: It is worth it even on earth?

A: Yes, even on earth, because the saints are terribly happy. The two groups of people that haunt my memory and stand out as incredibly happy, truly happy, deeply happy, are the two most ascetical groups that I know. One is a group of Carmelite nuns in Danvers, Massachusetts, who live in almost perpetual silence. I was asked to give a talk to them; they gave a talk to me by their silence. And most of all, Mother Teresa's Missionaries of Charity. They have a house in Roxbury, which is the worst slum of Boston, and they pick up the pieces of the worst neighborhood, with the worst families, and they just do what they can. I was asked to give a talk to them, and they were just radiantly happy. They get up at four A.M., they each have one piece of clothing and almost no private property, and they eat very simply. They are radiantly happy. It works.

> The saints are terribly happy. The two groups of people that haunt my memory and stand out as incredibly happy, truly happy, deeply happy, are the two most ascetical groups that I know.

Q: I have a question I would like to limit to evil, rather than suffering. You mentioned that in the Bible, God doesn't give us a reason for the existence of evil. He didn't give Job a reason; he doesn't give us a reason for his reason. In your tremendous study and the amount of thought that you have put toward the subject, have you personally found an answer for this, and if so, where? And if not, does that lead you somewhere else?

A: Let me just give you a partial answer to that question. As a philosopher, I was always bothered by the book of Job. I knew it was a classic—I *felt* it was a classic—but I was bothered by the fact that God didn't answer any of Job's questions. I said, "Yes, God has the right to do that, but I don't like that." Job cops out too easily: "Yes, God, anything you say." I don't like slimy, pious worms who say, "Okay, anything, step on me." I guess I'm too much of a New Yorker, and Job is such a New Yorker—until the end. He shakes his fist in God's face and says, "You bloody butcher, how can you get away with this? I demand some explanations." That is kind of impious maybe, but we can identify with that. Then, at the end, what a disappointment—all of these great questions are not answered.

So, I said that is a failure of dramatic art. The character of Job changes too quickly in the end. The author of the book of Job, I thought, did to Job what Peter Jackson, the director of the movie, did to Faramir in *The Two Towers*—which is inexcusable.* He is a hero, not a villain. However, reading Martin Buber—I think it was *I and Thou*—convinced me that I was utterly wrong. Buber is commenting on God's pronouncement of judgment at the end of Job; the three friends of Job, who are perfectly orthodox theologians, say, in tedious repetition, "God is great and God is good, let us thank him for our food. Amen." They utter no heresy, yet they are condemned.

Job, on the other hand, who flirts with heresy and blasphemy—"God, you are an arbitrary despot. I hate you. Get off my back"—is approved. God says—I think the words are "I am angry at you and your three friends. . . ." He blames "Bildad the Shuhite," the smallest man in the Bible, "for not speaking rightly about me, as my servant Job has." But they had spoken perfectly rightly about God, and Job had spoken wrongly.

"Wrong," says Buber. Since God is the Thou who can only be addressed and not expressed and since God's divinely revealed name is *I Am*, not *It Is*, therefore, Job, who talks to God, pleases God, unlike the three friends, who never talk to God, never pray, and never talk about him and thus do not please God.

I said, "That's right." Suppose I was teaching a class, and two of my students interrupted my lecture by breaking out into loud, animated conversation about the professor: "Do you think Professor Kreeft is crazy?" "No." "Yes, he is." "No, he isn't."

---

* This is a reference to the deviation from the original Tolkien plot in which Faramir realizes that the ring is a thing of evil and should not be used. Thus, he is not tempted to hold on to the ring but sends Frodo, Sam, and Gollum on their way. Peter Jackson has Faramir bring them to Gondor and only later release them.

"Wait a minute!" I would say. "Hello, I'm here." I wouldn't be offended that they thought I was crazy. That is quite reasonable, but not that you would talk about me in front of me without realizing that I'm here. Well, that's what we're doing to God all the time.

"God this, God that." "Hi, troops, I am here. Why aren't you talking to me?" Talking—that's what Job did. That's what God wants. I think that is very profound.

Q: Are you saying that you think evil exists or possibly exists so that we will pay better attention to God, so that we will engage God?

A: We are such fools that I have to admit that's true. C. S. Lewis puts it this way in *The Problem of Pain*: "God whispers to us in our pleasures, but shouts to us in our pains." It is this megaphone that rouses a deaf world.

Q: If you accept a theistic framework, is asking, "Why?" tantamount to a lack of trust in God's sovereignty?

A: Just the opposite.

Q: To make it practical, to give an example, one that I have wrestled with, is Eric Liddell. Eric Liddell, as you know from *Chariots of Fire*, ran and won the Olympic gold, and then what most people forget is that afterward, he left and went to Shantung Compound, which is the title of another great book by Gilkey. He suffered and died there. So, overlaying your framework of suffering on top of that, is all we are left with that God will have a greater purpose or is there another answer to that question?

A: If you weren't deeply connected with God, you wouldn't be asking him, "Why?" If you had left him, there would be no concern. The question "Why?" if asked from the heart, presupposes a relationship. It wants to add reason to faith. There is some faith there—faith, not just as thought but as personal trust. Then, that faith is ignorant. Since it is accompanied by love, it wants to know more. We want to know more about him; so we keep asking God, "Why this and why that?" That is very good. Jesus never once discouraged that kind of question. That is just intellectual honesty.

Q: Coming from the seat of Northern philosophy in Boston, can you give us New Yorkers, who experienced 9/11, some philosophical reference and reflection?

A: Can you be more specific so that I can be?

Q: Many people have lost a chance of hope. Many people have found a chance of hope, and many are still looking for that chance of hope.

A: I think great good and great evil, great pleasure and great pain, always give us a choice. We can be more wise and hopeful and good in the presence of either one, or we can be less. Let's first take great good. A wonderful thing happens, and we can say, "Oh, now I can relax; everything is all right; no more questions." No, no, no, a wonderful thing happens: "Where did this come from? Thanks be to God. Wow. This is a message from heaven." It is a pointing finger that points beyond itself.

> I think great good and great evil, great pleasure and great pain, always give us a choice. We can be more wise and hopeful and good in the presence of either one, or we can be less.

Similarly with evil. Evil just happens. I have a picture on my office wall; maybe some of you have seen it. It's about something that happened, I think, toward the end of the nineteenth century in Paris. There is a two-story railroad station, and a locomotive plunged through the second story and fell down into the street, and there it is at an angle. A great, big steam locomotive and a single word on it—*shit*. That is not blasphemous; it is only obscene. It is an offense against good taste but not against good religion. That is one answer to evil, and that is counterproductive. It doesn't do any good. But, on the other hand, what happened on 9/11 is evil. It shows me that evil is real. I am now wise. It shows me that I must have solidarity with my brothers and sisters in fighting it. So, I become more courageous.

The response in uniting New York and America, and even the world, certainly did an enormous amount of good. I won't say it did more good than the thousands of lives that were snuffed out, but evil always rebounds. Evil always has some good fruit. I think of God as something like a French chef who uses decayed vegetables to flavor foods wonderfully. The evil always has some good purpose.

Q: I have a question about evil and suffering and the difficulty of taking a perspective on it in a culture that's gripped with fear—which I see America as being at present. Do you think that could at all skew a perspective that you might take on evil and suffering? In other words, to the extent that you might even gather together in a really nice place like this and start talking about it as if it were something definitely real, as opposed to what somebody else might say it has been. The undercurrent of what I am asking is, is there a concern that there is an exclusion of a nontheistic perspective, of a nonphilosophical perspective? A perspective that takes into account psychological data, which I noticed you kind of pooh-poohed.

A: Not data; don't fault the data. The theories.

Q: There is a lot of data and support of the contention that reminders of mortality actually lead to strengthening of bonding to cultural worldviews, for instance. So, do you think that there is some degree of relativity, and do you think that your view is colored by your worldview and your biases and perhaps even by your own development?

A: Of course it is.

Q: I am just wondering if you see how that colors your perspective on suffering.

A: That's what a worldview is. A worldview isn't a factual detail. It's a picture of the whole. It's a map that puts the details in a certain order, and everybody has one. Nobody can avoid one, even those who oppose worldviews. That is itself a worldview.

Q: So, how does that affect your perspective on suffering and evil?

A: It gives me light. It's a flashlight. The data are the same. You and I both know the data. We interpret the why. There are two different reasons why two different people interpret the same data very differently.

One of them comes from the person—your character, your personality, your proclivities, your fears, your desires, your opinions. The other might come from objective truth. There might be a light that shines in one mind and not the other. Or, more likely, a light that shines in both minds, but differently, so that you see something that is really there that I don't, and I see something that is really there and you don't.

For instance, let's say that I, as a typical theist, would say, "Death is great, because it leads to heaven." I am omitting a whole lot. Death is an atrocity. Death is an enemy before it is a friend. It can be a friend, even if there is no life after death, because life on earth forever without death would be like eggs going rotten. I might not see that as someone who doesn't believe in life after death does see it. So, since I am sensitive to that data, I have to listen more to you.

Q: So, you are still looking at forever; maybe there is just forever.

A: Yes. We all have to be open to all the data we can, but it seems to me that we have to be looking for *truth*, not just comparing opinions. Comparing opinions is just sort of internal mental masturbation—playing with opinions.

Q: Maybe it's all we have.

A: If that is all we have, then we are like those two people in the *New Yorker* cartoon some years ago on a desert island, starving. A message in the bottle comes. There is hope. They open the message, they read it, and their faces fall. The caption says, "It's only from us."

Q: It may be Harvey; it may be Harvey.

A: Well, if it is Harvey, we are in for it, but at least you can still make a Pascal's wager. There is no conclusive case that it is only Harvey. So, if both options are equally intellectually respectable, what would you gain by the despair and the emptiness by opting for it? At least Pascal's wager makes sense, doesn't it?

Q: I don't look at things only in terms of loss and gain.

A: No, neither do I. That comes second. The most important question is truth. If you would give me a tremendous psychological gain, an immense amount of happiness at the expense of truth or an immense amount of truth at the expense of happiness, that would be a hard choice. But I would, at least, want to choose truth, rather than happiness.

William James divided all minds into the tender-minded and the tough-minded. The tender-minded seek happiness and ideals and comfort and integration and all that sort of thing. The tough-minded seek facts. He said that a tough-minded person and a tender-minded person can't understand each other and can't really have an argument. I think he's a little wrong there, because deep down, I think we're all tough-minded. For instance, this is a wonderful place, but does anybody really think this is heaven and that I'm God? If you thought that this was heaven and I was God and this was the beatific vision, would you be happy? If happiness is all you want, why would you believe that, because we know that it is not true, stupid. See, truth trumps happiness. So, one, truth; two, happiness.

Q: I wonder if you might briefly contrast Kierkegaard's balancing act of faith with nature's nihilistic will to power.

A: In twenty-five words or less, Kierkegaard's faith is not a balancing act; it is a leap—a definite commitment with all of his heart, but in a lot of darkness. Nietzsche made the opposite leap. He said, "I will now disprove the existence of all gods. If there were gods, how could I bear not to be a god? Consequently, there are no gods." That is faith, but it is the opposite faith. It makes no sense. It is Lucifer's faith—"Better to reign in hell than serve in heaven." I think when Nietzsche goes into hell, he will sing the words from Sinatra's song "I did it my way."

Q: Maybe I just misunderstood you. You are talking about the whole idea of either the result of evil or the result of suffering producing something good.

I have also heard this philosophy called the Fortunate Fall—that it is a good thing that Adam and Eve sinned, because then God could send his Son. But that doesn't seem to make sense. You also might have said something answering that other question about when you referenced death. I am just really confused.

A: If it is fortunate or good, then why not do it? If God brings good out of evil, then why not supply him with a lot of evil, because we're not the General and we're not advising the General. We are foot soldiers, and we have been given our marching orders. There is good, and there is evil. There is right, and there is wrong. Fight for the right and against the wrong. We're also given little clues about the general strategy. God says, "Even when you do wrong, I can make good out of it." That's dangerous. It's wonderful, but it's dangerous and can't substitute for the first thing. We know very clearly our marching orders. So, let's go out and do them.

The Importance
of Fatherhood

PAUL VITZ

March 25, 2004

Introduction

Good evening, I am Eric Metaxas, and welcome to Socrates in the City, the thinking person's alternative to standing in front of Trump Tower and having your picture taken.

By the way, in passing, I want to publicly thank Donald Trump for adding to the aesthetic value of Fifth Avenue with that fabulous banner. It's so charming that it really is almost Dickensian. It's just wonderful to have somebody scowling at you from a building, isn't it?*

Anyway, it is a pleasure to be here tonight and to see all of you. As many of you already know, the idea behind these Socrates in the City events comes from Socrates's famous maxim that the "unexamined life is not worth living." It follows logically that the unexamined maxim is not worth remembering. So, I think the fact that this Socratic maxim has been remembered for lo, these twenty-five centuries means that it has been examined and been worth remembering, although I am not sure if that is true, because I really can't remember.

Anyway, our thesis here at Socrates in the City is that the illustrious inhabitants of our fair city—that's us—are less likely to lead examined lives

---

* A massive advertising banner for *The Apprentice* starring Donald Trump hung from the Trump building located just across Fifth Avenue from the University Club, at which this event was held.

than people in other parts of the world, principally because we New Yorkers are very, very good at distracting ourselves with high-flying careers and low-flying entertainments. I am not certain that this is true. I have no data, but it is a thesis. And I will be sticking with this for the remainder of the evening. So, please humor me.

In any case, over the last five years, we have scoured the known world for brilliant thinkers who have led particularly examined lives so that they might share the benefit of their examinations with us here in our unexamined burg, as it were. Of course, we inevitably have had to look far beyond New York City for these thinkers—the thesis again being that New Yorkers are, by definition, too successful and too distracted and too ambitious to ever attain the level of self-examination and philosophical brilliance necessary to address one of these august gatherings we like to call Socrates in the City.

Here at Socrates, we have had speakers from everywhere but New York. We have had speakers from Boston, actually three: Dr. Armand Nicholi, who spoke on C. S. Lewis and Sigmund Freud and teaches at the Harvard Medical School; Dr. Thomas Howard on *Chance or the Dance?*, from Saint John's Seminary in Boston; and the illustrious Dr. Peter Kreeft, who is a philosophy professor at Boston College. So, three from Boston, none from New York. We have had three speakers from the Washington, DC, area: David Aikman, the journalist and former senior editor at *Time*; we had Frederica Mathewes-Green just a couple of months ago; and of course, we have had Os Guinness, who has spoken at something like eight Socrates events now. That is a world record, I believe—a Guinness world record.

We have had speakers from Boston, speakers from Washington, DC, and we even have had a speaker come to us from merry olde England, and not just an Englishman but a bona fide Knight of the British Empire, Sir John Polkinghorne. But as I say, we have never looked to our own here in Gotham for a Socrates speaker. Until tonight, my friends.

The presumption had been, as I said, that there simply did not exist a New Yorker of such brilliance and erudition and self-examination as to warrant an invitation to our happy convocation.

So, that was my presumption, and, dare I say, the presumption of more folks than would care to admit. Some of them are perhaps in this very room.

But on behalf of all those whose presumption that was, let me tonight say that in the person of Dr. Paul Vitz, we present our admission of error and our most profound apologies. That's right. Horrid as it is to fathom, Dr. Paul Vitz is that extraordinarily rare New Yorker who is able to live, indeed thrive, amidst the inescapable din and the infinite enticements of this great city—and yet to be a self-examined soul.

And for this, my fellow New Yorkers, I think he deserves some kind of prize. Unfortunately, we have no prizes to give away tonight, save one, that being an attentive audience, which is to say, all of you. Yes, you, ladies and gentlemen, are that prize of which I speak. Doesn't that make you feel good? Perhaps it just makes you feel cheap. In any case, that is the situation.

So, now, a word of introduction about our indigenous speaker, Dr. Paul Vitz. Dr. Vitz lives right here in the belly of the unexamined beast that is New York City. He is a professor of psychology at New York University, which is also located in that self-same unexamined beast's belly. Dr. Vitz is a senior scholar at the Institute for the Psychological Sciences, and he is the author of hundreds of articles and several books, among them *Psychology as Religion: The Cult of Self-Worship*; *Faith of the Fatherless: The Psychology of Atheism*—he will be touching on that thesis today, among other things; *Sigmund Freud's Christian Unconscious*; and others. Most of these books are available at our book table at a reasonable discount, and I am sure Dr. Vitz will be happy to autograph them for you, if you ask nicely.

Dr. Vitz lives here in New York, in Greenwich Village, with his wife, who is a professor of French, also at New York University. They have six children, and I would assume that this alone gives Dr. Vitz all the credentials he needs to say something worth hearing on the subject of fatherhood.

Fatherhood is one of those subjects that seems, at least in my lifetime anyway, to be somewhat neglected. We hear a lot about motherhood these days, but fatherhood seems somehow to have gone, shall we say, out of vogue. The happy images that we would get of fatherhood from such past movies as *Life with Father* and such TV series as *Father Knows Best* and *Leave It to Beaver*, however unrealistic they might have been, nonetheless had their fingers on the idealized essence of fatherhood, and I think it is safe to say those images could be reassuring in a good way.

But the four-decade backlash against these images sometimes gives us a contemporary view of fatherhood that, on the fictional side, would be Al Bundy and Homer Simpson and on the nonfictional side would give us something like, for example, Michael Jackson hanging Junior over a balcony at a fancy high-rise hotel—not exactly the kind of thing that Andy Griffith or Robert Young would have done. They certainly would not have made their children wear masks.*

But, in any case, things have changed. I think some of these changes make me long for what Dr. Vitz has to say on the subject of fatherhood, whatever that will be.

And now, ladies and gentlemen, Dr. Paul Vitz.

---

* The late pop star and singer Michael Jackson was in the habit of appearing in public with his children wearing masks, and in 2002 he famously shocked his fans when he impulsively dangled his infant son, Prince, from the fourth-floor balcony of the high-rise Hotel Adlon in Berlin, Germany.

Talk

—————

Trust New York to come up with an introduction like that. I mean, really. It is true I'm a New Yorker. I've lived in the City now for almost forty years, and whether I'm up to all those adjectives, that's another thing for you to judge later. I'm not so sure, but I hope to hold up Manhattan in this list of speakers.

It's not just a pleasure to be here, but it's also a challenge. I don't think I've ever addressed an audience of the kind you were described as, and it looks like you really are. I met some of you beforehand. You come from different countries. Some of you have very odd names; some of you have very familiar names. But I expect that there is a little bit of the world here tonight, not just New York in a parochial sense.

What I'm going to talk about is the general theme of fatherhood. I think that I can show, with a few comments and analysis, that the crisis of our culture today is in important respects a crisis in the family. But at the center of the crisis in the family is a crisis in what it is to be a father. We've lost this understanding of the capstone, in my judgment, of what it is to be a man, because I think all men are called to be fathers. Now, I don't necessarily mean they are called to be biological fathers. I mean that

> **At the center of the crisis in the family is a crisis in what it is to be a father. We've lost this understanding of the capstone, in my judgment, of what it is to be a man.**

they're called to be fathers to at least some of the younger people in their life.

But I want to introduce this with a remark from the ancient Hebrew Scriptures where they say that "the sins of the fathers" go on for generations, sometimes for three or perhaps for seven. It is interesting that they only speak, so far as I know, about the sins of the fathers being perpetuated onto their children.

Now, I don't want to suggest that mothers aren't capable of sinning or of not being good mothers. But there is something very profoundly true about the scriptural observation. First of all, I think mothers are much more reliable at being mothers than fathers are at being fathers. There are many, many more "good enough" mothers, relatively speaking. So they're less likely, I think, to be causing damage to their children. I know there are exceptions. After all, I've been an active therapist for years, and I certainly know people who have had serious trouble with their mothers. But in general, mothers are much more reliable at being mothers than fathers are at being fathers. Second, if a mother is not reliable, usually it shows up very soon when the child is young, and other women who observe it—the grandmother, the sister—step in and help out. You find substitute mothers and foster mothers coming in quickly, if the mother is one of those who are truly unsatisfactory.

And finally, there's another reason why these comments from the Jewish Scriptures are correct, and that is, if the mother really fails and there's nobody else to pick it up—if mothering fails—the children are so damaged that they can't pass their sins on to anybody, that is, they're not out there functioning. They may be withdrawn, they may be in a mental institution, and they may be so frightened or anxious that as members of society, they simply fail. Or let's say that the children got into some socially destructive mode, when they got a little bit older. So, in a certain sense, the sins of the mother are much less likely—even if they do occur—to be passed on to subsequent generations.

And so, they speak of the sins of the fathers, and what happens is something like this: The child has a good enough mother, and then the father comes along and fails in some substantial way; perhaps he's an alcoholic, or he abandons them and runs off with another woman. In fact, one of the tragic ways in which a father can fail when the child is young is simply to die, and the child feels abandoned. Young children don't understand death as an accident; they just feel purposely abandoned. There are ways to overcome this to some degree, but for some of the people we will look at, their failed father was a dead father—a dead father who was not later replaced in any way by a new substitute father.

What is the father's major function? I'll talk about some of the data later, but the father is a kind of Mr. Outside, while the mother is Mrs. Inside. She forms the basic character, the emotional life, the interpersonal responsiveness of the child, much more than the father. But the father introduces the child much more often to the outside world. The father symbolizes the structure of that world, of law and order, of the activities, of the things that you get involved in when you leave the home.

What happens when the child is functioning okay because of having a good enough mother but has a bad father? Very often, the child will get out into that world and cause a lot of trouble, because the father hasn't been there. In fact, in social science, probably the most reliably documented piece of evidence is the effect of bad fathering on children; we can see it in various pathological indices. It's unbelievable that this information has been around for over fifty years in extremely substantial ways, but it continues to get little attention.

Let me mention in summary what some of these indices are: Researchers have found that the father makes major contributions to the child's development, especially to individual identity and social identity. The father helps the child to separate psychologically from the mother, teaches the child much more to control its impulses, especially in the case of small boys and older boys as well. The father serves as a buffer from the mother's attention and keeps the child from being overly emotionally bound to the mother. "This often happens when the mother really has no one else to get involved with, because the father has abandoned her. The father is very instrumental in the development of the intellectual life and the outside activities of the children and in their respect for the outside world in terms of law and order."

The most common finding is the tendency to criminality in boys and young men who didn't have fathers. It's so common that it's a cliché. We see it over and over again. Our prisons are filled with young men who didn't have functioning fathers. This is a common response to a lack of discipline and fathering. These young men also lack an understanding of the outside world and often have a kind of incompetence in dealing with it that leads to anger and a rage, and it shows. They often run into a bunch of other young men like themselves, and pretty soon you've got a gang with all of its well-known problems.

By the way, when the father is present, the children end up with higher cognitive capacities, higher IQs. In addition, when the father is in the family, the children are more likely to be employed, make more money and more often succeed in life. This is true for both the boys and the girls.

We've all heard about something called "the Mozart effect." I'm not talking about the effect of his music on your brain but about the effect of Mozart's father. Mozart was the product of his father's devoted attention, though perhaps a little bit too intense. In fact, history is filled with children like that. There's Pascal, whose father spent his time at home, schooling the young genius, and there was John Stuart Mill with his father, James Mill. At age three, young Mill was learning Greek. His father focused intensely on him. In the athletic world today, we have many outstanding athletes whose fathers were important to their success. Michael Jordan talks about his father as having helped him, as having modeled for him, as having led him. For Supreme Court justice Clarence Thomas, it was his deeply involved grandfather. And when it isn't a father, it's a coach, or a teacher or another substitute father.

Many times, young women who are very successful show the same phenomenon. They have a strong sense that their father is with them and has broken the barriers down for them. I don't know all of the examples. Recently I saw in the paper an article involving a very successful, wealthy New Yorker who is the head of Citigroup—Sandy Weill. I've never met him, but there was a picture of him with his daughter. They were smiling next to each other. The daughter had just had her first IPO. He was right there with her, giving her support. This is one of the things that fathers do for their children.

But returning to criminality: This is perhaps the major way in which failed fathers pass on their sins to the next generation. There are plenty of poor environments where the fathers are present and there is no criminality. We think of criminal behavior as somehow related to ghettos or the inner city or something like that. When the social scientists take out whether the father is present and the whole issue of the stability of the family, there are no ethnic, racial, linguistic, or cultural factors related to criminal behavior. It is family structure that counts, and the crucial family person that isn't there is the father. The mother may be there, but she commonly struggles through welfare; if she has a job, the children get farmed out to daycare. Either way, there's a big price to pay for the children.

We all know that it's very hard to raise kids and you need at least two adults. It's nice to have the roles differentiated. Of course, they're not going to be always differentiated in the same way. There will be generally some common things that both parents do. The most reliable thing that fathers do—99 percent of women seem to agree on this—is to take out the garbage.

Other than that, maybe the man will be in charge of finances, but maybe not. But almost always, the package of different things done by the husband and the wife will have a clear male and female character to them, even though certain particulars will not be sex typed. Obviously, sometimes you trade off, but there's the need for two roles. Usually, the father represents authority and serious discipline. A lot of his authority is just in his size. You have to remember what it's like to be a little child. Your father is big, and he's sort of scary. His voice is a little scary and he's got a beard and he's scratchy and he smells more. When he looks at you and shouts, you shape up. You're scared, and you figure you can't always count on your mom to save you; indeed, often she has told Dad what you did wrong!

So, that's part of his function, and it's a very important one in which the boy, especially, learns limits and discipline and learns the meaning of self-control. He learns it not just because his father tries to teach him that but also because his father *shows* him.

As an introduction to my next topic, I'd like to say that what we have in our society now has been a failure of fatherhood. There's some evidence—though it's not on television yet—but there's some evidence of a revival of an intellectual interest in fatherhood; for example, "the fatherhood initiative." Various books are coming out on the topic of fathers from thoughtful intellectuals, think tanks and so forth. What we're trying to do is to rediscover intellectually what was known in the past intuitively and was just part of tradition. Modernism, of course, is often about challenging tradition. Likewise, postmodernism, which is really just late modernism, reliably questions and rejects traditions. But a new major era seems to be just beginning in the shadow of the old and dying modernism.

I have a name for it, for what it's worth. I call it *trans-modernism*. We're moving into a new historical period in which we will rediscover the validity of a lot of our traditional understanding, but we're going to discover it intellectually. We're going to discover it in the language of today, which is science, and in the present case, social science. We're going to understand the sensible reasons why many of these traditions evolved. In the past, people couldn't speak about traditions; it was just what your people always did. But now I propose that we will learn why so many traditions were sound, and, in particular, we are learning why fatherhood is so important for the health of children, families, and society—indeed why being a father is good for each man. I think it's very important for individual men to have this understanding, because fatherhood is the way a man fulfills his manhood. If you think you're fulfilled as a man because you're living like James Bond, you're out of your mind. He's the guy without any bonds with anyone. Maybe I'm dating myself. Do people still watch James Bond?

The famous and wise psychologist Eric Erikson has well described genuine maturity as centered on generativity, contributing to the lives of others and involving self-sacrifice, not searching for your own personal pleasure as our consumer and media-saturated culture implies.

The world is hungry for examples of nonselfish men.

The point is you've got to go beyond that, and it comes from being able, as a man, to sacrifice for others. The world is hungry for examples of nonselfish men. I'll come back to that later.

Now, I want to get to a related topic, which I began coming across about ten years ago or so. I was doing some work on the lives of famous atheists—just reading about them and so on. Over and over, I kept finding bad relationships with their fathers, and I said, "Hey, maybe there's something going on here." Then I found, of all things, a comment by Sigmund Freud, which I'll slightly paraphrase—it's almost identical. He said, "Nothing is more common than for a young person to lose faith in God when he loses respect for his father."

That was Sigmund Freud, but he never followed that up. It was just one of his brilliant cast-asides. But he did go on to say that our psychological approach to God in the West is first through our own psychological relationship to our father. And so, if God is like our father and our father is an SOB, you don't want to have anything to do with God, in plain and simple language.

With this understanding in mind, it's interesting to look at the lives of famous atheists. You have to remember that the psychology of a dysfunctional father was affecting them when they were children, well before they became famous atheists. And keep in mind that a child only wants his father to love him and to be there with him in the family, and when's he treated badly, this can set in motion a long-term resentment. [All of the following material about atheists is treated in a scholarly fashion in Dr. Vitz's book *Faith of the Fatherless: The Psychology of Atheism.* Dallas, TX: Spence, 1999.]

Here are some of the examples. I looked at almost all of what are generally understood to be the most famous atheists in the West. Here's an interesting one—Ludwig Feuerbach. Maybe you've never heard of Feuerbach. He was a German philosopher who wrote his atheistic works in the 1840s. He exercised considerable influence on Karl Marx, who just gobbled him up. Feuerbach argued that God didn't exist, that he was just a projection of human, psychological concerns of various types. He obviously was ahead of Freud on this issue.

What was Feuerbach's childhood like? His father and his mother were married and had a number of children; his father was a famous jurist, lawyer, and professor at a nearby university. When the boy was twelve or thirteen—and this is now in the 1820s, a much more conservative environment than now, but even today, imagine this happening to your own family—young Feuerbach's father abandoned the family and took up living with another woman in a nearby village.

The other woman was the wife of his father's best friend.

Feuerbach Sr. lived with this woman a number of years. I don't know what the best friend was doing about all this—that wasn't in the biographies—and he had a child by this woman. This would have been an enormous scandal; everyone would have been talking about it and known about it, since Feuerbach Sr. was a prominent person. It was a clear rejection and abandonment of his family.

After about three years or so, the woman he was living with died. So, senior Feuerbach came back to the family to live. Young Feuerbach's mother must have been a very patient and kind woman—or perhaps very weak. Biographers mention only the basic facts; they don't talk about what the psychology was like of living with this notorious scandal. The father also had a nickname. It was "Vesuvius." He obviously blew up and exploded often. He sounds like a real nice guy.

All right, one atheist, one bad father. Let's look at a few more. Let's take Schopenhauer. The situation is very different, but again we see the failed father element. Schopenhauer had a very bad relationship with his mother. His mother was nasty to him all his life and said, "I didn't want you, and you ruined my life." The father was a well-to-do merchant; the parents traveled and often went to England. Most of the time they traveled without young Schopenhauer, and Schopenhauer was left at home with a nanny here and a nanny there. It's not just the poor; it's the rich as well who abandon their children. Then for about two or three years, he stayed in the same place with his family and had a nice relationship with his father, but continued the bad relationship with his mother. Then his father left again when both parents went to another country. When Schopenhauer was sixteen—this is in Germany—his father came back and started a new business, and he had young Schopenhauer work with him. Then, the father committed suicide.

Schopenhauer talks about how devastated he was by the feeling of abandonment. This is one of the things about suicide that is so profound. Suicides never seem to factor in the feeling of rejection and hostility and abandonment that they create in the lives of those they leave behind. Shortly after that, Schopenhauer became an atheist and later famous for being the great pessimist.

How about some others? Let's take Hobbes. He was probably an atheist, probably one of the first. At that time, it was a little dangerous politically to be an atheist; so, he kind of covered his tracks and said, "Oh, I'm a materialist." But, in fact, he was almost certainly an atheist.

When he was a boy, his father was an Anglican clergyman but wasn't a very good one. He was famous for falling asleep in his own services, and he also had an irascible temper. When Hobbes was probably around three or four, his father had a fight in front of his small church with another clergyman, knocked him down, and beat him up. Then Hobbes Sr. fled, and his family never saw him again. So, a father abandoning—yet *again*. Hobbes is well known for his anticlerical sentiments, in addition to being a materialist/atheist.

There are many others. Freud himself fits his own model. Freud did not respect his father. He saw his father, who was a religious, liberal Enlighten-ment Jew, as weak in a number of ways.

All of his biographers are aware that Sigmund Freud saw his father as weak in response to anti-Semitism. There is a famous incident in which his father was walking down the street and someone called him a "dirty Jew," knocked his hat off, and essentially gave him a big challenge. Sigmund asked, "What did you do, Father?" He replied, "I just picked up my hat and walked away." Perhaps this was when Freud as a young person lost respect and stopped believing in God, who was clearly associated for Freud with his father. Sig-mund Freud was a complicated man, a difficult man, but he was also a coura-geous man and admired bravery.

In addition, in two letters that Freud wrote to a colleague during the 1890s when he was in the midst of his own personal psychoanalysis, he stated that his father was a sexual pervert. (The point that he was a pervert was deleted from the original publication of the letters.) Freud said that symptoms of his father's sexual perversion could be seen in his younger sisters. I don't want to condemn even Freud's father, but in Freud's judgment, it's clear that he saw his father as some kind of sexual pervert and as a coward.

Here is another example: Voltaire. Voltaire was probably not an atheist; perhaps rather a Deist, but in his case it was hard to tell. We do know that Voltaire really disliked his father. In his letters he never said anything nice about him; he said many nasty things. But, of course, the crucial thing that Voltaire did was to reject his father's name, and he invented the name *Voltaire*. He gave himself that name and thus implicitly said: "I don't want to be con-nected to my father and his family and name. I'm to be known as *Voltaire*." Everybody knows him by that name, but nobody knows quite where the name came from.

It's also interesting to me that the first published play that Voltaire wrote as a young man in his twenties was titled *Oedipe* (*Oedipus*). It was a thinly dis-guised redoing of the Oedipus myth in the context of killing God and killing the king (the king being a father figure and someone that, if you're mad at your father, you can also hate).

One of the most powerful and rich examples of our thesis was Friedrich Nietzsche. His father died when he was four, and he never really got over it. When Nietzsche said, "God is dead," he was really saying, "Dad is dead." He never claims that his atheism was a rational thing. He said he knew it by instinct. His own unconscious mind knew it, but he saw his father's death as abandonment. His father became sickly over two or three years and then died. He talks about this in his memoirs and autobiographical material a great deal. It was really a major event in his life, and he had no other men in his family to come in to be substitute fathers.

Now, two contemporary figures. One is Madalyn Murray O'Hair. Most of you know about her. She was president of the American Atheists. She was the woman responsible for getting prayers taken out of the public schools in the 1960s, and we do know something about her background.

One of her sons wrote about Madalyn's relationship with her father, saying that he was present when Madalyn picked up a ten-inch butcher knife and threatened her father with the words: "I want to kill you; I want to dance on your grave." We don't know what was responsible for that, but, in general, daughters don't feel like doing that to their father. Presumably, something caused it, but we do not know what it might have been.

And then there are Sartre, Hume, Bertrand Russell, and many others who fit the pattern of the dead father and the absence of any good substitute father. There is one interesting case that took place here in October concerning a New Yorker, a successful psychologist named Albert Ellis. He's probably eighty or more now. He has his own institute in the City. He's a real New Yorker. He was born and raised in New York, and he founded a school of psychology called "rational emotive behavioral therapy." It's a kind of cognitive therapy aimed at changing your thoughts and behaviors and your emotions. It has been quite influential.

It's not just believers who have a motive for believing in God. Unbelievers can have a motive for *not* believing in God.

I knew nothing about him. I just happened to be at a place where we were both speaking. While he was there, I summarized some of my evidence that bad fathers had been an emotional contributor to the lives of many atheists, and he heard me.

At this conference, he was present as an atheist arguing against belief in God, and I was presenting an interpretation of some of the motives behind the atheists' beliefs. In other words, it's not just believers who have a motive for believing in God. Unbelievers can have a motive for *not* believing in God. I spelled out what I called the "bad father hypothesis."

After we both finished speaking, we walked along together as we left the podium. He looked at me and said, "Well, that's interesting, but you know, I had a good relationship with my father." And I said, "Well, a psychological hypothesis rarely fits one hundred percent of the cases. If you're right thirty or forty percent of the time, if you found a factor that works even that well, that's pretty good."

I went back to New York. I had written up my talk, and a friend of mine who was an editor asked me to send it to him, and I did.

About a month later, we were talking, and he said, "Oh, by the way, Paul, that paper you wrote fits Albert Ellis perfectly." And I said, "George, this can't be. He heard me read that or most of it. And he said he had a good relationship with his father." And my friend said, "Well, look, Paul, we're publishing his biography, and last night I was reading the page proofs. Go read it." So, I read it.

Young Albert and his brother were abandoned by their father. His mother was mentally not functioning very well, and the father—this was in New York in the twenties and thirties—was a philanderer. He played around and wasn't around much, and then, after a while, completely abandoned the family. Once in a while, Albert would see him on the street or something like that. Young Albert and his brother toughed it out. They took care of their mother. They put themselves through City University, and Albert ended up getting a PhD. As a result of all of this, Albert Ellis is one of the classic tough, old-fashioned New Yorkers. He grew up on the street, but he was a very smart intellectual, too. It's an unusual combination and probably doesn't happen much anymore.

However, Albert must have been angry at his father. Imagine: This is the late twenties and early thirties, and then the Depression comes on. Your father isn't there. He's left you and the family, and he's with other women, and once in a while, as a kid of eight, ten, twelve, you see him. You're going to be very disappointed, perhaps enraged. *This is not what fathers are supposed to be and do, especially then at that period.*

So, those are some of the examples of atheists with bad fathers. There are many other people that I could mention in support of the bad or absent father theory. I even know some famous psychologists that fit the theory well.

In my study, I put together a kind of historical control group, where I looked at the fathers of famous theists who lived in the same country and during the same historical period as the atheists. These were philosophers, and others who publically stood for God, often with arguments but in other ways as well. The first one is Pascal, who lived in France during a time of great skepticism about God. His mother died when he was three, and his father homeschooled him—that wasn't the term they used then, but the father educated young Pascal and his sister hour after hour, year after year.

Other examples of theists with good fathers include G. K. Chesterton, who said, "You know, I had a happy childhood. I'm sorry to disappoint all the people looking for problems in people's lives. But I had a happy childhood." One of the reasons he had had such a good one was that his father stayed home a great deal and spent time with his children. He played with them and made up games with them and read to them. I guess that you could say, "They really bonded."

Here are some others that had good fathers. Edmund Burke, the great conservative thinker, had a pretty good father, but he also had a substitute father, an uncle, who was very important to him. This is something to keep in mind. Nietzsche didn't have a substitute father. Freud didn't, but Burke did. He had an uncle. He often lived with him and was devoted to him all of his life. Burke said his uncle was "the best man I've ever known."

Another example is Wilberforce, the great evangelical English Protestant who was responsible for getting rid of slavery in England, the first country to ban it. He spent his whole life focused on the issue of banning slavery. Until young Wilberforce was nine years old, he had had a pretty normal family life, but then his father died. The mother didn't know what to do; so, she sent her son to live with an aunt and an uncle who were, I think, Methodists, but were called *Enthusiasts* at the time. He lived with them for a couple of years. One of the people he met there was a close friend of his aunt and uncle—a man by the name of John Newton.

In case you've forgotten who John Newton was, he wrote the famous song "Amazing Grace." John Newton had been a slaver, the captain of a slaving ship, and later he became a Christian and strongly rejected and repented of his earlier life. "Amazing Grace" was about his own transformation from the wretch he had been. It is in this new family, that young Wilberforce learned about the issue of slavery when he was a boy. Then his mother got upset, because this enthusiastic religious environment disturbed her—she thought it was too extreme and she brought her son back home. William Wilberforce said he wept as if he was leaving his father and mother when he left the home of his aunt and uncle.

Wilberforce was a well-to-do young man. He went to Cambridge. Then, at age twenty, he decided to run for Parliament. He won a seat and remained there for the rest of his life. He had a kind of secondary religious re-conversion in his twenties. After many years of working against the English slave trade, he was finally able to get it abolished in England and throughout the British Empire.

Wilberforce had five sons, to whom he was devoted. A sign of this is that four of them became clergymen. We have the letters he wrote them; they are moving letters of love and support. He often mentioned his prayers for them and his desire to see each one of them. This wasn't in just one letter. The letters came month after month over the years—there are whole volumes of them. For each of his children, he would set aside certain hours of the day to reflect on them and pray for them.

Another major theist with a good father was Thomas Reid, one of the great Scottish philosophers. Yet another among many is Moses Mendelssohn. He's our first Jewish philosopher on the theist side. He had a good relationship with his father, and he took the name of *Mendel sohn*—the son of Mendel. His father's name was Mendel. (In this case, he is the opposite of Voltaire.)

For Jewish theists, there were often many rabbis and other scholars around who served as father figures for them and gave them a positive view of what it was to be a father. Here, too, family members could be important. Martin Buber had a substitute father who was his grandfather.

An interesting example of a theist is Walker Percy. (I'm jumping around a bit so as not to present only philosophers.) Walker Percy, a well-known Southern novelist, had serious odds against him. His grandfather had committed suicide, and his father was subject to depression and was sent away to a mental institution. Then his father committed suicide by shooting himself. So, now Walker was alone with his brother and his mother. A few years later, his mother was killed in an auto accident where suicide was suspected.

Young Walker was then essentially adopted by his uncle, who devoted his life to Walker and his brother. The uncle was a small-time businessman and a poet, a great reader of literature. He dedicated his life to educating the two boys, and the result was that we got a good novelist with a positive attitude toward God and religion, instead of maybe another suicide or another atheistic writer. The point I'm trying to make is that fathers, including substitute fathers, have an enormous impact on the religious and emotional lives of their children.

There are also cases where you have a religious father who is kind of hostile, angry, who talks the talk but doesn't walk the walk. This very commonly causes rejection of the faith of their father. This can be true even with ministers' sons. When the minister neglects his own family or is a bully or commits suicide, a great resentment develops, and it can lead to ministers' sons becoming atheists, skeptics, and agnostics.

I want to give another example of an atheist's father and his son and what happened. Consider the minor philosopher James Mill and his son, John Stuart Mill, a truly major philosopher. James Mill was militantly atheistic. I couldn't find out much about his background. The biographical record only says that his father was probably an alcoholic. That isn't substantial enough information, but in any case James Mill was a very serious atheist, and he was also devoted to his son. So, while he taught his son atheism, intellectually speaking, he also showed him a father's love and support. The two messages were at cross purposes, just as when, on the one hand, you have a minister who talks God and love and then on the other hand acts like the devil. With the Mills, we have a father who talks and teaches atheism but shows love and support.

The net result was that during his life, John Stuart Mill published nothing about religion. After his death, when some of his works dealing with religion finally came out, many thought he was going to turn out to be another militant atheist. He was not religious, but he was really rather tolerant toward religion. We can say that psychologically, this is a kind of compromise between the two positions.

Let's return to fathers. If you're going to take away one message from my talk, it is this: You fathers are of great importance in forming the religious attitude of your children. As we have seen, many an atheist was damaged by negative personal relationships, especially with a father or a father figure. Of course, for some atheists, their position is solely about reason and evidence and the intellectual life, but for many others, there is an important emotional substrate, an irrational component—certainly there was with Nietzsche—and these emotions are really guiding them.

And as already noted, if we consider criminal behavior and absent or dysfunctional fathers, we can clearly see how fathers pass their sins on to their sons and daughters, too.

In summary, I think all this evidence should be a call to men to rediscover what fatherhood is about. It is about helping other people, leading them in a self-sacrificing way. Yes, it's about self-sacrifice. That's the only way you earn genuine respect, and when men do that, the public responds. The wife responds; the children respond.

It's about self-sacrifice. That's the only way you earn genuine respect, and when men do that, the public responds. The wife responds; the children respond.

After 9/11, one of the reasons we responded so positively to the firemen and their deaths was that we saw self-sacrifice by manly men who weren't in it for the money, weren't in it like the CEO who needs more than enough money to work for his company. They weren't in it for themselves. That is why all these jaded New Yorkers on 9/11 stood and applauded when the firemen went by.

This is what the world wants, and this is what fathers are called to be. It's not an issue of changing the country or anything like that. You want to change your own life. This is the way to live the better life as an adult man—by being some kind of father. You can focus on your own children or on those others outside of your family.

I'm a grandfather now; I'm getting to be a geezer. Grandchildren are another kind who need fathers. The point is that there are plenty of people who need fathering, who need your help, your support. And when you're through with fathering, not only will they be happy and much better for it, so will you.

Q & A
___

Eric Metaxas: To think he was in New York City right under our noses for these four years—it makes no sense. We have some time for questions and answers.

Q: Thank you for a wonderful talk. I can understand how the message of self-sacrifice is one that people hearing it can put into effect right away as fathers. I am wondering if you have any thoughts about how your findings may be used in talking to atheists about God.

A: Many atheists, as I have said, are really greatly disappointed in what the meaning of God and fatherhood is for their life. Some of them also have an intellectual issue. That is a separate thing. By the way, I was an atheist for twenty years; I am not hostile to atheists in principle.

The way is to show them a good father figure—somebody who is clearly not in it for himself, who is in it in a self-sacrificial way. We have lots of models of that in the faith. That was one of the meanings of the Passion of Christ; I am referring to the suffering he endured—his death for our sake. But the point is to show to the atheists people who demonstrate the kind of father they didn't have.

Sometimes you can speak to them in a different way. This occurred once with a man who had had a very bad, nasty father and was very resentful of it but was now married and had three or four children. I gave him a challenge. I said, "Okay, be the father you never had and always wanted. In doing that, you will get what you didn't originally have." It is always about showing self-sacrificial love. That is what it is, and you have to show it. We need a culture that gives more examples of this.

Q: I would like to follow up on the theme of self-sacrifice. You mentioned courage and heroism and the firefighters. I have seen this in a lot of military families where the father was a hero and the children will replicate that heroism, and the grandchildren will replicate that heroism, and so on. I am wondering if you have any thoughts on the way this positive reinforcement happens within a family and how it is also connected with personal recklessness, because there is an element of recklessness in courage and heroism.

A: Those are tough questions. As far as the modeling in the family goes, one example I can share is of a family I knew where the father had died. So, there is a question of how the death is treated in the family. I mean, how the father is treated, and it is important—a number of widows that I have talked to were aware of this—that when the father had been a good man and although he was dead for whatever reason (accident or war or illness), they kept his memory alive as being good. It was very important that he not be seen as invisible or in some other negative understanding. This happens in military families too, because of the death rate. The issue of what we mean by bravery is a special topic. I don't know enough about it to be able to say anything I think useful.

Q: You mentioned a number of names. I have done a lot of miscellaneous reading, not spending my time more constructively in pool halls. What do you think of Kierkegaard, Francis of Assisi, and Anna Freud? The first two had bad relations with their father, and Anna Freud was totally, as I am sure you know, devoted to her father. And I could even throw in Saint Augustine, who had a terrible relationship with his father.

A: In the book, I wrote a whole chapter or section on Kierkegaard, and it is clear that when Kierkegaard had a falling-out with his father—when he was seventeen or eighteen, just as he was going to college—that he lost his faith. And it was with the restoration of a positive relationship with his father shortly before his father died that Kierkegaard came back to the faith. He explicitly stated my own hypothesis in his writings at that time. I would have to find the quotes for you.

Anna Freud was close to her father and admired him very much and was responsible, for example, for making those letters delete the reference to the grandfather being a pervert. But I don't know—there are a lot of complicated biographical interpretations of the Sigmund–Anna Freud relationship. Some people say it was positive and strong, and I lean toward that, but there is another position according to which it was a kind of incestuous relationship based on the fact that Sigmund Freud psychoanalyzed his own daughter. Let me explain that in psychoanalysis, you can't become a psychoanalyst unless you go through your training period, which involves your being psychoanalyzed by an older psychoanalyst.

It has always been the tradition that the older psychoanalyst should not be a member of your own family, the reason being, of course, that in classical psychoanalysis, the Oedipus complex is about the childhood relationship of a sexual kind with both parents. Freud made an exception to that rule with respect to his daughter Anna. He was her training analyst. You can see it is not an obvious call. It was indeed unusual, even inappropriate. But as far as I know, she was not anything like a militant atheist, and certainly consciously, she respected her father, defended him and admired him. Therefore, she should follow in the natural model of being sort of like her father, but more in the John Stuart Mill mold.

In the case of Saint Francis of Assisi, he had a bad relationship with his father. He even took off the clothes that his father had given him, publicly, in the town square—but the bishop was present and re-clothed him by wrapping his mantle around him. The bishop, representing God, became Francis's father.

As for Saint Augustine, I can only speculate that his long avoidance of accepting God and Christ had some connection to his rather dysfunctional father but that substitute fathers may have eventually helped him to convert. We know that Ambrose became a major new father figure for Augustine, in Milan—another bishop as father. In addition, his mother, who came to be known as Saint Monica, was an unusually holy and prayerful person. She alone was a powerful influence. In any case, we must not forget that my hypothesis about bad fathers is not applicable to all cases and that in all cases there is free will, which is a central reality. My hypothesis is only about a major underlying pressure that depending on the person's free choice may or may not be determinative.

Q: Regarding Anna Freud: Well, just before she died, she was crippled. She had saved this tattered old raincoat, and every day her nurse would take her out. She was in London at the time when Freud ended his life. She would be wrapped up in that raincoat that she had saved for forty or fifty years.

A: It was her father's?

Q: Yes. I read the book *Freud Was Wrong*. It was a very interesting book, and I am sure you have read it. It was very, very moving.

A: She was deeply attached to him. The question of the nature of that attachment is what people talk about.

Q: You spoke earlier about reaffirming a relationship with children in the sense that if you are a father not intricately involved in a child's life, yet at the same time intricately involved in other people's lives, you can be a prolific speaker and an enthusiastic, uplifting person to other people. How can you relate that to your own children, and do you find it hard to be able to do that? How can you do that?

A: I am going to give some very unpsychological comment on that. The man should have enough humility to listen to his wife.

Q: Say no more, thank you.

A: Now, she has to not be too naggy and all of that. But he has got to listen.

Q: You spoke about Albert Ellis. Why do you think that he "made it" and toughed it out, after he had the womanizing father? Where did his strength come from, if he had all of these things against him as a child, with his mother not being emotionally there, dysfunctional, and his father being absent?

A: First of all, partly I don't know. Partly, I would propose that some children have a capacity for resilience, a certain kind of strength, and the third thing was his brother. The two of them were very bonded and have remained so throughout their lives. They formed a little team. He had someone to talk to and to work with. So, I would say it is partly that he probably had the temperament of this type of toughness that some people have, so that they can deal with certain kinds of stresses and strains better than others. And partly he had his brother.

Q: So, you believe that it is fundamentally maybe from conception?

A: One's temperament can be a factor. I don't think that Albert Ellis would have made a good artist or poet. He probably wasn't sensitive enough for that; that is another capacity, and he didn't have that temperament. If he had, he might have collapsed under the absence of social support. But he had a temperament that allowed him, for whatever reason, to be strong, as well as having the support from his brother.

That is the best I can guess. This is why biography eventually always has certain ambiguous and uncertain elements. We have to remember that in all lives there are those points where there is freedom. There are points where you decide to choose your understanding of your father as an SOB, instead of choosing to say, "I will find a way to find something better to replace you with." There are always times when you have some freedom, and that is a mysterious component in these cases as well. So, I am not being a total determinist. I am talking about things that push you in certain directions. Nevertheless, a person can choose to resist that push.

Can an Atheist Be a Good Citizen?

FR. RICHARD JOHN NEUHAUS

September 22, 2004

Introduction

G ood evening, and welcome to Socrates in the City, the thinking person's alternative to having yourself surgically altered to look like a jungle cat.

I am Eric Metaxas, and for those of you unfamiliar with Socrates in the City, let me explain a bit. The Greek philosopher Socrates said rather famously that "the unexamined life is not worth living." Of course, that's nonsense, but he was living in a different time, and that's just the way they thought back then. Thank you for laughing. Of course, it is eternally true that the unexamined life is not worth living.

We at Socrates in the City thought it a good idea to facilitate the examination of our lives, as Socrates said. So, we frequently, monthly now, invite brilliant minds who are also brilliant speakers—as there are many brilliant minds that are not brilliant speakers—to come and address us on some of the big and provocative questions of human existence, such as the existence of God, the nature of God, the nature of faith, the relationship between faith and science, the problems of evil and suffering, and the question of human nature. No question is too large for us here at Socrates in the City, although I confess we've stayed out of the whole Swift Boat controversy.*

---

* During the 2004 presidential campaign, the Swift Boat Veterans for Truth, a group of 527 Vietnam War veterans, called into question the war medals given to John Kerry, the Democratic Party candidate for president.

Tonight, of course, we will be hearing from Father Richard John Neuhaus on the fabulously provocative subject of whether an atheist can be a good citizen. I think the short answer might be *yes*, but I look forward to Father Neuhaus's more in-depth and nuanced thinking on this subject.

Father Neuhaus is someone whose work I've been following and someone I've been admiring for a number of years. Please don't let that throw you. He's a good egg, nonetheless, and I suggest that you stay.

I would, of course, be remiss in failing to mention that tonight's festivities, which are heavily subsidized, are brought to you by Bounty, the quicker picker-upper. Also by Amana, makers of the Amana Radar Range: If it doesn't say, "Amana," it's not a Radar Range. By the way, you can find out more about SITC and how to help support us at www.socratesinthecity.com. Isn't it fascinating the way the Internet has changed our lives? I actually got this haircut off the Internet, but I don't want to go into that.

The fabulous piano music you've been listening to tonight is courtesy of Ms. Sue Song, to whom we are always grateful. Sue has been with us for almost every single Socrates event. So, I really am just tremendously grateful. I've tried many times to get other musicians to give Sue a break, but it never really works out. They always cancel at the last minute.

I was close to getting the hip-hop artist Fat Joe to be here tonight, but something came up at the last minute. There is a quote from his song "Lean Back," which I thought was appropriate for the evening:

My fellas don't dance
They just pull up they pants
And do the rock-a-way.

We look forward to getting Fat Joe for a future event. Enough nonsense. At last, let me tell you about our guest of honor, Father Richard John Neuhaus. We are sincerely thrilled to have him with us tonight at Socrates in the City.

For those of you unfamiliar with his work, let me just say a few words. First of all, Father Neuhaus lives right here in New York City. He is acclaimed as one of the foremost authorities on the role of religion in the contemporary world. He is president of the Institute on Religion and Public Life, a nonpartisan interreligious and educational institute here in New York City. He is editor in chief of the Institute's publication *First Things*, a monthly journal of religion and public life. I had the august privilege of appearing in that great magazine just a few years back; so, I'm a little biased in thinking it an organ of exquisite aesthetic and moral taste. But it is, of course. Seriously though, it's a fabulous magazine.

Over the years, Father Neuhaus has played a leadership role in organizations dealing with civil rights, international justice, and ecumenism. If you're not familiar with ecumenism, you can see me after class, and I can tell you what that is. Father Neuhaus has been the recipient of numerous honors from universities and other institutions, including the John Paul II Award for Religious Freedom. He has held presidential appointments in the Carter, Reagan, and first Bush administrations. In a survey of national leadership, *U.S. News and World Report* named Father Neuhaus "one of the thirty-two most influential intellectuals in America."

In a survey of national leadership, *U.S. News and World Report* named Father Neuhaus "one of the thirty-two most influential intellectuals in America." Of course, I always want to know who was thirty-three. It's got to kill that guy, whoever it is.

Of course, I always want to know who was thirty-three. It's got to kill that guy, whoever it is.

In September 1991, Father Neuhaus was ordained a priest of the Archdiocese of New York. Among his best-known books are *The Naked Public Square: Religion and Democracy in America*, *The Catholic Moment: The Paradox of the Church in the Postmodern World*, and with Rabbi Leon Klenicki, *Believing Today: Jew and Christian in Conversation*. In 1995, Father Neuhaus edited, along with my former boss Charles Colson, the book called *Evangelicals and Catholics Together: Toward a Common Mission*. His most recent book, which I know we have copies of this evening, is *As I Lay Dying: Meditations upon Returning*.

I could go on and on, and, of course, I have, and I apologize. So, let's get down to business here, and let me introduce someone that I'm very proud to have with us here tonight—and thrilled to count among us here in Manhattan generally—Father Richard John Neuhaus.

Talk

Thank you, Eric. What a marvelous introduction. I almost feel guilty for interrupting him. He wonders who was number thirty-three. I wonder how *U.S. News and World Report* would know.

I should say, "The unexamined life is not worth living." Some of you may want to look up on the *First Things* web site, www.firstthings.com, a marvelous article by one of our regular contributors Gilbert Meilander, a Lutheran ethicist, titled "The Examined Life Is Not Worth Living." It's a very clever, interesting, and rewarding turn on the difference between the Socratic and the Christian understandings of knowledge. What else?

The title is "Can an Atheist Be a Good Citizen?" I had thought of choosing something mildly controversial, but I decided to go with this title. Now, I don't want you to stay in suspense as to the answer to the question; I would very much like to answer the question in the affirmative. That is the decent and tolerant thing to do. Before we can answer the question, we should first determine what is meant by *atheism*, and second, we must inquire more closely into what is required in being a good citizen. There is atheism, and there is atheism. The Greek *atheos*—what did it mean? It meant "one who is without God"; it had less to do with whether one believed in God in the sense that we use that word today than whether one believed in reverencing the gods of the city or of the empire.

For his perceived disbelief in the gods, Socrates was charged with atheism. The early Christians were charged with atheism for their insistence that there is no god other than the God of Israel, whom Jesus called *Father* and who brings all other gods and goddesses and deities under judgment.

In the eyes of the ancients, to be *atheos* was to be outside the civilizational circle of the *civitas*, the civilized community. To be an atheist was to be subversive. The atheist was a security risk, if not a traitor. Christians were thought to be atheists precisely because they professed the God who judges and debunks the false gods of the community.

In the classical world, then, the answer to our question was decisively in the negative. No, an atheist could *not* be a good citizen, but those whom they called *atheists*, we do not usually call *atheists* today. Those whom we call *atheists* in the modern period believe they are denying what earlier atheists, such as Christians, affirmed. That is to say, they deny the reality of what they understand believing Jews and Christians and Muslims to mean by God. This form of atheism is a post-Enlightenment and largely nineteenth-century phenomenon. It developed a vocabulary that was strongly prejudiced against those who believe in God. Note that the very term *believer* is used to describe a person who is persuaded of the reality of God. The alternative to being a believer, of course, is to be a "knower."

Similarly, a curious usage developed with respect to the categories of faith and reason, the subjective and the objective, and, in the realm of morals, a very sharp distinction between fact and value. *Belief, faith, subjectivity, and values*—these were the soft and dubious words relevant to affirming the reality of God. On the other hand, *knowledge, reason, objectivity, and fact*—these were the hard and certain words relevant to denying God. This tendentious vocabulary of modern unbelief is still very, very much with us today, and against such tendentious vocabulary, one must argue, as the great Michael Polanyi does in his classic work *Personal Knowledge*, that everyone who thinks is a believer—the atheist no less than those whom we conventionally call *believers*.

Necessarily following from such distortive distinctions are common assumptions about what is public and what is private. One recalls Alfred North Whitehead's axiom that "religion is what man does with his solitariness." Even one so religiously musical, so to speak, as William James could write, "Religion shall mean for us the feelings, acts and experiences of individual men in their solitude." In this construal of matters, we witness a radical departure from the public nature of religion, whether that religion has to do with the ancient gods of the city or with the biblical Lord who rules over the nations.

The gods of the city and the God of the Bible are emphatically public. The confinement of the question of God or the gods to the private sphere constitutes what might be described as *political atheism*. Many today who are believers in private, and very devout believers in private, have been persuaded or intimidated into accepting political atheism. All of that powerfully contributes to what I have elsewhere described as "the naked public square." Political atheism is a subspecies of practical or methodological atheism, which is, quite simply, the assumption that we can get along with the business at hand without addressing the question of God, one way or another.

> **Many today who are believers in private, and very devout believers in private, have been persuaded or intimidated into accepting political atheism.**

Here the classic anecdote—familiar to many of you, I'm sure—is the response of the Marquis de Laplace to Napoleon Bonaparte. Napoleon observed that Laplace had written a huge book on a system of the universe without mentioning the Author of the universe, to which Laplace replied, "Sire, I had no need of that hypothesis." When God has become a hypothesis, we have traveled a very long way from both the gods of the ancient city and the God of the Bible. Yet that distance was necessary to the emergence of what the modern world calls *atheism*. The remarkable thing is that the defenders of religion so uncritically accepted the terms of the debate set by the Enlightenment *philosophes* and their later imitators.

Not all of them, thank God, recall Pascal's assertion of his belief in "the God of Abraham, the God of Isaac, the God of Jacob, not of philosophers and scholars." Modern atheism is the product, in largest part, not so much of anti-religion as of religion's replacement of the God of Abraham with the god of the philosophers—and of the philosophers' consequent rejection of that *ersatz* god. Descartes determined that he would accept as true nothing that could be reasonably doubted, and Christians of the time set about to prove that the existence of God could not be reasonably doubted. Thus did the defenders of religion set faith against the doubt that is an integral and necessary part of the movement toward faith.

The very phrase that is much debated, *the existence of God*, gave away the game—as though God were one existent among other existents, one entity among other entities, one actor among other actors, whose actions must conform to standards that we have determined in advance are appropriate to being God. The Transcendent, the Ineffable, the totally Other, the God who acts in history, was tamed and domesticated in order to meet the philosopher's job description for the post of God, and not surprisingly, the philosophers decided that the candidates recommended by the friends of religion did not qualify for the post.

The American part of the story is well told by James Turner of the University of Michigan, in a wonderful book called *Without God, Without Creed: The Origins of Unbelief in America*: "The natural parents of modern unbelief turn out to have been the guardians of belief," says Turner. Many thinking people came at last "to realize that it was religion, not science or social change, that gave birth to unbelief. Having made God more and more like man—intellectually, morally, emotionally—the shapers of religion made it feasible to abandon God, to believe simply in man." Turner's judgment is relentless. He goes on: "In trying to adapt their religious beliefs to socioeconomic change, to new moral challenges, to novel problems of knowledge, to the tightening standards of science, the defenders of God slowly strangled Him. If anyone is to be arraigned," says Turner, "if anyone is to be arraigned for deicide, it is not Charles Darwin, but his famous adversary Bishop Samuel Wilberforce, not the godless Robert Ingersoll but the godly Beecher family."

Now, in response to that kind of reductionist Protestantism, H. L. Mencken observed, "The chief contribution of [liberal] Protestantism is its massive proof that God is a bore." That's unfair, of course, as Mencken was almost always unfair, but it is not untouched by truth. The god that was trimmed, accommodated, and retooled to be deemed respectable by the "modern mind" was increasingly uninteresting, because unnecessary.

Dietrich Bonhoeffer, the great German Lutheran pastor and martyr under Adolf Hitler, described that god as a "god of the gaps," a god invoked to fill in those pieces of reality that human knowledge and control had not yet mastered. H. Richard Niebuhr, the elder—and some would say wiser—

brother of Reinhold Niebuhr, is well known for his withering depiction of the gospel of liberal Christianity. He said it depicts a god that without wrath "brought men without sin, into a kingdom without judgment, through the ministrations of a Christ without a Cross." It's very perceptive. Absent are sin and divine judgment and redemption. It is not surprising that people came to dismiss the idea of God, not because it is implausible but because it is superfluous—and yes, Mencken, finally boring.

In the varieties of atheism in the modern world, there is also the more determined materialist who asserts that there simply is nothing and can be nothing outside a closed and all-encompassing reality of matter and motion. This was the position of the late and unlamented "dialectical materialism," as it was called, of Communism. It is the position of some scientists today, especially those in the biological sciences who are wedded to Darwinism as a comprehensive belief system. Physicists, as it turns out, are increasingly and generally open to the metaphysical, and I warmly recommend in that connection, if you haven't read it, the critique of Richard Dawkins's atheism by the physicist Stephen Barr, in the current issue of *First Things*.

Perhaps more commonly, one encounters varieties of logical positivism, as it is called, that hold that since assertions about God are not empirically verifiable—or, for that matter, falsifiable—they are simply meaningless. In a similar vein, analytical philosophers would instruct us that "God talk" is, quite precisely, nonsense. This is not atheism in the sense to which we have become accustomed, since it claims that denying God is as much nonsense as affirming God. However, it is atheism in the original sense of *atheos*, of being without God.

Then there is the much more radical position that denies not only the possibility of truth claims about God but the possibility of truth claims at all, at least as "truth" usually has been understood in our civilizational history. A prominent proponent of this view in America is Richard Rorty. Please take note that this is not atheism that pits reason against a possible knowledge of God. This is the atheism of unreason.

Richard Rorty is sometimes portrayed, and frequently portrays himself, as something of an eccentric gadfly. In fact, along with Derrida, Foucault, and other Heideggerian epigones of Nietzsche, Rorty is the guru of an academic establishment of great influence in our intellectual culture.

Here we encounter the partisans, the apostles, of a relativism that denies it is relativism, because it denies that there is any alternative to relativism, and therefore, the term *relativism* is meaningless. They are, as they say, radically anti-foundationalist. That is to say, they contend that there are no conclusive arguments underlying our assertions about truth, except the conclusive argument that there are no conclusive arguments underlying our assertions about truth. Now, to put it too briefly, but not, I think, inaccurately, "truth" is, in this view, what the relevant community of discourse agrees to say is truth. The goal in this way of thinking is self-actualization, indeed, self-creation. The successful life is the life lived as a *novum*, an unprecedented thing, a thing never before, an autobiography that has escaped what Richard Rorty calls the "used vocabularies of the past."

Now, this disposition has its academic strongholds in literary criticism and sectors of philosophy, but it undergirds assumptions that are very, very widespread in our intellectual culture. In some variations, it is frankly asserted that arguments claiming to deal with truth are but disguised strategies for the exercise of will and the quest for power. Whether the issue is gender, sexual orientation, or race, we are told that the purpose is to change the ideational "power structure," which is presumably presently controlled by oppressors who disingenuously try to protect the status quo by appeals to objective truth and intersubjective reason.

But, you might be asking, are such people like Richard Rorty et al. really atheists? You might ask them, in which case, I can tell you by experience, that they typically will brush aside the question as "not serious," for the theism upon which atheism depends is, in their view, not serious. As with *relativism* and *irrationality*, so also with *atheism*; the words make sense only in relation to the opposites from which they are derived. Of course, privately, or for purposes of a particular community's identity, any words might be deemed useful. One might even find it meaningful to speak about "Nature and Nature's God," as the Declaration of Independence does. People in this view can be permitted to talk that way, so long as they understand that such talk has no public purchase, no claim on anyone's attention. What Rorty calls and admires as "the liberal ironist" can employ any vocabulary, no matter how fantastical, so long as he does not insist that it is true in a way that claims the attention of others or limits their "novel vocabularies."

There is, indeed, irony in the fact that some who think of themselves as theists, as believers in God, eagerly embrace the deconstructionism of this operative atheism. Today's cultural scene, as we all know, is awash in what are called "new spiritualities." A recent anthology of what is called "America's new spiritual voices" includes contributions promoting witchcraft, ecological mysticism, devotion to sundry gods and goddesses, and something very charming—and if I had the time, I would look into it—presenting itself as Zen physio-psychoanalysis. All are deemed to be usable vocabularies for the creation of the self.

Now, sometimes, these so-called new spiritualities are more socialized, more communal in nature, being focused less on the inner truth than on the ultimate truth of our sociology and of our encountering God in the other. My friend Cardinal Avery Dulles was speaking in a parish one time, and there was a large banner in the chancery where he was speaking. The banner said, "God is other people." Cardinal Dulles says he fervently wished that he had had a Magic Marker at that point so that he could have put an emphatic comma after the word *other*: "God is Other, people."

However variously expressed, it is evident that many of the burgeoning "spiritualities" in contemporary culture are, in fact, richly religionized forms of atheism. There is additional irony. Beyond pop spiritualities and Rortian nihilism, a serious argument is made today against a version of rationality upon which Enlightenment atheism was once premised. Here one thinks, for example, of Alasdair MacIntyre, and especially of his marvelous book *Three Rival Versions of Moral Enquiry*.

MacIntyre effectively polemicizes against the version of rationality that understands itself to be universal and disinterested and autonomous and transcending tradition. Our situation, MacIntyre says, is one rather of traditions of rationality in conflict, in rivalry. MacIntyre's favorite tradition is Thomism and its synthesis of Aristotle and Augustine, but he is prepared to join forces with the Richard Rortys in debunking the hegemonic pretensions of the so-called autonomous and foundational reason that has so long dominated our elite intellectual culture. The idea is that after the great debunking and all cards of rival tradition are put on the table, then we can all have at it in a level playing field. Presumably, the tradition that can provide the best account of reality, that is most persuasive to most people, will win out.

I have enormous respect for Alasdair MacIntyre, but I think this is a risky game. It is a game in which many Christians and observant Jews are engaged today. It is true that in exposing the fallacious value-neutrality or claims to value-neutrality of autonomous, traditionless reason, that intellectual discourse is opened up to the arguments of an eminently reasonable theism. But, in the resulting free-for-all, it is open to so much else. It is made vulnerable to the Nietzschean will to power that often sets the rules, and those rules are designed to preclude the return of the gods or God in a manner that claims public allegiance. For one tradition of reason, Thomism, for example, to form a coalition, even a temporary coalition, with unreason in order to undo another tradition of reason, such as that of the autonomous mind, is a perilous tactic.

Yet, something like this may be the future of our intellectual culture. In our universities, Christians, Jews, and, increasingly, Muslims will be free to contend for their truths—just as Marxists, of whom there are, indeed, a great many left, and Nietzscheans and devotees of the Great Earth Goddess are free to contend for their "truths." It is a matter of equal-opportunity propaganda. But—and again, there is delicious irony here—the old methodological atheism and value-neutrality, against which the revolution was launched, may, nonetheless, prevail.

There is, I believe, reason to fear that a reasoned faith in God, when it plays by the rules of the atheism of unreason, will be corrupted and eviscerated.

In other words, every party will be permitted to contend for *their* truths so long as they acknowledge that they are *their* truths and not *the* truth. Each will be permitted to propagandize. Indeed, each will *have* to propagandize if it is to hold its own, because it is acknowledged in advance that there is no common ground for the alternative to propaganda. And the alternative to propaganda is reasonable discourse.

But there is, I believe, reason to fear that a reasoned faith in God, when it plays by the rules of the atheism of unreason, will be corrupted and eviscerated. The method becomes the message. Contemporary Christian theology—Protestant and Catholic in its many variations—already provides all too many instances of the peddling of truths that are in the service of truths other than the truth of the God of Israel.

Now, I have touched briefly on some of the many faces of atheism—of living and thinking *atheos*, without God or the gods. There is the atheism of the early Christians, who posited God against the gods. There is the atheism of Enlightenment rationalists, who, committed to indubitable certainty, rejected the god whom religionists designed to fit that criterion. There is the practical atheism of Laplace, who had "no need of that hypothesis" in order to get on with what he had to do. There is the weary atheism of those who grew bored with liberalism's god created in the image and likeness of good liberals. There is the more thorough atheism of Nietzschean will to power, and finally there is the atheism of putative theists who peddle religious truths that are "true for you, if you find it useful to believe them true."

We come back then to the question "Can these atheists be good citizens?" It depends, I suppose, by what is meant by *good citizenship*. We may safely assume that the great majority of those who say they are atheists abide by the laws, pay their taxes, and may even be congenial and helpful neighbors. But can a person who does not acknowledge that he is accountable to a truth higher than the self— a truth that is not dependent upon the self—really be trusted?

John Locke, among many, many other worthies, thought the answer to that was no. However confused was Locke's theology, he and others were sure that the social contract was based upon nature, based upon the way the world really is. They were convinced that respect for a higher judgment, even an eternal judgment, was essential to good citizenship. It follows that an atheist could not be trusted to be a good citizen, according to Locke and others, and therefore could not be a citizen at all. Locke is rightly celebrated as a champion of religious toleration but not of irreligion. John Locke wrote, "Those are not at all to be tolerated who deny the being of a God"—this in his famous letter concerning toleration. "Promises, covenants and oaths, which are the bonds of human society, can have no hold upon an atheist. The taking away of God, through but even thought, dissolves all." *The taking away of God dissolves all.* Every text is susceptible to becoming pretext; every interpretation, a strategy; and every oath, a deceit.

James Madison, in his famed *Memorial and Remonstrance Against Religious Assessments* of 1785, wrote to similar effect with regard to religious freedom. It is always being forgotten that for Madison and the other founders, religious freedom is an inalienable right that is premised upon an inalienable duty. Madison wrote: "It is the duty of every man to render to the Creator such homage and such only as he believes to be acceptable to him. This duty is precedent, both in order of time and in degree of obligation, to the claims of Civil Society."

Then there follows a passage that could hardly be more pertinent to the question that brings us together. James Madison wrote: "Before any man can be considered as a member of Civil Society, he must be considered as a subject of the Governor of the Universe. And if a member of Civil Society, who enters into any subordinate association, he must always do it with a reservation of his duty to the General Authority; much more," says Madison, "must every man who becomes a member of any particular Civil Society, do it with a saving of his final allegiance to the Universal Sovereign."

In our founding period, state constitutions could and did exclude atheists from public office. It is well worth recalling, however, how much the founders had in common with respect to religious and philosophical beliefs. While a few, Jefferson notably, were sympathetic to milder or stronger versions of Deism, the fact is that most were rigorous Calvinists in the Puritan tradition, and almost all assumed a clearly Christian and a clearly Protestant Christian construal of reality. In the language of philosophical discourse, the founders were "moral realists," which is to say, they assumed the reality of a good not of their own contriving. This is amply demonstrated from many, many sources, not least, of course, the Declaration and the Constitution and especially the Preamble to the Constitution.

The good, what was called *the good*, was for the founders a reality not of their own inventing, nor was it merely the so-called conventionalism of received moral tradition. The founders' notion of the social contract was not a truncated and mechanistic contrivance of calculated self-interest. Their understanding was much more in the nature of a compact, premised upon a sense of covenantal purpose guiding what they called this *novus ordo seclorum*, this "new order of the ages." That understanding of a covenant encompassing the contract was, in a time of supreme testing for America, brought to full and magisterial articulation by Abraham Lincoln. The Constitution, he proposed, represented not a deal struck but a nation "so conceived and so dedicated."

In such a nation, an atheist, I would suggest, can be a citizen, but not a *good* citizen, for a good citizen does more than abide by the laws. A good citizen is able to give an account, a morally compelling account, of the regime—of the constitutional order of which he is part. He is able to justify its defense against its enemies and to convincingly recommend its virtues to citizens of the next generation so that they, in turn, can transmit that regime to citizens yet unborn. This regime, this order of liberal democracy, of republican self-governance, is not self-evidently good and just. An account, a moral account, must be given. Reasons must be given, and they must be reasons that draw authority from that which is higher than ourselves, our own convenience, our own conventions. They must be able to draw authority from that which transcends us, from that to which we are ultimately obliged.

Those who believe in the God of Abraham, Isaac, Jacob, and Jesus turn out to be the best citizens. Those who were once called *atheists*, the Christians, are now the reliable defenders not of the gods but of the good reasons for this regime of ordered liberty. Such people are the best citizens, not in spite of but *because* of their loyalty to this political order, a loyalty that is qualified by a loyalty to a higher order. Among the best of the good reasons they give in justifying this regime is that it is a regime that makes a sharply limited claim upon the loyalty of its citizens. The ultimate allegiance of the faithful is not to the regime or to its constituting texts but to the City of God and the sacred texts that guide our path toward that end for which we were created.

And so, such citizens are *dual* citizens in a regime that, as Madison and others well understood, was designed for such dual citizenship. When the regime forgets itself and tries to reestablish the gods of the *civitas*, even if it is in the name of liberal democracy, then the followers of the God of Abraham have no choice but to be faithful and, in being faithful, to run the risk of once again being called atheists.

As for what is meant by *atheism* in the modern era, the conclusion is that the American experiment in constitutional democracy was not conceived and dedicated by atheists and cannot today be conceived and dedicated anew by atheists. In times of testing—and every time is a time of testing for this experiment in ordered liberty—a morally convincing account must be given. You may well ask, "Convincing to whom?" One obvious answer in a democracy, although not the only answer, is this: A morally convincing account must be given to a majority of our fellow citizens. Giving such an account is required of good citizens, and that is why, I reluctantly conclude, atheists cannot be good citizens. Thank you.

Q & A

Thank you so much, Father Neuhaus. We have a few minutes for questions and answers. I hope that a few people out there have good questions. If anyone would be brave enough to ask the first question, it doesn't have to relate to anything that you just heard; just any question would be fine.

Q: This is about the question of secularism as it relates to what is happening today in Iraq and France with the two French journalists who are being held hostage, and it's about the demand that France abrogate its law forbidding the wearing of Muslim head scarves, Jewish headgear, and Christian crosses in France's public schools. Do you have any thoughts on this problem?

A: Yes—surprise, surprise—I do. France has a peculiar tradition stemming from 1789, in the French Revolution, of a laicist passion, a laicist—anticlerical, anti-Christian, and most specifically anti-Catholic—character. This has now extended to Islam for very good reasons, because the presence of Islam, not only in France, but in Germany and in other places, poses the very real prospect of what a recent book calls *Eurabia*, that is to say, the reality of Islam becoming, in public and in law, the dominant cultural and religious force in France and Germany and some of the other countries.

Those of you who read *First Things* know that I hold Bernard Lewis in highest regard for his writings on the clash of civilization between Islam and Christianity in the West. Bernard Lewis, a very cautious, scholarly, and prudent man, recently observed, after a long, long reluctance to say it, that in his judgment, by the end of this century, most of Europe will be Muslim. Just the demographic, cultural, political realities suggest that. If that happens, that is a development of monumental importance for the future of Western civilization, for the future of the Christian Gospel, and for the future of the role of America in the world.

Q: In *Thus Spoke Zarathustra*, Nietzsche somewhat lamented the situation, in the early part of the century, with God and religion being on the wane, as he saw it. He said that it was an awesome task to try to replace religious values with a set of values of your own. I was wondering, if one were able to do that as an atheist, then could an atheist be a good citizen?

A: I think the answer continues to be *no*, because all of us are contextualized, which is simply to say that we are all parts of a particular cultural, political, social circumstance. To be a good citizen, and I hope throughout my talk it is apparent, I was talking about being a good American citizen. Now, one might change the argument significantly relative to other circumstances politically and culturally.

I think Nietzsche was a genius, which should be needless to say—a mad genius perhaps to the end of his life, truly mad by any criterion—but he firmly, unlike many atheists, firmly rejected a specifically Christian God, the God of the Cross, as the God of underlings and weaklings, who were not worthy of what human beings, in his understanding, are capable of being. We know the values with which Nietzsche replaced the vacuum, after he had swept the field of Christian morality and Christian faith.

While it would be reckless—and some people have very recklessly drawn a direct line connecting the dots between Nietzsche and the Third Reich and Adolf Hitler—there is no denying that the chief ideologist of the Nazi movement did see in Nietzsche a kind of veneer of philosophical justification for what they were doing. When you create a vacuum, when you create what I call "the naked public square"—a public life denuded of the moral discourse, including the moral discourse that is religiously grounded in a society—then you have destroyed the very bonds of what Lincoln called the "mystic cords" that bind us together with the dead and with those not yet born.

So, even if one believed the American experiment and the American constitutional order are fundamentally, wrongly founded—and there are people who believe that, even some Christians and others—we still have no choice in our historical moment but to accept responsibility in our context, in a very keen awareness of our obligation to both those who have gone before us and those who will come after us.

Q: As someone who has been both Lutheran and Catholic, I was curious to know if you could recommend any resources that set out as fairly as possible the positions on both sides and the arguments or evidence that each side marshals.

A: There are a host of good things. Most of them tend to be, up until the last couple of decades, highly polemical and distortive and almost by definition unfair. A lot in the ecumenical era to which Eric referred tends to the opposite in fudging and gliding over differences of very great importance.

A particular book that deals specifically with this is reviewed in the current issue of *First Things*. Almost everything you would be interested in is in *First Things*. On the specific and very important Catholic/Protestant difference on what we understand Mary to be and the role of Mary in the faith, it's written by an Evangelical by the name of Gustafson and Longenecker, a Catholic. Again, go to the web site of *First Things*. It is a font of wisdom!

Q: In over-identifying the faith with empire, there can be gross misrepresentations of the kingdom in terms of its political, economic ramifications. Therefore, in radical Reformation history, there's also been resistance to identification with the existing status quo. So, the flip side of your question is if atheists don't necessarily make good citizens, do the rest of the people, the fifty percent that are warming the pews, the theists, necessarily make good citizens?

A: Obviously, not necessarily at all. I did a lecture somewhere some years ago on this title, and Jules Feiffer, the cartoonist for *The Nation*, got wind of this.

I guess it was a news story or whatever, and he did a full-page cartoon ridiculing the argument that I was making. It listed, one after the other, all kinds of religious leaders and prominent Christians who had done terrible and criminal things in the course of the last several months. Of course, I would expect that the overwhelming majority of people in our jails are believing Christians, although there is an unusually high incidence of Muslims. So, we're not saying that all Christians are good citizens.

I thought you were going to ask a different and a very important question, and that is the degree to which there is a danger that we identify our responsibility to the American experiment with a notion of America's providential purpose, or "manifest destiny," in the world. The answer is *yes*. That is always a danger and has at times been a danger, but I would say today, the greater danger is that we have forgotten that there *is* an understanding of Providence in Christian history and in Christian theology and that we believe in a God who is active in history, although we do not discern his purposes with any degree of precision with regard to particular political, historical world events.

Therefore, it is very important, to my mind, that we continue to have in the Pledge of Allegiance "under God." These "trivial symbolic things" of "ceremonial deism," as the Supreme Court says, are things of extraordinary importance, because they symbolize not that America as a nation is somehow favored and privileged and elected as Israel or the Church is elected, but rather exactly that America is under judgment. To be under God is to be under both his mercy and his judgment. It's a matter of vital importance to the revitalization of the American liberal experiment and democracy—if, indeed, it can be revitalized—that we have, as the founders had, that sense of historical and moral responsibility to that which transcends us.

Q: I'm an elected lay leader with the congregation at the Cathedral of Saint John the Divine, which makes me an Episcopalian/Anglican. While we are a large denomination, some ninety million around the world, we would be deluding ourselves if we did not link that size to the expansion of the British Empire and its political growth and the idea that the Church moves slightly one inch behind the armies. One could say that a lot of the map of religions around the world has been linked to the mighty power of Rome and Constantinople. My question is, is atheism not necessarily always linked to theology and complex issues, but in some cases is simply a fatigue of the church-and-state relationship and the battles therein and what has come out of it in a very nonreligious sense over history?

A: Yes, I think the answer to your question is right. One of the reasons for the comparative vitality of religion and of Christianity, specifically in this country, is that we have not had a state church. The Church has unwisely, in my judgment, in times of history, allied itself with state power. Now, at the same time, you have to put yourself into the historical circumstance of the people involved. For example, it's very easy today to—and almost all theologians and religious thinkers [do]—condemn, dismiss out of hand, Constantinianism, the fourth-century quasi-establishment of Christianity as the religion of the Roman Empire.

Here we come to the question of Providence and how hidden and mysterious are God's ways. Did not God use that association in remarkable ways for good—in a whole realm of areas? Similarly, did not God possibly use the British Empire for good in ways that may have been much, much better than the intentions or the motives of the people that were running the empire?

I would suggest my disposition is that of Saint Augustine in the fifth century. It is not true, as many people think, that when Augustine was writing *The City of God*, the Roman Empire was falling around him. It was in trouble, but he still thought it was strong and had a great future. Yet he had this powerful sense—which gets back to what I talked about as his dual citizenship and is very consonant with what Madison is saying in the *Memorial and Remonstrance*—that we live in two communities, two cities, or, as Augustine put it, "the City of Man and the City of God." They are not neatly separated; they are entangled in very, very troubling, and sometimes confusing and conflicted, ways. The City of Man, whether it be the Roman Empire, whether it be American liberal democracy, whether it be anything else, is always going to be the kingdom of what Augustine called the *libido dominandi*—the lust for power and glory—and that will always be the case.

And yet, there are some cities of man that are better than others, some ways that are better ordered than others. It is my belief and conviction—but this is a political historical judgment, not a theological judgment—that the American experiment is well ordered for its potentiality for doing justice both to human dignity and the right order in society and to the freedom of the Church to flourish as its own mission requires.

Q: As a preacher of the Gospel myself, I was preparing a sermon to be delivered at the Duke University Chapel about the law of God, or the command of God, concerning the love for one's enemy and proper conduct toward one's enemy. I was trying to find voices, testimonies, witnesses who would speak for God in such a human situation. I found five voices from my reading of the newspaper and listening to C-SPAN and the network news against state-sponsored torture or state-permitted torture or torture allowed to take place under unheeding or inattentive commanders.

Not one of those five voices came from within the Church. Four of them were—I don't know what they were, but certainly not observant Jews or Christians. The fifth one is well known for his atheism in your second sense. This was very disappointing to me. It seems to me that the Church has failed us in this time of international crisis. I offer that as a witness and wonder what you would say about it.

A: I confess I'm a little surprised, because I could give you a list of, had we time, five hundred writers, theologians, bishops, et cetera, who would very strongly and compellingly make the case against torture ever being morally permissible. I'm troubled that Alan Dershowitz of Harvard Law School, who is not an observant Jew, has written, I think, a deeply, deeply wrongheaded book urging us to get used to the idea that we are going to have to accommodate ourselves to torture as a normal means of waging war against terror, et cetera. I'm sorry to say that some of my friends at *Commentary* magazine have written in a similar vein.

I think they're wrong, and certainly the teaching of the Catholic Church is that torture—the deliberate infliction of pain and humiliation upon others with the intent to degradate them—that is, to violate their human dignity—is always and everywhere wrong. We must never get used to it, and we must never—contra Alan Dershowitz—let ourselves experiment with the limits. Sinful human beings that we are—and sin-riddled institutions, as all political and military and police institutions also are—we human beings cannot be trusted with experimenting with torture.

Q: This question is in terms of our own spiritual journeys. I am Catholic, and most of the time, I worship in a Catholic parish. My own sister became a Presbyterian minister. I was wondering what, after seventeen years as a Lutheran, was the major focus in your becoming an ordained Catholic priest.

A: As you might imagine, it's a long story, but very simply, I entered into full communion with the Catholic Church in order to become more fully the Christian that I was as a Lutheran. I became a Catholic when I could no longer explain to myself or to others why I was not a Catholic.

Q: In the light of Lincoln's great word on that "mystic" thread that we should try to discern, what would you say about the current political election?

A: At one aspect of that, of course, is the very lively interest around the belated, but increasingly bold, initiatives of the Catholic bishops with respect to public figures, politicians, and others who openly, persistently, publicly, defiantly reject the Church's teaching with respect to the defense of the innocent in the case of abortion, euthanasia, and embryonic stem-cell research. My own view is that the bishops are at long last doing their job. The Catholic position is that nobody can tell you, the Church cannot tell you, how to vote, for example.

It is orthodox, rock-bottom-firm Catholic teaching that a person must act in accord with his conscience. At the same time, it is rock-bottom Catholic teaching that a person must *form* his conscience rightly. In the formation of conscience, the first responsibility of bishops is to defend and articulate the fullness of the faith without compromise. That is what the whole controversy is about. It ought not to be controversial at all.

> It is orthodox, rock-bottom-firm Catholic teaching that a person must act in accord with his conscience. At the same time, it is rock-bottom Catholic teaching that a person must *form* his conscience rightly.

In 1984, you recall that then-representative Geraldine Ferraro* was running

---

* Geraldine Ferraro, who was an attorney, a member of the United States House of Representatives, a Democrat Party member, and the first woman vice-presidential candidate, died on March 26, 2011.

as vice president and said publicly on a number of occasions that there is more than one Catholic position on abortion and that you can be pro-abortion and a faithful Catholic. To that, my late dear and much-missed friend John O'Connor, who had ordained me to the priesthood—and some people, of course, accused him of meddling in politics and violating "church and state," which was all nonsense—very carefully, very lucidly, very calmly said, "The issue that Representative Ferraro has put on the public table is what is Catholic teaching, and I, being the archbishop of New York, feel I should perhaps be allowed to say something about that. Among the things I have to say is that what Ms. Ferraro is saying is simply not true. That's not Catholic teaching."

That's what the Catholics are doing now. If you have a Catholic that says, "I am a good Catholic and I also stand before NARAL and Planned Parenthood, their meetings, and pledge allegiance to their cause, which is explicitly and overtly premised against, in hostility to, the Catholic Church," it just creates scandal. That's the Catholic phrase, which doesn't mean scandal as in sex-abuse scandal or bank robberies or whatever. *Scandal* means to confuse the faithful about the truth.

The bishops have the obligation then to encounter that person, engage that person in dialogue and persuasion, and to try to move that person toward recognition of his or her error and to repentance and amendment of life. The bishops' statement in June is very careful about this and allows for a lot of perplexities and prudential judgment of bishops in particular circumstances.

But, at some point, if that person persistently, publicly, defiantly says, "I reject the Church's teaching that abortion [for example] is intrinsically evil—that it is always and everywhere evil—to deliberately take an innocent human life," then at some point that person has to be told persuasively, compellingly, lovingly, "My friend, you are jeopardizing your relationship with the Church, and, if Catholics are right about this, your relationship with God. This is a very solemn thing, and you should not present yourself at the Eucharist, at the Holy Communion, which is the central act of representing one's full communion with solidarity with the faith of the Church, until you've taken care of this problem."

That's the pastoral responsibility of the bishops, and if it has political fallout one way or another, that finally is the responsibility of those who take an extremist—don't-give-an-inch litmus test—position with regard to the support of the unlimited abortion license.

Who Are We?
C. S. Lewis and the
Question of Man

———

JEAN BETHKE ELSHTAIN

———

September 29, 2005

Introduction

I am Eric Metaxas. Good evening, and welcome to Socrates in the City, the thinking person's alternative to the Oxonian Society. It is a very cheap shot to say that. I am referring to an article in *The New York Times* yesterday about the Oxonian Society. It claimed that the Oxonian Society had no legitimate connection to Oxford.

The Oxonian Society meets here in New York in clubs like this and counts among its speakers such luminaries as Sharon Stone. It's a very elite sort of thing.

I wanted to point out that Socrates in the City is really not like the Oxonian Society, because we have some very real connections to Oxford. Indeed, it was at Oxford this summer that I met our speaker tonight, Dr. Jean Bethke Elshtain. Her talk at Oxford was so wonderful I thought, *Hey, let's get her to come and speak at Socrates in the City in New York City*, and here we are.

Socrates in the City has other connections to Oxford, and I want to mention some of those tonight. For example, our previous Socrates speaker, Joe Loconte, who is right here in the front row—our alumni speakers' area— Joe and I had the high privilege of being asked to debate at the Oxford Union last spring, and we took them up on that. We gave them what-for. It was an extraordinary thing. We have photos to prove it, the black-tie dinner beforehand and so on. Many of our previous Socrates speakers have attended Oxford University or, in fact, have taught there or do teach there.

So, as I say, unlike the Oxonian Society, which was really taken to task in *The New York Times* yesterday, Socrates in the City has very legitimate connections to Oxford. But our name is Socrates in the City, and we have no real connection to Socrates.

That's our particular disconnect. They have their disconnect; that's our disconnect. The point is that like the Oxonian Society, we are a bunch of wine-bibbers and poseurs who get intellectual big shots like Sir John Polkinghorne and Dr. Elshtain to provide us with some sort of intellectual cover and respectability. I don't know if I mentioned Sharon Stone, but we are going to get her eventually.

Seriously, folks, we like to kid. Tonight, we proudly welcome Dr. Jean Bethke Elshtain of the University of Chicago, where she is a professor of political and social ethics. Her résumé is so impressive and her accomplishments so vast that I had better cut the chitchat and plunge right in, because I really want to get to those accomplishments.

Her bio says that she is a political philosopher whose work shows the connections between our political and our ethical convictions. Her tools in showing this connection sometimes include an electron microscope. Can you hear the crickets? That is really reaching very far for a joke. Basically, I wanted to say that it is hard to see that connection between the political and the ethical. But, you know, if I really have to explain it to you, either it is a bad joke or you are unworthy of the joke, and I think it's perhaps a little bit of both.

Professor Elshtain holds *nine* honorary degrees—surely not simultaneously. That is physically impossible. I understand that even Andre the Giant in his prime could only hold six, unless you don't mean that *literally*.

Anyway, Dr. Elshtain is the Laura Spelman Rockefeller Professor of Social and Political Ethics at the University of Chicago and has been in that post since 1995. She also has taught at the University of Massachusetts and Vanderbilt, and has been a visiting professor at Harvard and Yale.

Professor Elshtain holds *nine* honorary degrees—surely not simultaneously. That is physically impossible. I understand that even Andre the Giant in his prime could only hold six, unless you don't mean that *literally*.

I should mention, incidentally, that I'm currently working on getting my honorary doctorate.

In 1996, Dr. Elshtain was elected a fellow of the American Academy of Arts and Sciences. She is the author of many books and was the contributing editor for *The New Republic*, before it became a scandal sheet. I'm sorry, that's the *Enquirer*. I always get them mixed up.

Professor Elshtain has been a fellow at the Institute for Advanced Study at Princeton. Nothing to sneeze at there. She is also a Guggenheim fellow, a fellow of the National Humanities Center, and in 2003–2004 held the Maguire Chair in Ethics and American History at the Library of Congress. Who can forget the old Maguire Chair at the Library of Congress? I believe the cushions are stuffed with horsehair, are they not?

Professor Elshtain also serves on the Scholars Council at the Library of Congress and is the recipient of the Ellen Gregg Ingalls Award for Excellence in Classroom Teaching, the highest award for undergraduate teaching at Vanderbilt University. Again, nothing to sneeze at. But perhaps the most impressive of all these amazingly impressive accomplishments is that in 2005–2006—that is *this* year, of course—Professor Elshtain will deliver the extremely prestigious Gifford Lectures at the University of Edinburgh. That is just an extraordinary honor. Previous Gifford lecturers have included Alfred North Whitehead, William James, Albert Schweitzer, Niels Bohr, Hannah Arendt, and Reinhold Niebuhr.

But seriously, these are hugely prestigious! If you're asked to deliver the Gifford Lectures, you become so intellectually respectable it hurts. It hurts me just to think about this. So, thank you for lending some gravitas and respectability to this cheesy little ad-hoc, feel-good-about-ourselves, wine-bibbing group. Thank you very much, Dr. Elshtain, we owe you one.

Now, I've noticed that whenever the Gifford Lectures are mentioned, they always have to mention the names that I just mentioned. But they don't mention *all* the names of the previous people who have been asked to deliver the Gifford Lectures, and I think there is good reason for that. For example, one of them is Noam Chomsky.

Also, and this is hard to believe, but Charo was a Gifford lecturer. They obviously don't mention that, because that is not going to make you look very good. They also don't mention that Harvey Keitel and Moms Mabley were previous Gifford lecturers. And it gets even more depressing—recently, Curtis Sliwa and John Gotti Jr. were both mentioned as Gifford lecturers

So, when you really know the full picture, these much-vaunted Gifford lecturers are not so impressive after all. It is very easy to sound impressive when we are selective about whom we mention in association with something. Another example that you always hear: Stephen Hawking is said to occupy the Lucasian Chair of Mathematics at Cambridge. Then they inevitably say, "which was formerly held by Sir Isaac Newton." We always hear that—"the Lucasian Chair of Mathematics at Cambridge, previously held by Sir Isaac Newton."

Well, I don't want to break it to any fans of Stephen Hawking here, but Sir Isaac Newton did not exactly leave the chair ten minutes before Stephen Hawking occupied it. No, you see, history tells us Sir Isaac Newton resigned his chair in 1701, leaving an alarming gap of 278 years between his occupying it and Sir Stephen Hawking's occupying it. Additionally, history tells us that between 1701 and 1979 many terrible, unworthy persons occupied that self-same Lucasian chair—persons whom Sir Stephen Hawking's sycophantic biographers would have us conveniently forget.

We know, for example, that not long after Sir Isaac Newton vacated the chair, it was occupied by several fishwives of ill repute, followed by a vulgar cobbler with scrofula. Most disturbingly, it was for many years occupied by an incontinent charwoman. So, the next time you hear about the Lucasian Chair of Mathematics, don't be impressed by that either.

Where were we? Oh, yes, we are here at the Union Club to hear Dr. Jean Bethke Elshtain. She will be speaking tonight on the question "Who are we?" We ask the big questions. We have asked, "What is the nature of evil? Where do we come from? Where are we going? Is there a God? If there is a God, what is God like? What do different worldviews say about evil?"

Tonight, we ask, "Who are we?" and we will hear from Dr. Elshtain on that. I had the privilege of hearing tonight's talk in Oxford at a C. S. Lewis conference this past summer. So, without further ado, it is my very distinct pleasure to introduce Dr. Jean Bethke Elshtain.

Talk

W ell, thank you so much, Eric, for this invitation. As some of you may know, Eric is a very persuasive person. Once he got on my case, I knew that I had to give in, and sooner or later I had to say *yes*. It so happened that I knew I was going to be in New York for another reason; so, this worked out rather well. Now, let me just plunge into this—alas—very sobering topic.

In March of this year, the prestigious *New England Journal of Medicine* published an essay on euthanizing handicapped newborns that incorporated something called the Dutch Groningen Protocol for such procedures. *The New York Times Magazine* on July 10, 2005, reprinted those protocols under the heading "Euthanasia for babies: is this humane or barbaric?"

Now, this way of presenting alternatives in a guise of putative neutrality, of course, is typical of much current opinion. I suspect that all of us know the average reader of *The New York Times* prefers to choose the humane, not barbaric, alternative, and the humane course, it turns out, is the one that favors infanticide, *if* the Groningen Protocols are followed. Euthanizing babies under such circumstances is the way of reason, we're told, and those who say we must not cross that line advance what the author calls *sentiment*, which he equates to nonreason.

The essayist, a fellow named Jim Holt, asks his readers to imagine a heated dining-room-table argument about such matters: "The way of reason involves unflinching honesty, rather than shrouding such matters in casuistry as in the United States. For moral sentiments are inertial, resisting the force of moral reason," and the essay concludes in this way: "Just quote Verhagen's"—Verhagen is the Dutch doctor who identifies himself as a pro-infant euthanasia practitioner—"description of the medically induced infant deaths over which he has presided: 'It's beautiful in a way. It is after they die that you see them relaxed for the first time.' And even the most spirited dinner-table debate over moral progress will, for a moment, fall silent."

The author, Mr. Holt, wants us to imagine the hushed atmosphere as one in which diners are overwhelmed by the vision of peace at last for infants born with deformities or certain ailments. I suspect that most of us gathered here in this room would fall silent from the horror of it all—basically the dictum "Let's give these perturbed spirits peace at last. Let's kill them." Holt also seems to believe that brutal candor about such matters is the ethically preferred route—"Yes, I'm killing them, and that's the right thing to do"—rather than the kind of muddling through that may involve allowing, let's say, multiply handicapped infants to die rather than using heroic measures, for example. That is presented as casuistic confusion. So, any course that reflects our moral uneasiness is dishonest, and any course that candidly makes it possible to kill is honest and reasoned.

I worry that, in the name of reason, we may be eliminating whole categories of human beings.

Now, is anyone in this room familiar with C. S. Lewis? Does anyone doubt what he might say about this, about the way in which darkness becomes light and healers become killers? Those of you, and I'm not assuming this for anyone in the room, but those of you who may be somewhat familiar with my work know that these are issues that have long troubled me. I worry that, in the name of reason, we may be eliminating whole categories of human beings.

For example, so overwhelming is our current animus against the less than perfect that nearly 90 percent of pregnancies that test for Down syndrome are aborted in the United States today. All of this comes under the rubric of choice, and it is under the notion of expanding choice that we are busily narrowing our definition of humanity and, along the way, a felt responsibility to create welcoming environments for all children.

When we aim to eliminate—whether through euthanasia or systematic selective abortion of flawed fetuses—one version of humanity, perhaps suffering humanity, but humanity, nonetheless, we dare to constrict the boundaries of the moral community.

In his *Ethics*, Dietrich Bonhoeffer, the anti-Nazi theologian who was hanged by the Gestapo in the closing days of World War II, insisted that the most radical excision of the integrity and right of natural life is what he called *arbitrary killing*. He defined that as "the deliberate destruction of innocent life," and he goes on to say, "The right to live is a matter of essence." It is not a socially imposed value. There is a truth claim there that holds no matter what, Bonheoffer says, "for even the most wretched life is worth living before God."

As with Dietrich Bonheoffer, C. S. Lewis was writing under the shadows of Nazism and Stalinism. His essay "The Abolition of Man" appeared in 1944, subtitled "Reflections on Education with Special Reference to the Teaching of English in the Upper Forms of School." This essay would seem to have very little to do with the grave matters with which I have begun. Not so. It turns out that Lewis sees pernicious tendencies in, of all places, elementary school textbooks. At first this is puzzling, but it quickly makes sense. The general cultural milieu—a culture's mores, as Alexis de Tocqueville, author of the great classic work *Of Democracy in America*, might put it—is always embedded in and embodied in the books that we require our children to read, the books that we use to teach them.

So, what on earth was going on with English textbooks, such that the great C. S. Lewis would take note of them? First, he detects an embrace of subjectivism, which means—speaking epistemologically—the embrace of both positivism and emotivism. That will become clear as I go along, I promise. The year 1944 and the immediate postwar decades were the heyday of this approach. It had clearly made its way into elementary schools, even as it was the dominant approach to the teaching of philosophy at Great Britain's elite institutions of higher learning.

So, we have the reduction of values to the subjective feelings of the speaker—that *sentiment* opposed to reason, if you will, of which the *New York Times* piece spoke. That view that moral claims are reduced to subjective feelings leads to the embrace, or is itself a fruit of the embrace, of two interlocked propositions. Lewis summarizes them this way: "First, that all sentences containing a predicate of values are statements about the emotional state of the speaker, and second, that all such statements are unimportant."

"One need not refer"—he goes on to the general philosophy at work—"that all values are subjective and trivial in order to promulgate this philosophy." Indeed, he tells us, many textbook authors probably do not recognize what they are doing to the schoolchild, and certainly, "the schoolchild cannot know what is being done to him. In this way, another portion of the human heritage has been quietly taken from schoolchildren before they are old enough to understand."

Let me provide an illustration of this general approach from my own experience. When our daughter, Jenny, was in fifth grade in a progressive public school in the town in which we then lived, one of those bucolic New England college towns in which the university students outnumber the permanent residents, she was required to complete a worksheet distinguishing fact from value. Values, of course, are defined as subjective opinions having *no* cognitive content. They are unreasoned. This is that positivism and emotivism of which Lewis spoke.

Jenny read aloud as she was doing this, and as she was trying to figure out this worksheet, I began to rant, as I tend to do when I am confronted with this sort of thing. Finally, to help her understand, I said, "Well, Jenny, if I say something is wrong, does that mean I am stating a fact or a value?"—values, remember, being the things that we all have, and we can't really distinguish between them because they all come out of the same subjectivist stew.

Predictably, Jenny answered, "A value." So far, so good. I was leading her someplace. I continued: "Well, Martin Luther King Jr. said slavery and segregation were wrong. Suppose there's somebody who says slavery is good, and we, in fact, should have more of it. Couldn't we say he is wrong and Martin Luther King Jr. is right and that slavery and segregation are bad and that that isn't just Martin Luther King Jr.'s opinion?"

Jenny was stumped for a moment. She was clearly bothered by this, and then she said, "Well, I think slavery's wrong too, but that is just my opinion."

Now, as you might guess, our discussion didn't end there, but this experience reinforces Lewis's claim of the pervasiveness of the sorts of teaching that he indicts in his essay. For Lewis, when ordinary human feelings are set up as contrary to reason, we are on dangerous ground, indeed, for a botched treatment of basic human emotion is not only bad literature, he tells us, but is morally treacherous to boot: "By starving the sensibility of our pupils, we only make them easier prey to the propagandist when he comes."

Lewis insists that in Platonic, Aristotelian, Stoic, Christian, and some Eastern religion, one finds in common, in his words, "the doctrine of objective value—the belief that certain attitudes are really true and others are really false to the kind of things the universe is and the kinds of things we are." He refers to this collective understanding of transcultural, universal values and claims simply as the *Tao* [traditional morality]. "Thus, emotional states can be either reasonable or unreasonable. They are not opposed to reason, for one must not traffic in false distinctions among reason and emotion and sentiment." In the positivism that he is criticizing, by contrast, "the world of facts without one trace of value and the world of feelings without one trace of truth or falsehood, justice or injustice, confront one another, and no rapprochement is possible. It is all a ghastly simplicity."

When I was a graduate student in the late sixties, early seventies, this "ghastly simplicity" was, in fact, the reigning approach in political science. To tell you the truth, I never quite got it, which is one reason, no doubt, that I became a political philosopher. We're a sort of lower order of being within the world of political science, because we persist in asking these bizarre questions about justice and decency and truth and so on and so forth. The approach to political science dictates the severance of these questions of value from questions of fact.

In my youthful optimism in the late sixties, early seventies, I had, for a time, believed that the decisive critiques of this approach mounted by thinkers like the philosophers Charles Taylor and Alasdair MacIntyre had finally pounded the nails into the coffin of positivism in the human sciences. It turns out it wasn't so. This approach reappeared with gusto in the current dominant approach in the social sciences, which is so-called *rational choice theory*.

Now is not the time, I realize, to unpack rational choice, or *rat choice*, as some of us prefer to call it, in any detail, but, suffice it to say, expanded as an entire worldview, rather than utilized as a more modest approach to a finite series of economic decision-making processes, *rat choice* trivializes all statements of values. They have no truth warrant or claim. It enshrines a reductive view of the human person as the sum total of his or her subjective preferences, his or her calculations of marginal utility. Within this world, everything, in principle, can be commodified. Everything, in principle, has a price rather than a value. Any restrictions societies draw on where human preference might take us are really arbitrary—there are no intrinsic goods or evils. Nothing is valued for its own sake.

So, for example, we may value babies in a certain way. It is an ancient sentiment, and we get very emotional about it, but this is a claim that has no rational content in this view, and you could as well commodify our understanding of babies and have, as a number of very well-known and distinguished adherents have argued, a market in babies where people that did not want their babies could advertise and sell their child to the highest bidder. Every value at face value is a preference, and it is describable in the language of maximizing utility.

Let me give you another example of this. When I was teaching at a particular university, not the place where I am now, an eager, young political science candidate gave his required job talk. He was one of those folks who probably had not had much choice about the training—mal-education—that he had been subjected to.

Everything to him was a preference. There was no other way to talk about politics or the moral life. So, when he completed his remarks, which were about American political life, I asked him the following: "When Martin Luther King Jr. delivered his great speech, he cried, 'I have a dream,' not 'I have a preference.' How do you explain this? Is there a difference?"

He was a little bit flustered, and then he said, "Well, what King was calling a dream is really a preference," to which I responded, "Then there's no difference in principle between King's dream and a debate about alterations in the price of utilities, for example."

This candidate's way of thinking makes a hash of our moral sentiments and of our God-given capacity to reason about that which is true and that which is good and that which is worthy. This surely is what C. S. Lewis feared in 1944; he feared that something precious and irreparable was being lost. And as in 1944, those debunking the normative status and truth warrants of claims of value were tacitly promoting values of their own.

Writes Lewis, "A great many of those who 'debunk' traditional or (as they would say) 'sentimental' values have background values of their own which they believe to be immune from the debunking process." One thinks of the fundamentalist skeptic who is skeptical of everything save his fundamentalism or the proclaimer of moral relativism who relativizes everything save his claim to moral relativism. So, in Lewis's epoch and ours, what matters is not the dignity of each and every human life, but rather a variety of things, including—and it pertains to my topic—the preservation of species, and newborns with major disabilities will never do that. They have no instrumental value. They will never maximize their reproductive potential. So, they lack value.

Two, they will never contribute to production. They will be worthless in "the marketplace." That too means they are without value. We might arbitrarily attach value to them, but that is emotive and not reasoned. It is interesting and troubling that we are in an age of human rights par excellence, and yet there are forces at work in our world that undermine a rock-bottom claim of human dignity that alone can ground a robust, sustainable regime of human rights.

Certain excisions of our humanity are obvious; for example, [the late] Osama bin Laden's claim that Americans, Jews, and infidels, which includes all Muslims that don't agree with him, can be slaughtered whenever and wherever they are to be found—men, women, children, armed or unarmed. We see the problem immediately: entire categories of humanity stripped of all rights in the rhetoric and the practices of those enflamed by this rhetoric, as Americans learned so tragically on 9/11 and as our British brothers and sisters learned on 7/7—people being indiscriminately killed because of who they are.

There are other forces undermining the ground of human dignity by eroding the full force of our humanity, whether whole or broken, normal or abnormal, young or old. Population biology and econometric perspectives are just two of the ways we have devised to do this. These approaches have worked their way into medical thought and practice and into medical ethics. I know this rather well, because I cross the street to go to the medical school at the University of Chicago from time to time to do a seminar for the students

It is interesting and troubling that we are in an age of human rights par excellence, and yet there are forces at work in our world that undermine a rock-bottom claim of human dignity that alone can ground a robust, sustainable regime of human rights.

who are taking a required course in medical ethics, and I keep telling them to throw out the textbook because it is false to the complexities of moral life.

I appreciate that many who share the view that seriously deformed infants should be euthanized will be horrified by my remarks. They, they will insist, are trying to be decent and human, trying to prevent "useless" suffering—a bit of an odd locution because it suggests that there is useful human suffering— but euthanasia enthusiasts would never accept this possibility.

Those working to counter the forces of utilitarianism and positivism should acknowledge these urgencies. The people who oppose this are not monsters, for the most part, though there are surely those who handle needles, like Dr. Jack Kevorkian—*Dr. Death*, as he actually liked to be called, who are, or were, deeply disturbed. Instead, I suggest most people embracing this perspective want to do the right thing.

Lewis understood this. He understood that various ideologies—including some contemporary right-to-die ideologies—are arbitrarily wrenched from their context in the whole, and here his reference point is to those truths that he has discussed, that he calls the Tao. Remember those universal truths. When these ideologies are wrenched from that context, he says, "they are swollen to madness in their isolation, and in this way, claims to human values are weakened or reduced to superstition." The Nietzschean ethic can be accepted only if we are ready to scrap traditional morals as a mere error and then to put ourselves in a position where we can find no ground for any value judgments at all.

At this point in his essay, Lewis turns explicitly to our conquest of nature, the way people in his era heralded man's triumph over nature's arbitrariness. His examples of this are going to sound archaic and very quaint to you, but his examples—and each one would warrant a fuller discussion—are the airplane, the wireless, and the contraceptive.

I want to take up contraception—"What's his beef about that?"—for closer examination. The living, Lewis argued, deny existence to the not-living through this method. Here is his real concern—that this is simply selective breeding with nature as its instrument. Those may seem harsh words, but consider that this exercise of power—perhaps better put, the way this power can be exercised and even promoted by states—implies the power to make one's descendants what one pleases, "for each new power won by man is a power over man as well. Each advance leaves him weaker as well as stronger. . . . The final stage is come when Man by eugenics, pre-natal conditioning, and by an education and propaganda based on a[n allegedly] perfect applied psychology, has obtained full control over himself. Human nature will be the last part of Nature to surrender to Man."

Lewis—remember he is writing in the era of Nazi eugenics policy and is very concerned about these developments—held out hope that "the benefi-cent obstinacy of real mothers, real nurses, and (above all) real children" might preserve "the human race in such sanity as it still possesses. But the man-moulders of the new age will be armed with the powers of an omnicom-petent state and an irresistible scientific technique: we shall get at last a race of conditioners who really can cut out all posterity in what shape they please."

It is extraordinary how prescient Lewis is on this issue, because if you read the material coming out of genomics, you begin to see in the language of "positive genetic enhancement," precisely the desire to mold human beings to our specifications. No one wants to say *eugenics*, because of its association with horrific historical events; nevertheless, you can see this enthusiasm about someday perfectly controlling the kinds of human beings we produce.

Lewis's reference point, as I pointed out, and that of his readers, would have been national socialist Germany with its cruelly enforced eugenics. I doubt that many in his own country thought their society might one day wander into this particular danger zone and that it would be not under the banner of totalitarian-ism but under the rubric of human choice and freedom.

As Lewis fretted about post-humanity, we have our own apostles, as you know, of the post-human future. In 1944, when C. S. Lewis wrote of the abolition of man, he was not trafficking in metaphor. He really meant the abolition of a human understanding of the human person, as we have known it; he meant the end of humanity as we know it, brought about by humanity itself, by our inability to limit what Saint Augustine called the *libido dominandi*, the lust to dominate, including dominating our own natures. This [lust] can take

> In 1944, when C. S. Lewis wrote of the abolition of man, he was not trafficking in metaphor. He really meant the abolition of a human understanding of the human person, as we have known it; he meant the end of humanity as we know it, brought about by humanity itself.

such obviously disgusting and evil forms as gulags and death camps, but it can also appear in other guises and in the name of doing good.

I want you to understand I am not trafficking in moral equivalences, nor saying that contemporary positive eugenics is identical to the eugenics project of states like the Nazi state. But I am alerting us to the very real dangers in our world at the moment. Current projects of self-overcoming are tricky to get at precisely, because they are not so manifestly hideous as the horrors of twentieth-century totalitarianism. That is precisely because they present themselves to us in the dominant language of our culture: *choice, consent, freedom*—and precisely because they promise an escape from the human condition into a realm of mere mastery, which is where a lot among us would like to be. So, we are readily beguiled with the promises of a new self.

Consider that we are in the throes of genetic fundamentalism/DNA fundamentalism and a structure of biological obsession with genetics that undermines a recognition of the fullness and limitations of human embodiment. One premise driving the Human Genome Project was the notion that one day we might intervene in order to promote perfect, if not better, human "products." Promoters of this development run to the ecstatic and still do. For example, a 1986 pronouncement by a geneticist that the Human Genome Project is "the holy grail of human genetics, the ultimate answer to the commandment to 'know thyself.'" If you wanted to ask this gentleman, "Who are we?" the answer would be, "You're your genes. And nothing more than that."

I also believe that nowadays we are loath to grant the status of given-ness to any aspect of ourselves. We don't like that way of talking; it suggests there are things we can't manipulate and we can't change, despite the fact that anyone who has been in contact with a human baby knows that there is a body there—a wriggling, complex little body that comes programmed with all sorts of delicately calibrated reactions to the human relationships that nature presumes will be the matrix of child nurture.

If we think about bodies concretely in this way, then we are compelled to ask ourselves about the world these little bodies enter—not "Is this little body perfect?" according to some ideal of what perfection is. But is the world in which this little body has appeared welcoming and warm, responsively attuned to the uniqueness of this particular child who is bound to be, as we all are, less than perfect?

If we tilt in a bio-constructivist direction, one in which the body is raw material to be worked on and worked over, then the surroundings in which bodies are situated fade, and the perfect body gets enshrined as a kind of messianic project.

Here's just one example: "We must inevitably start to choose our descendants by permitting or preventing the births of our own children according to their medical prognosis, thus selecting the lives to come." The argument in this particular essay [by a current bio-constructivist author] was that so long as society doesn't cramp our freedom of action, we're going to stay on the road of progress and will exercise sovereign choice over birth by consigning to death or nonexistence those with a less-than-stellar potential for a life "not marred by an excess of pain or disability." As you can see, that is an extraordinarily slippery way to put it: "an excess of pain or disability."

On one of the occasions this last year when I was in London, there were a couple of cases that had really hit the paper. One was of a woman who had resisted her ob-gyn practitioner who was insistent that she should abort because the sonogram indicated that her child would have a cleft palate. This is now being considered by some as one of those imperfections that means this child should not even be born. The doctor, by the way, did not deny it.

What C. S. Lewis called the *extreme rationality*—"a kind of narrow notion of rationality that consigns to the dustbin of history all claims of intrinsic value," as those embracing such truth cannot allegedly meet certain standards of a rationalistic defense of those values. This winds up promoting a subjectivism of values that, it believes, are somehow more honest, and "when this happens, those whose values triumph will be those who possess the most overwhelming will to power."

By contrast, according to Lewis, "A dogmatic belief in objective value is necessary to the very idea of a rule [way of life] which is not tyranny or an obedience which is not slavery." We seem to have moved rather far from the real-world drama of disabled newborns being intentionally euthanized. But, I hope, if I have done my job at all competently, that you can see in the celebration of deliberate infanticide as the courageous, reasonable thing to do or what reason "dictates" the sort of thing that C. S. Lewis warned us against in 1944.

Why not love this helpless being in the time God has given her? What can this disabled newborn teach us about grace and beauty and human life, about *caritas*, about love and charity? Why can we not ameliorate pain and discomfort without believing we must either use extraordinary measures to keep alive or else boldly kill?

In conclusion, I want to tell you a story. Last year, the eighteen-year-old son of one of my cousins died. He was supposed to die when he was an infant, before he became a year old certainly. He had been born anencephalic. He could never speak, he could never feed himself, he couldn't sit, he couldn't crawl, he couldn't walk. He couldn't do any of the normal things human beings generally do or learn to do.

According to the doctors, there was no "there" there. Aaron was definitely a candidate for infanticide. Certainly, if you follow Peter Singer at Princeton, he should have been euthanized at birth. According to Singer, parents can make that decision even after birth. But to anyone who met him, Aaron was a beautiful child with the biggest blue eyes and the most strikingly dark eyelashes imaginable. He stared out at the world, making no apparent distinctions, until his mother came into view. And then his face—the only words you can think of, and you would use these same words, if you had seen him—would beam or his face would light up. There is no other way to put it. He knew her and he loved her and I would defy anyone to claim otherwise. Her love and care and devotion kept him going for eighteen years.

When he died, an entire family—parents, siblings, grandparents, aunts, uncles, cousins, and a wider community—grieved their loss.

My cousin Paula Jean never once bemoaned her fate or wondered what it might have been if this child had been born a different kind of Aaron. Aaron had been given to her, and she would do her job joyfully. In those eighteen years, this young man, who could not move on his own, never once developed a bedsore. Those of you who have ever tended an infirm person know how difficult it is to prevent these kinds of things from happening.

The story of Aaron and Paula Jean is an amazing story of human grace and human endurance. I think it tells us that we have within us the strength to do the things that the wider culture tells us we cannot do or should not do. I ask you to contrast *this* with a vision of peace promulgated by the euthanasia doctor.

There are two contrasting images of the human future embedded here, one in which human beings will write, perhaps, the decisive chapter in the story of whether we will abolish man, the human person, that is, obliterate what makes us truly human, or whether we will love and cherish our humanity, however wretched, however broken.

Q & A

Q: I was very touched by what you said. I have a master's degree in special education with an emphasis in mental retardation, and I have spent most of my entire adult life working with children that were seriously disabled. I had a lot of children with Down syndrome in my classes over the years, and they gave me a great deal more than I gave them.

Mother Teresa said a nation that accepts abortion is not teaching its citizens how to love. I think she has also said, "We have to love until it hurts." My question to you is, do you think we are a nation that either does not know how to love or is so terrified of it that we just don't do it anymore, because to love means we have to die to ourselves constantly?

A: It's a provocative question. Let me approach it in two parts. One is your statement about what you received from these children and the Down syndrome children and so on. That kind of observation, as you may know, is a very common one with people who actually spend time with and work with these children. I think it is very easy to eliminate the category when you don't have any concrete experience of Down syndrome children. So, I thank you for sharing that observation.

I have been especially interested over the years that a number of my students, when a certain discussion would be proffered, would come up to me after class and say, "I have a Down syndrome brother or a Down syndrome sister." It was fascinating to me how many of them wanted to go into fields that had to do with the care and the tending and the treatment of children and adults with disabilities. It enhanced, and this leads directly to the second response to you, their sense of a moral obligation and purpose and, I think that one could say, expanded their capacity to love those who are, in some significant ways, quite different from us. They are human beings, but they are human beings created differently, if you will.

Love is a complicated thing and involves a certain capacity to give of oneself. I think that the last four decades in American life, that notion itself has come into ill repute, because we seem to have a kind of zero-sum understanding of the "self" itself.

That leads me to the question about knowing how to love. Love is a complicated thing and involves a certain capacity to give of oneself. I think that the last four decades in American life, that notion itself has come into ill repute, because we seem to have a kind of zero-sum understanding of the "self" itself. That is, if I give some of myself to another, it is a loss for me. If I give 10 percent, I am only 90 percent left for who I am. There is an equation of self-giving with self-abnegation that constrains, in palpable ways, our capacity to give of ourselves and to receive at the same time, because our abstract view is that we will get nothing—we will just give, give, give, and get nothing out of it. What one receives, of course, is not quantifiable.

It would make no sense to the person concerned with maximizing utilities at all. You should see those people try to think about Christian martyrdom, for example—dying for one's faith. Some of the absolutely hilarious notions about how the person is maximizing his or her utilities by bravely going to death rather than to recant the faith: maximizing the utility of a preference for an afterlife or some bizarre notion. They just cannot deal with certain very powerful, fundamental human things, and love is one of them.

So, to the extent that the views I have talked about become ever more widespread and deepened in the culture, I fear that you may be right, that we can be very sentimental and romantic about love, but the hard work of giving and receiving I think we're frightened of.

Q: I go to one of the medical schools here in town. It's very much like what C. S. Lewis talked about where you have the assumptions presented to you but never the arguments. Everything from electrons and neurons to today's discussion of end-of-life decisions with the reasonable decision being to pull the plug as soon as possible and the "unreasonable" decision being to make unreasonable measures to hold on to life.

I don't know that Lewis's essay ever affected how anything was taught in the upper forms of schools in the forties. My question is, is there anything else that can be done? In a year I'll be running around like crazy and staying up to all hours. I'm not sure I'll be able to make a philosophical defense of whatever decision I would like to make [regarding end-of-life decisions] in the face of a medical community that doesn't understand it.

Are there resources available for actually building a philosophical underpinning so that you can make an argument when the time comes at three A.M. and you're being pushed by someone who has a high level of authority over you?

A: You're in a pickle. I understand a bit of what you're going through. My kid brother is an MD, and I have some sense of how grueling that is and how little time there is—in fact, almost no time. The possible time for reflection is eclipsed quite radically; so, I understand the situation that you are in.

I would say that by the time it gets to the actual decisions that you are confronted with in medical school, where, as I indicated, the time for reflection is so truncated, it's probably too late. That is, that certain frameworks of understanding and ideas, which are alternatives to the dominant one that you've discussed have to be present as possibilities, it seems to me, as possibilities in the culture, even if they are not taught in the textbooks. This is one reason why Lewis said that his hope lay in real mothers and real nurses. He's referring to nannies that did some of his child rearing in the UK, and to real children, who burst through these categories with their aliveness and complexity.

You are dealing with people who are in a situation where it is easy to define them reductively as their ailment and to forget or to lose a wider sense of humanity, which, remember at the beginning I said, would caution us about physician-assisted euthanasia and also caution us about certain situations, about a kind of endless prolongation of life where the person is clearly terminal. I think that can have its own form of cruelty attached to it, because the person is so thoroughly medicalized and is simply given the panoply of equipment, removed from the touch and the care, often, of loved ones. So, your task is a big one.

If you don't have one of these at your medical school, you could start a group for Christian physicians. There is such a group at the University of Chicago Medical School, wanting to go beyond their training and consideration of some of the medical dilemmas that will be presented to them, and they provide one another with support. This is a very difficult thing to do as a lone project.

Some sustainable support would be of enormous help to you. So, I can only wish you good luck. It's hard to persevere against the driving force that you are confronted with. I very much understand that. But I think sometimes, just piercing through the fog and saying, "Hang on, what are we doing here? Let's think about it," can have a bracing effect, a salutary effect. People say, "Gee, you know . . . hmmm . . . I wonder. . . ." They're forced, perhaps—no guarantee—to reflect on what it is they are doing.

The political philosopher Hannah Arendt argued very eloquently that the task of the political theorist is not to tell people what to do but to help people to think about what they're doing. I suspect that is the task of so many of you in this room in your own respective vocations. Try to get people just to think for a moment about what they are doing.

Q: My question is about human fertility control. If you really think about it, I think all human marriages employ some degree of fertility control, both in the selection of a marriage partner and also by various means in the marital act that would consciously limit the children that are born, usually for economic reasons or something else.

So, would you consider this to be a standard by which all of us stand condemned, since this is a conscious choice in which we are deciding who should be the yet-to-be-born, or would you locate the wrong elsewhere?

A: Obviously, C. S. Lewis isn't here, but would that he were. It would be much more interesting than having me standing here to discuss these things with you. I suspect that he wasn't so much issuing a general statement about couples limiting birth within a marital relationship as he was very concerned about the *philosophy* that was being promoted in tandem with couples' decisions to do that—that is, the notion that we are most human when we are fully in control of things, that we are most human when we can decide who lives and who dies. Obviously, when a couple is using some form of, let's call it *birth limitation*, instead of *control*—I don't like that word *control* very much—it begins with different assumptions.

Let me just tell you something: When the birth-control movement emerged in the early twentieth century, it was also a eugenics movement, as many of you surely know. Margaret Sanger, who was the big apostle of birth control in the United States, was a eugenicist and had a journal preaching eugenics. Jews weren't supposed to have many kids, and people from southern Europe were not supposed to reproduce freely and were inferior. She pushed for limited immigration quotas for "less worthy people" from certain parts of Europe and all the rest.

So, there is that kind of thing in the background that Lewis knew about. Then you have Nazi eugenics in the foreground. I think that it's the notion of control, especially as he tells it, when you have an unholy alliance of a certain set of unprincipled scientists and an omnicompetent state, that's where the *gravamen* [essential element] of the argument lies. To the extent that human beings immerse themselves in this philosophy, I think he would tell us that it is extraordinarily corrupting. I don't think he would stand in front of a couple who has three children and think, *That's enough*. I don't think he would say, "Shame on you, you should have ten." He wouldn't do that. I think it is the wider philosophical surround within which things happen that he is trying to get at, I suspect, because he certainly didn't ever write against birth limitation.

Q: I want to put forward a distinction between value and values. One of my favorite stories is the Grand Inquisitor, where Jesus comes back to the earth and is immediately arrested and told, "How dare you come back? The responsibility you gave to individuals crushes them; so, we the Church have taken on that responsibility for ourselves and given them values so they don't have the responsibility to create them themselves." One of Dostoevsky's friends, Solovyov, also said that love, which, I think, is the point, as the first questioner indicated, is the recognition of the absolute value of the other. So, could the idea that an individual has objective value still be a value that we come to subjectively as a community, as an individual?

A: Let me clarify. The distinction, let's say, between subjective, as in your understanding of your own approach to or awareness of certain issues, of course, simply means that you are a subject and you're thinking about these things. Let's distinguish between that and the kind of subjectivism that Lewis was criticizing.

I suspect that the way he would talk about it would be to say that subjectivism presumes that each of us is in our own isolated little world of entirely and uniquely subjective values. These differ from person to person, and there is no way to adjudicate between them. So, it's that kind of subjectivism he is concerned with and that undermines these claims of value, as you talked about it.

If we lived in a society in which there was a way people could connect certain awarenesses that they have, let's call it a *subjective value,* to this wider notion of objective value, then I don't think we would have the problem that Lewis is talking about here. I think it is the *disconnect.* Subjectivism triumphs when people have relinquished the notion that there *really are* claims of value, *really are* things that are true and things that are false, as Lewis says, to the kind of universe we live in and the kinds of creatures that we are. It is that disconnect that is very worrying.

I should tell you that in my own classes, I prefer to talk about moral norms or imperatives even more than value or values, precisely because of the subjectivist spin that these have received and because values came in with a triumph of a certain kind of market language. Things have a value, that is, a price. So, the fact that we talk about these issues in that language now sort of slants things or tilts things a certain way. That is a whole other topic, and we are not going to solve that problem tonight. It is another one of those issues that clusters, you know, to the questions that I am talking about tonight.

Q: My question has to do with something that is current and very much present in front of us and one that you as a political philosopher comment upon—the election today of our new Supreme Court chief justice and how the culture wars are now couching this debate for the next appointee, who will be obviously an arbiter of a constitution which this country was based upon. Remember that we are standing in a club that in 1862, supported the South and Judah Benjamin, as the mayor of New York wanted to secede from the Union. In light of that and in light of the culture wars, can you speak to how we should couch those issues as we go forward and decide on our next justice?

A: I am probably skating on thin ice, but I'm going to answer your question anyway. I think Judge Roberts obviously did a very elegant job talking about the role of the judge, and the judge, in a sense, is someone who is obliged to respect a certain fundamental structure of the law. As you know, embedded within the U.S. Constitution are some of these universal propositions about the human person and the kind of government that should follow, given these understandings of the human person.

I was struck by the Senate hearings. I was at a conference in DC, and I wasn't liking it so much. So, every chance I could get, I would run to my hotel room and turn on C-SPAN. One of the things that really struck me—and it actually ties to what I said tonight, which is why I decided I would have a go with your question—was the fact that given his stellar qualifications, given his intellect, given his respect for the Constitution, those who clearly had problems with him fell back on the notion he was deficient in feeling. Did you pick that up? *He's deficient in feeling.*

So, they are accepting the reason/feeling split. Maybe the smartest guy that ever came down the pike, but "Boy, what about your heart?" as Senator Schumer put it. In fact, he said, "You may be the most powerful intellect ever to come before this committee, but I want to know about your *heart.*"

What that meant was "You don't ooze sentiment the way we think people should." That's a way of saying that the kind of objective status of claims embedded in the law is not enough; you've got to prove that you can go on *Oprah* and weep on cue. I think that that corrupts our public discourse, because any person can do that if called upon to do it. By the way, the law is supposed to protect us against a momentary deluge of an excess of feelings of that sort.

There is a way in which the law at its best should embody reasoned emotion. Certainly, our founders believed that, when they were talking about human freedom and human liberty and human dignity and all the rest.

But I think the view that splits reason and feelings is, in fact, rife in the culture and promotes and preserves precisely the ideas that Lewis is criticizing in his 1944 essay.

Q: You promised a sobering talk, and I think you delivered it. It seems that the general trajectory that you're painting—continuing Lewis's description— is one of decline. I was wondering what you see in the culture at large that is heading in the other direction? Is there a path to combat this decline, not just in individual lives but in the broader culture?

A: Regarding the troubles that C. S. Lewis saw in his society in 1944—mind you, this is a society that had stood up against the Nazis when nobody else was doing it. So, there was still some robustness there, and he accepted that, but he saw these other troubling signs.

I'm going to tell you something that struck me recently about possible sources of renewal and a kind of revivification of a certain hope, including a hope that links us from generation to generation, because one of the characteristics of many of the developments I was criticizing is a kind of attitude, a kind of *presentism*: "The world starts with me; it will end with me. I am not acknowledging my indebtedness to the past, and I don't much care about what is going to happen in the future, because I won't be here anyway."

I think that we are part of a great sort of chain of humanity; as Bernard of Chartres said, "I stand on the shoulders of giants." I didn't invent this all by myself. That, I thought, came through so powerfully in Pope John Paul II's funeral and this outpouring of humanity that took the media utterly by surprise. By then, it shouldn't have taken them by surprise, because it happened every time he did anything. But what struck me were the millions of young people who turned up and stayed there under these very difficult conditions for days, in order that they could be present.

Something was calling to them. He somehow spoke to them, even in his infirm old age, with the Parkinson's and all the rest. If we could think this through with you—it would be a very interesting exercise considering what that embodied and what hope that represented—we could see some possible sparks for a certain kind of renewal of our humanity more fully understood, which is what Lewis is talking about.

Q: I have a question about what your depth of knowledge is about the medical imperative, about the mission of any doctor. I happen to be one, and I have seen suffering. I've been in the units where children are being preserved at extensive costs, and I am in favor of it, but again, the mythology of the omnipotent doctor does vex me, because I wish I were omnipotent. I do work with children who are emotionally and intellectually impaired. So, I wonder about our resources and why our society, if we do want to support someone like C. S. Lewis, can't give us the resources.

A: As I told you, I trek over to the medical school from time to time, not every day. I have a kid brother who is a doctor, read a lot of stuff, and I certainly do know that the number one promise that a physician makes is to do no harm. What I wanted to suggest in my talk is that *harm* is a complicated and slippery word, and there are various ways that harm can be done. We justify it or we comfort ourselves by saying, "I'm doing the right thing. I'm easing suffering. I'm doing this; I'm doing that."

One other thing to conclude is that much of the pressure put on doctors comes from patients. That is, patients have imbibed a view of the omnipotence of the doctor and have put pressure on doctors in all kinds of ways. I saw that in an oncology ward, when I was being the spokesperson for a colleague who was a Czech émigré and had no family and who was dying of a very pernicious, aggressive form of leukemia. I spent a lot of time in there. Doctors at times pushed things beyond what families thought would be best. At times, the doctors were ready to say, "We need to let the person go, and you have to think of ways to take leave," but they felt pressured by the families to keep going against all hope.

So, this is a wider cultural set of assumptions that gets reflected in a variety of ways in each of our vocations and, obviously, in a particularly powerful way in the medical profession.

The Good Life: Seeking Purpose, Meaning, and Truth in Your Life

CHARLES W. COLSON

May 24, 2006

Introduction

Welcome to Socrates in the City, the thinking man's alternative to jeering Barry Bonds.* Okay, sorry, but there's something about Barry Bonds that I need to get off my chest. I will feel better. So, thank you for being my 320 therapists.

I am Eric Metaxas, but before I introduce our speaker, I want to say that the Bonds thing is very troubling to me. It's a conundrum. If I were Selig, the commissioner, I think I would take the gas pipe [i.e., commit suicide], if you could find one in 2006. I don't think they exist anymore.

Seriously, what does Bud Selig do about Barry Bonds and the big numbers that he has put up? He has just hit the iconic 714; he's just achieved it, and yet we know there's a problem. But I've come up with a solution. You guys can just take it and do what you want with it.

Okay, here's my solution. I was an English major in college; that's why I can't get a job. I read *The Scarlet Letter*, and I believe Nathaniel Hawthorne has given us a clue as to what might be done. My suggestion is for Selig to call a press conference and to announce that our long national nightmare is over.

There's a little Watergate-era joke for the speaker. How many people

---

* At the time of this lecture, Barry Bonds had recently surpassed Babe Ruth's historic mark of 714 career home runs. In 2007, Bonds was involved in a steroids scandal, sullying his achievement and status as a sports figure.

remember Gerry Ford? Talk about a guy with an asterisk, but that's another story.

But my solution is this: Selig should announce that the solution is for Bonds to keep his numbers, but for the rest of his career, for the rest of his life, in the off-season as well, until the end, he has to wear—yes, you've guessed it—a scarlet asterisk!

I just want you to think about that, because for the rest of the summer, this question is going to be burning, and people are going to be asking, "What to do, what to do?" What would you do if *you* were Bud Selig? My answer? Pin a scarlet asterisk right on the uniform.

Well, we've solved that. I feel better. So, let's change the subject. I have to say it's extraordinary to see such a huge Socrates in the City crowd. For those of you who are new to Socrates in the City, we're, of course, a society of jugglers and magicians who gather to share tips on juggling and magic—and to make fun of David Blaine.

Of course, that's not true. Socrates in the City is a speakers' series, and a wonderful speakers' series. It's inspired by Socrates's maxim that "the unexamined life is not worth living." I agree with that. I think most thinking people agree with that, and it struck me and some friends of mine that those of us who live in New York City lead particularly unexamined lives. I'm not going to mention any names. Jim Lane, for example.

I apologize, Jim; I'm sorry, but the point is that not just my friends but New Yorkers in general lead famously unexamined lives. So, some friends of mine and I thought we should do something about that, and we decided to have a speakers' series where we would have brilliant thinkers who are also— and this is rare—great speakers, opining on the very big issues of life, on the big and controversial questions that everyone dodges, especially if they are running for public office.

The big questions of life: Does life have meaning? Is there a God? If there is, can we know God? What about evil? Raising all of these big questions— that is what we're about at Socrates in the City—and trying to start a conversation about them, because we think they're important for us to think about, and also, I think that they all have great answers. Most people don't know that they have great answers, but they do. That's what we're about here at Socrates in the City.

We have had many fabulous speakers. Tonight, of course, our very special guest is my former boss and my former and current hero, Charles Colson.

But I have to confess that when I walked in here tonight, I was a little confused. This is actually very embarrassing, but I didn't realize the speaker tonight actually was Chuck Colson. I thought the speaker tonight—this is crazy—was Chaka Khan, the singer. Do you know her? I've been confusing them for a long time, and it's very embarrassing because they're really quite different.

But I'm not alone. A lot of people confuse Chuck Colson with Chaka Khan. First of all, the name is remarkably similar. So, a lot of people get confused. Very few people will admit to it, because it is rather embarrassing, but I don't mind admitting to it. Even when I worked for Chuck Colson, I often confused him with Chaka Khan. That *was* embarrassing.

The first few times he didn't seem to pick up on it, and I was really thanking God for that. But I thought, *I have got to do something about this, because it keeps happening.* So, I came up with a little crib sheet, which I sort of palmed like a magician, listing all the differences between Chuck Colson and Chaka Khan.

I know nobody is going to admit it, but I know half of you can't tell them apart. So, now, to help you, I'm going to just give you a few ways that they're different. Actually, three ways they are different.

Okay, first of all, number one: Chuck Colson is the founder of Prison Fellowship; Chaka Khan is the high priestess of *funk*.

Is that helpful? Good.

Number two: Back in 1973, Chuck Colson was special counsel to President Nixon. But in 1973, Chaka Khan was lead singer for Rufus. Aren't these helpful?

And finally, number three: Chuck Colson was the winner of the Templeton Prize in religion, and Chaka Khan was the winner of a Grammy Award for "Tell Me Something Good," which was actually written by Stevie Wonder, if you didn't know that.

So, I hope that has been a helpful primer to all of you on the difference between Chuck Colson—who is here tonight—and Chaka Khan, who is actually *not* here tonight. Chaka Khan is a singer of funk. Chuck Colson is *not* a singer of funk, although I have to say, Chuck, if Stevie Wonder wrote you a song, you could probably really break out with a big hit. Who knows?

Oh my, I just said, "Break out," didn't I? Susanne warned me, "Whatever you say, Eric, don't use that prison lingo thing, because it rubs Chuck the wrong way," and now I've just said, "Break out." I'm so sorry! You know, I should say this to all of you for future reference. Guys like Chuck, who've been on the *inside*, do not appreciate it when guys like us on the *outside* try to use prison lingo. So, if you're around Chuck, I'm just telling you, don't call prison by any of its colorful names to try and impress him. Like *pokey*. Or *the big house*. Please try to resist.

He also hates *hoosegow*—and will blow a stack if you call it the *jug* or the *can* or the *cooler* or whatever. All right, this is getting out of hand. I apologize. I'd better stop before somebody uses a shiv on me or before the screws get wind of what's cooking here. I think I'd just better get serious and move on. Forgive me.

I think you know how seriously happy I am tonight. To have Chuck Colson with us at Socrates in the City is just tremendous. It was not easy to get Chuck to come. To be honest, Chuck doesn't like me very much. So, I pretended to be someone else, and voilà! He's here.

No, seriously, I am thrilled. Most of you are familiar, of course, with Chuck's story. I don't want to steal his thunder, but he did work, of course, in the Nixon White House and ended up in prison for a Watergate-related offense. But nothing could've been a bigger blessing for the world, because Chuck Colson had a powerful transformation in his life and he found meaning—actual meaning in a way that he never had before—and the best part was that it was also very real and that he felt a compulsion to share what he had found not only with others but with prisoners all over the globe, to show that their lives have genuine meaning.

Anyone who has a heart for those who suffer, for those in prison, has his finger on the pulse of what life's all about, even if you don't know what life is about. You know that it is somehow very close to suffering, to understanding the meaning of suffering, and to being with those who suffer.

So, we're going to hear tonight from Chuck on the subject of his book *The Good Life: Seeking Purpose, Meaning, and Truth in Your Life*. I don't think we've ever had a title that was more at the very core of what Socrates in the City is all about. We're usually a little bit more oblique, but Chuck happens to have written a book that is right on the nose about who we are at Socrates in the City.

As I have mentioned, I had the privilege of working for Chuck a number of years ago. The reason I wanted to work for him was because I had read some of his books, which we have at the book table here tonight. I beg you to grab one—or two or five—and take it home and read it and give it to your friends. There are very few people who write books quite like Chuck does.

He is one of the few public individuals who has been willing to talk about the big questions and take the grief that comes with publicly talking about the big questions and meaning and wrestling with those thorny issues that they are. But I am personally very, very grateful that he has. His books have meant a lot to me and have helped me personally figure out the meaning of life.

I have to say a few years ago I was privileged to accompany Chuck to the prison in Danbury, Connecticut, with some friends. I grew up in Danbury, spent years there, and had never been past the prison gates until two years ago when I visited with Chuck. There's no question that it was absolutely among the most meaningful days of my life.

If you're interested in visiting a prison or learning more about prison fellowship ministries, don't hesitate. Run. You will be very glad you did.

As I also mentioned, Chuck served in the Nixon White House and has written many books. He's the host of *BreakPoint Radio*, a daily commentary on world issues. He is also, as I mentioned, the winner in 1993 of the very prestigious Templeton Prize in religion. People always claim prizes are prestigious, but some actually are. This is one of the actually prestigious ones. On and on it goes.

Perhaps one of the most impressive things, and I will close with this, about Chuck's innumerable accomplishments is that he has done virtually all of it without steroids.

Ladies and gentlemen, join me in giving a Socrates in the City welcome to my friend Chuck Colson.

Perhaps one of the most impressive things, and I will close with this, about Chuck's innumerable accomplishments is that he has done virtually all of it without steroids.

Talk

I'm absolutely delighted to be here. I must say I've been doing this now for almost thirty-three years. I've been to 5,702 rubber-chicken dinners and done many after-dinner speeches and occasions like this. I've spoken at Guild Hall and at Buckingham Palace—I've been all over the world. But normally, you sit there and you think, *Will this guy ever finish the introduction?* The more you've accomplished in your life, the longer the introductions go. It's really tough on the speaker to keep hearing all that stuff. Tonight was the freshest, most creative introduction I think I've *ever* had.

I honestly was sitting there hoping he wouldn't quit. I've heard myself, and I'm not fresh to me anymore, but he is absolutely terrific. What a great job. Thank you, Eric.

Last summer, Eric and I were in England for a lecture series at Oxford's C. S. Lewis Institute. This kind of ministry that I'm in can puff you up, but God has ways of bringing you back to earth. After I had spoken in the morning—great crowd, great experience—Eric and I (and I think Jim Lane had arranged this) got together a bunch of the scholars at Oxford and a group of Christian religious leaders who were in Oxford for these conferences. We all had lunch together in one of the dining rooms of one of the old colleges. If you ever walk through the campus of Oxford, you know these Gothic buildings and the beautiful mahogany-paneled walls and can feel the centuries going past you as you walk through the corridors.

We sat at this great table and listened to some of the people who were in a group called *Oxford Analytica*, dons at Oxford analyzing events and sending the information out all over the world. It was the most stimulating two hours I think I've spent. But I was in a hurry to get back for the afternoon session, because Antony Flew was speaking later at Oxford. He was the world's leading philosopher of atheism; so, I wanted to get back and hear him.

I left the dining hall exhilarated by all the ideas that had been discussed at the table for two hours. When I got out onto the street, I realized it was two o'clock in the afternoon, nine o'clock back home. I call my wife, Patty, at home every day, and so, I took the phone out and dialed our home number.

Just as I got her on the phone, I turned into the main street of Oxford, and a woman came along. What stood out was that she was wearing big, bouncing, white athletic shoes and hair going all over the place. She had that look I've seen a million times. When she saw me, she went, "*Huhhh*," and came right over. I was talking to Patty. So, I started walking a little faster, and the woman walked a little faster. Now she was looking right in my ear. I wear hearing aids; I'm not self-conscious about it, but she was staring at one of my hearing aids.

I told Patty, "I can't deal with this woman here." I hung up the phone and thought, *I'd better be nice*, because we had quite a distance to the corner, and God was convicting me. So, I started talking to the woman, but not much, because I spent the whole time listening to her telling me her entire life history and how much my books had meant. When we got to the corner, I really felt convicted, because I wasn't being nice now. So, I turned to her and said, "Ma'am, can I help you across the street?"

She said, "Oh, yes!" So, I took her arm, and we started across. Traffic was going in both directions, whizzing past. We got right in the middle of the street, and she stops. I could not move her—traffic on both sides. She was staring up at me, and then she said, "Mr. Colson, you're really a very handsome man." Anybody likes to hear that, and then she said, "But you're much older than I expected." No good deed goes unpunished, as the saying often goes.

I'm delighted to be here with Eric, with this venture of Socrates in the City. This is a wonderful thing, because the unexamined life is *not* worth living. Socrates was correct. I don't think any of us really live unexamined lives.

I think most of us ask the big questions; I think they're wired into us. We'll talk about that a little bit tonight. Most of us put them off, because we distract ourselves from them, because we often don't want to face them, but they're out there.

So, I commend Eric and his colleagues for doing this. It's a wonderful opportunity to get people together and hopefully have some intelligent discussion. I first met Eric a number of years ago—speaking of intelligent discussion—when I was speaking at Yale Law School on a subject that I had written about: why Yale can't teach the rule of law and why Yale Law School has undermined the rule of law. I thought that would be a riot. Actually, the hall was packed, and there were a bunch of people sitting in front from the town—Yale graduates like Eric and others.

One of the curses of modern education today is that people are told there is no truth and therefore there's nothing to argue about. The students all figured, "Well, this is what Colson thinks. Let him think it, but it's not what I think; it's not worth discussing." You really can't have a conversation unless you have some common standard of what you believe to be true so the questioning was really dull, except for Eric. He started popping up with all these great questions, and afterward I got him and thought, *If this guy is as smart as he seems*—and it wasn't much competition, because nobody was asking questions—*I had better get to know him better.*

That was the beginning of our friendship, which has now gone back many years. He worked with us in the ministry and did a wonderful job helping me with the radio program *BreakPoint*, which is now on a thousand stations across the country.

I also have with me Frank Cerutti, who is the vice president of Prison Fellowship and travels with me a great deal. Several people asked me as we were milling around the crowd whether they could get involved in the ministry locally or whether we do something in Rikers Island; yes, we do. We have a wonderful ministry on Rikers Island. But if you're interested, our executive director for the City [New York City] is Ryan Myers. Stand up, Ryan, so they can see you, and if you're interested in going to the—the only phrase that Eric didn't come up with is the most common one among prisoners—*the slammer*, because the door slams behind you. So, if you're interested in going to the slammer, see him or see Frank.

One of the things about my life—those of you who know much of my story will know it has been a roller coaster certainly, but one of the things that I think my life illustrates is what a paradox life is. It's never the way we think it's going to be, and sometimes the worst things we do turn out to be the best things, while the things we think are the best sometimes turn out to be the worst.

About a year ago, I got a phone call from Dan Rather's producer. It had just been announced that Rather was going off the air. Any of you who thinks there's not a God in heaven, look at that: Dan Rather was taken off the air! And the call was "Would you come on his program for one of his closing shows?" because he wanted to interview people who had been part of big stories he'd covered. I laughed uproariously.

I wanted nothing to do with Dan Rather. I went home and told my wife that night, "What do you think, honey? He wants me to come on his show. Can you imagine that? I told him, 'No way.'" She said—wives are wonderful this way—"That's not really very Christian, is it?"

They called again the next day, and I said, "Well, let me talk to Dan." So, I got him on the phone, and I ended up I doing it. It was an interesting experience, because I hadn't seen him in almost thirty years, and he was one of the guys that had run me out of town. He was going through some really deep waters, and we got into some fascinating conversation, but when he was running the cameras, he said, "Mr. Colson, you look so different than you did thirty years ago when I covered you, Watergate, and the White House."

I said, "I am! No, as a matter of fact, I thank God for Watergate." Dan Rather's eyes puffed. He didn't use this on the film—it died on the cutting-room floor, but he was staggered. "How could you thank God for Watergate?" But I honestly do.

As I look back on my life, I realize that all the things I'd sought in power and prestige, in influencing government, I never found—and then to go to prison, where everything that I'd worked for was in a shambles and the president whom I knew and served and loved was being impeached and resigned instead of being impeached. And suddenly, it was all gone.

It was tough to be in prison, period, particularly if you're a high government official, because a lot of the guys look at you and think you're the one that put them in prison, and so I had threats on my life. It's not a pleasant experience. You get there, and everything you've owned is taken away from you—all your clothes, all your possessions, your rings. You're handed a pair of underpants. Mine had five numbers stenciled on it. I knew I was the sixth person putting them on and sleeping in a dormitory at night. I'd been in the marines; I'd lived in everything, but you never really get used to the desolate life of a prisoner and the pervasive sense of hopelessness and despair.

The thing that was really most difficult for me was the realization that when I was a little kid starting out, the grandson of immigrants, earned a scholarship to Brown University, the first person in my family to go to college, I had thought, *I'm just going to get ahead, and someday I'm going to get to the top and have power and influence people's lives.* I was a political idealist. I had studied political philosophy at Brown. I was really interested in this. So, I thought, *I can get into government and really affect how people live.*

Many people go into politics for idealistic reasons, despite what you're reading about some of the bad apples in Washington these days. They're really going into it because they want to serve; they want to do something good for their country, and I did.

Here in prison I'm thinking all of that has been devastated now. I'm public enemy number one; I'm the number one scoundrel of Watergate. I'll never have the chance to do the things I thought were really important in life. That, to me, was the most despairing thing in prison.

I'd look around seeing these other guys lying on their bunks, their bodies corroding and souls dying in prison. Little did I dream that I would get out of prison and God would use my life to start a movement, which is now in 113 countries around the world with hundreds of thousands of volunteers, seven million kids getting Angel Tree gifts at Christmastime—this huge movement—and every step of the way, I've seen God orchestrate it.

Many of you who are in this room who are probably unbelievers may be wondering when I say "the sovereignty of God," and you're probably thinking, *Well, that's God talk.* It's not God talk. I have to tell you: Suspend your disbelief like when you read a novel. Suspend your disbelief for a moment till we get through this talk, because, I have to tell you, I have watched this happen. Most of the good things that have happened in my life—I didn't plan them. They were circumstances, and the strangest set of circumstances over thirty years is how this movement has spread all around the world.

And so, I come away from that with the realization that sometimes the worst things which happen to you turn out to be the best things. A devotion I love to read in the morning says that suffering is the school of faith. I don't know how Peter Kreeft dealt with it when he was here, but it's something C. S. Lewis talked about. Suffering is something like God's megaphone. He gets our attention that way. Out of suffering can come redemption in ways that we don't understand. Sometimes the worst things that happen to us turn out to be the very best. If—as I believe—God is sovereign, then there's really *never* cause for despair.

Often you find the meaning of life in crisis when you're forced to face those big questions and really think hard about them in the face of everything in life falling apart in front of you. What I've discovered over all these years as I've lived this life—first in political power in the office next to the president of the United States, then in a jail cell, and now traveling around the world from prison to prison and different kinds of people that I've met from every walk of life—is that we get deluded. Alexander Solzhenitsyn said this best when he was writing in *The Gulag Archipelago* about his experiences ten years in the gulag—*ten years*. He said, "Bless you, prison, bless you, for being in my life. For lying upon the rotting prison straw, I came to realize that the object of life is not prosperity, as we are made to believe, but the maturity of the human soul."

I would argue that the maturing of the soul is manifested when other people become more important than you. That's the most countercultural statement I will make tonight. We live in a self-absorbed, self-obsessed culture—the seventies was the "Me Decade"—and today, everything about the world revolves around us. This is a nation of 280 million imperial selves, and it's one of the reasons that we can never get together on political or social questions. It's the reason we're yelling at each other, because everybody considers him- or herself to be—in that abominable phrase out of a Supreme Court decision—"personally autonomous." I've discovered that that's the most bankrupt way to see life.

I live in a place called Naples, Florida, which is one of the garden spots of the world. It's an absolute nirvana for all golfers, and they all come there. They're all CEOs of major corporations, and they retire to Naples and this is "it"—twenty-seven golf courses and miles of sparkling beach and the best country clubs. I watch these guys; they're powerful people. They have this New York look on their face; they're determined. But now, all of a sudden, they start measuring their lives by how many golf games they can get in.

I often say to them, "Do you really want to live your life counting up the number of times you chase that little white ball around those greens?" And they kind of chuckle, but it's a nervous chuckle, because in six months they've realized how banal their lives are, and they've got beautiful homes—castles—and when they get bored with that, they build a bigger castle, and they're miserable. The object of life is not what we think it is, which is to achieve money, power, pleasure. That's not the holy grail. The object of life is the maturing of the soul, and you reflect that maturing of the soul when you care more for other people than yourself.

> **The object of life is the maturing of the soul, and you reflect that maturing of the soul when you care more for other people than yourself.**

I had to cross this Rubicon in my life, because I was a self-centered, hard-driving, hard-charging guy. *Now* I get my joy not out of those kinds of things—the Templeton Prize, which was a big thing, a million dollars; it went to Prison Fellowship. That was a great deal. They gave me a medal, and honestly, I was asking somebody the other day, "Where is that medal?" That doesn't mean a whole lot.

But I start thinking about guys like Danny Croce, who was in a prison in Plymouth, Massachusetts, and driving home drunk one night had killed a policeman. Desperate, he wanted to take his own life. He said he found a Bible and gave his life to Christ. He saw the prison chaplain and got his daughter enrolled in our Angel Tree program so she could get Christmas gifts at Christmas. His life started to change inside that prison. Then he heard about Chuck Colson Scholarships at Wheaton College; he got one and graduated in Bible and theology at the top of his class at Wheaton. He's back in that same prison in which he was an inmate, but now he's the chaplain in that prison for two thousand people.

Every time I see Danny or José Abrue—his wife, Myra, is here tonight—and hear their story, I realize how God took them and plucked them out of prison, turned them around, got them a beautiful home and a family. It's just about people whose lives were once wrecked. That gives me incredible joy.

Cherise, whom I just met in San Francisco recently, is a beautiful twenty-one-year-old African-American woman. She told the story that she was beaten by her father; there was a hole in the wall next to her bed, because he used to abuse her and throw things at her. She grew up in this home, which would redefine *dysfunctional* if you heard the kind of home she was in and what she was subjected to. When her father went away to prison, she got involved in Angel Tree and then got into one of our programs. This beautiful young woman came to Christ. She's now a senior at Berkeley and is going to attend Harvard graduate school.

Lives can be redeemed. When you put your head on the pillow at night and you're thinking about your life, that's what counts. What have you been able to do to help someone else get a little better break in life? It will mean far more to you when you're counting up, when you're keeping score, than the number of golf games, the size of your home, the sports cars. Far more.

Christianity, the Christian faith, I would argue, is a way of understanding life, not through your eyes but through God's eyes. That, I think, is the simplest way to explain it. Not my self-centered self looking at life, but how it must please God to see people who are on the margins of society—neglected, forgotten, the poor, the outcasts, the prisoners—get a chance. I go to a wonderful church and worship there every Sunday. I love it. But I also worship when I see somebody redeemed out of the gutter. That's worship in the fullest sense.

Now, some of you are sitting there, I suspect, saying, "Well, that's okay for Chuck Colson." I remember when I witnessed to a famous journalist. I won't use his name. He wanted to meet me one day. He was obsessed with God. So, we had lunch at a power restaurant in Washington, and he said, "You have the next hour to talk me into the existence of God." He ate while I talked and perspired.

The first thing I did was to tell him about my experience with Christ, and he said, "Oh, that's good. That's fine for you," he said. "I've got a friend in California. She's got crystals that got her off of drugs. That works too." So, some of you are, I suspect, just sitting there, because this is a normal reaction, and are saying to yourself, *Well, it worked for Chuck Colson. That's good, but what's that got to do with me?*

My argument would be that Christianity is not simply a personal experience, and I think 90 percent of the Christians—maybe some of you in this room who are believers—get this wrong. Rick Warren got it right. Why that book has sold twenty-eight million copies, I believe, is because the first sentence says, "It's not about you; it's about God." We think it's all about *us* getting the benefit of being Christians or going to church or getting moral teaching.

There are any of a number of things about what Christianity means to me personally, but I would argue that Christianity not only is important for you to find meaning and purpose in your own life, but it is vital to the good life corporately, that is, how we live our lives together.

I wrote a book with Nancy Pearcey and Harold Fickett called *How Now Shall We Live?* about five or six years ago that deals with how Christianity affects every single area of life. Abraham Kuyper, one of the great theologians at the turn of the century—1800s into the 1900s—was prime minister of Holland. When he dedicated the Free University at Amsterdam, he said, "In the total expanse of human life, there is not one square inch of which the Christ, who alone is sovereign, does not declare, 'That is mine!'"

Music, science, politics, even law—God has something to say about it, and when we understand what he has to say about it, here's my simple proposition that you can chew over. I'll add some things to explain it, and then if you've got time, if I provoked some thought, in the question period, ask me some questions about it: You can only make sense out of life when you see life through the lens of a biblical understanding of reality—what's called a *worldview*. That's not an esoteric term for professors on campuses; it's a very common term.

Everybody, every single one of you, in this room, has a worldview. A worldview, as C. S. Lewis explained it, is how the world works and how you fit in. It answers four basic questions:

"Where did we come from?" For the examined life, that's the first question you have to ask, because everything is going to turn on how you answer that question. If we came out of the primordial soup, as people believe today and as your kids are being taught in evolution courses in public schools, then there is no basis for human dignity. If we're created by a loving God, then we're invested with dignity.

"Why is there a mess in the world?" is the second question. Is there anybody here who doesn't believe that there is such a thing as sin or evil? Anybody here who doesn't believe the world is a mess? Life is a mess most of the time. You're struggling with things. You've everything put together, and the world rolls over on top of you. The wife of one of our associates was taken off to the hospital yesterday. They thought it was pneumonia. Now it turns out to be a punctured lung apparently and fluid in the body cavity, maybe cancer. One day you're healthy; one day you're not. "Why is there sin and suffering?" That question has plagued humanity from the beginning.

"Is there a way out?" If there *are* sin and suffering and you can answer where they come from, then "Is there a way out?" is the third question. So, how can I be redeemed? How are *we* to be redeemed? Every great thinker—Jesus included (and I would call him a great thinker)—has had an answer to that question. Every utopian promise has been a promise of redemption. Marx said, "Throw off the oppressors, throw off your chains, workers arise, and throw off your chains"; Freud said, "Get rid of all those childhood repressions; let your sexual desires be free, and you'll be free." Every philosophy has promised redemption.

Only one worldview says that you were created in the image of God and were made perfect to live forever in relationship with God, but sin entered the picture, and that was not because God gave our primeval ancestors a choice in the Garden, but since he loved us so much he gave us a free will. If we're made in his image, we have to have a free will. It's key that you understand that.

However, if you have a free will, it presupposes that you may choose, as Augustine put it, the nongood, instead of the good. Our first ancestors chose the nongood, and ever since, people have been choosing the nongood. Every day of the week, people choose the nongood; it results in sin and evil. We're responsible, but in the Christian understanding of things, we have redemption through Christ. The Cross means the atoning death of Jesus Christ on the Cross in our place.

I look back thirty-three years to a night in my friend's driveway when I first heard the Gospel. I first heard about Christianity in a serious way. I was a Christian like most Americans. I had grown up in America. I wasn't Jewish. I went to church twice a year; I must be a Christian. Then I heard the Gospel and understood that Christ had died for my sins—that was thirty-three years ago—and in a flood of tears, I called out to God. I didn't know the words or anything else. I think back on that every single day and realize that if it hadn't been for that night, and if it hadn't been for the fact of the Cross, that I would be dead today, because I would have suffocated in the stench of my own sins.

I think back and realize what Christ has taken away and forgiven me for, and I am so profoundly grateful that I will always do my duty because of that—gratitude, the mother of all virtues, as Chesterton said. That's Christian redemption.

Once you get through the questions of where we came from, about which there are profound debates, and of why there are sin and suffering, about which there are endless debates, and nobody's really got a very good answer; I've given you the best one I've got, then, when you look at the various redemptions that have been offered, I would simply say that if you want to know the tested truth about anything, including redemption—what is truth? Truth is that which conforms to reality—let's see which redemption works.

I've always said that if you wanted to see whether a worldview is true or not, test it out as you would test a road map. If you go to MapQuest to get driving instructions from here to Buffalo, you get the map and you follow it and you end up in Hartford. That's not a good map. You do it again, and you end up in Erie, Pennsylvania. That's not a good map. Finally, you get one that gets you to Buffalo. What do you call it? *True.* That's true. It reflects reality and a worldview. The whole purpose of life, in my opinion, is to search for a worldview that conforms to reality, one that is true.

I write this in *The Good Life* that my dream, when I practiced law, always was to argue a case before the Supreme Court. Then, I won a case in the court of appeals, the government appealed it, and it was going to the Supreme Court. I was going to argue it and was getting all boned up on it. I was so excited about that case, and then I got appointed to the government, to be special counsel to President Nixon. All of a sudden I was on the other side. I didn't get to argue the case. *Big* disappointment. So, I never argued a case before the Supreme Court, but I still dream about this and think that when I get to heaven, maybe God will let me argue a case before the Supreme Court the proposition of which is that there's only the biblical view of reality—created in the image of God, falling into sin by our own free will and creating sin in the world, and Christ redeeming us from that. And then there's the fourth question.

"Once redeemed, do I know what my purpose is in life?" My purpose is to try to help redeem that fallen culture and to do things in society that help to alleviate the consequences of sin and suffering. You can get up every morning and get really excited about that as a way of understanding your life as a purpose. It beats the stuffing out of what those executives that come down to Naples have to think about when they get up in the morning: "Why hasn't the gardener given me a better shrub-cutting today?"—and who are grumpy, out at the golf course at nine, hungover. That is no way to have purpose in life. A Christian worldview gives you great purpose.

I would like to take those four propositions: created in the image of God, fallen into sin ourselves by our own free will, redeemed by God's own intervention in our lives, and then a purpose to fulfill God's mandate to care for the creation and to care for the world. I'd like to argue before the Supreme Court and say, "That's the *only* worldview that works." Compare it to Confucianism, to Hinduism, to Buddhism, to Islam; compare it to any other philosophy. The others don't work.

Human history is the ash heap of all the promised utopian answers to human problems, every one of which had lead to tyranny. Look at the twentieth century. Every single one of the tyrants of the twentieth century promised to be a redeemer. It was a false redemption, a false promise. The blood ran through the killing fields of Cambodia and the gulags and the Holocaust as a consequence of the false redemption promises of tyrants. They've used promises to exploit people.

The only One who has never exploited people is the Prince of Peace, who offers redemption as a free gift. We're scandalized by it because it's free, and that is one reason the Gospel is rejected by so many so-called sophisticated people.

The only One who has never exploited people is the Prince of Peace, who offers redemption as a free gift. We're scandalized by it because it's free, and that is one reason the Gospel is rejected by so many so-called sophisticated people. It's just too simple, isn't it? It's too easy.

I would love to argue that case of comparing those worldviews, because today we are in a clash of worldviews, friends. Samuel Huntington had it right in the mid-nineties, when he wrote the book *The Clash of Civilizations and the Remaking of World Order*. Is there anybody here who read that book? Do you remember hearing about it at the time or reading the reviews in *The New York Times*? Samuel Huntington is a professor at Harvard. He wrote this book at a time when everybody said we had arrived at what Francis Fukuyama said was the end of history. Talk about utopians. The end of history!

Western liberal democracy is one of the great ideological contests to the twentieth century. People will live in peace and happiness ever after. Come 9/11, everybody went out and found Huntington's book, and what Huntington said is this: There are three great religious blocks in the world—Eastern religion; Islam, which stretches from Indonesia in the east to Nigeria in the west—some thirty-eight countries in Islam; and Western liberal democracy informed by Judeo-Christian truth. He said that the great dialectic of the twenty-first century, the great struggle, the battle of the twenty-first century, will be between Islam and the West. He wanted to say that Islam will win, because the West is decadent and Islam is monolithic and aggressive.

I don't buy that part of it, but that is what he said. After September 11, 2001, everyone realized this is really serious, and trust me: It *is* serious. I have studied as much about that as anything over the last five years, and I am convinced that Islamo-fascism is every bit as much of an evil as Nazi-fascism was. I'm convinced that it is an alien worldview that goes far beyond terrorism. I'm convinced we're grossly underestimating it. There are, by most counts, a 110 million jihadists among Muslims—most of whom are peace-loving people, admittedly, but there are some who are radicalized by the teachings of one Sayyid Qutb, in particular. When we look at the two worldviews, it's no contest.

Where did we come from? Both worldviews agree that we were created by God, but there the similarity ends. Islam says that Allah rules by fiat, and we don't say that. We say that God has spoken but offers us grace. Islam has no concept of grace. We believe that human beings are responsible for sin. We have fallen into sin. Islam is a utopian religion that believes human beings are basically good, and therefore, if we just do what Allah says, we'll live happily and peacefully ever after.

You can see how happily and peacefully all these Islamic republics around the world live—chopping off the hands of thieves and massacring people—a perfect formula for tyranny, no redemption. The Christian Gospel is nothing if it's not redemption.

In Islam, there is no redemption, unless you participate in the jihad, and then you end up in paradise with seventy-two virgins—a preposterous idea, preposterous distortion. The Koran was written over a period of thirty years, and it was written in bits and pieces and later assembled. It is absolutely rigid, because it was "dictated by God." It is very much unlike the Christian Bible and the Jewish Bible, which people believe were spoken by the inspiration of God but which are interpreted in the light of reason and understanding. Not so with Islam; that is why it's so harsh.

Islam advances by *jihad*, and Christians advance by making a great *proposal*: "Come to the wedding feast." "Come sit at the table" is an invitation. We're always accused of imposing things; we can't impose a thing. All we've got is a proposal given in love to a lost world with a broken heart. God calls us and says, "Come"—totally different than advancing by jihad.

Finally, Christianity is a pluralistic belief system. We believe that Christianity should have its day and place in the marketplace, but we firmly believe as modern Christians exactly what the founders said: "We hold these truths to be self-evident, that all men are created equal, that they are endowed by their Creator with certain unalienable Rights, that among these are Life, Liberty and the pursuit of Happiness." That applies to Jews and Muslims and Buddhists and Hindus and agnostics and atheists. Not so with Islam. Islam believes that until you are killed—if you're an infidel, and everyone in this room, as I look around, is probably an infidel, a Jew, a Christian, a non-Muslim—there cannot be peace, and Allah cannot reign. That is a vicious belief system, and it is theocratic; it does not believe in a state church, but it *does* believe in a church state. This is a totally alien worldview.

Equally alien and equally at play today is the battle between what I call *secular naturalism*, which is the rampant belief system in American life. It has arisen as a result of the relativism of the sixties and seventies; the idea is that there is no truth, no standard of truth, and thus we live by our own formulations of what is right and just and true, and we've come out of the primordial soup; so, there is no basis for human dignity. Thus, Peter Singer, distinguished professor of ethics at Princeton, can say that all species are alike. He advocated bestiality until he was challenged once in a debate by one of my colleagues who said to him, "But that's not giving the animal a choice."

Never underestimate the resourcefulness of a Princeton professor of ethics from Australia who is determined to impose his utilitarian system of ethics on us. Singer went back to the People for the Ethical Treatment of Animals and later on gave a speech in which he said, "Of course, animals have a choice; they can show affection." He also believes that babies should be killed by infanticide and old people should be left to die—after all, 80 percent of all medical expenditures are incurred during the last six months of people's lives; so, just stop treating them at six months before they die. Right? You just have to count backward; there are no problems with that. But he actually says that.

Singer also says to withdraw care from terminally ill people, or in the phrase that is so popular in American hospitals today—and doctors in the room will understand this: "*futile* care"—"*futile* to continue that care," which is a euphemism for saying, "Get the people who are on the margins of society out of the way." Stop and think about it. If the secular naturalist is right that we came as a result of a grand collision of atoms and all these random mutations, all of these billions of years later—which, by the way, if you were here for Polkinghorne's lecture, he absolutely refutes by looking at the human cell structure and the way in which information pours through the body—but if you believe secular naturalism, then what basis is there for ethics, traditional ethics, that there is a standard for right and wrong and a basis for human dignity? There is none.

So, what is your option? Your option is to do the greatest good for the greatest number and maximize the personal happiness of all species, which is precisely the operative definition of ethics among 80 percent of America's intellectual elite today. They won't say it quite that bluntly, but that's precisely what it is—John Stuart Mill's utilitarianism updated for the twenty-first century.

I am going to make one other very provocative statement, and then I'm going to quit. I want to make this without having to flesh it out, which is unfortunate, because I wish I had time to do it. As you can tell, I've got a couple of people in the room who've been through our Centurion Program in which we teach the biblical worldview—Chuck Stetson and Sheila Weber, of course; any other Centurions here? I've been teaching biblical worldview for the last three years to a hundred people who come in every year. You could really take a couple of hours on this, as I normally do, but I just want to make this statement because I want to throw this out for you to think about and in the question-and-answer session. If you want me to enlarge on it, I will.

So, here's my provocative statement. There are five things that are unique and distinctive about a Christian-informed view of reality. Just think about this. Number one is the concept of human dignity, which is why William Wilberforce, whose life we will be celebrating soon with the movie *Amazing Grace* on the two-hundredth anniversary of the abolition of the slave trade, did what he did. Wilberforce, the Christian, who worked tirelessly against all the powers of England to end that abominable practice, and not just Wilberforce two hundred years ago, but today, too—all the great human rights campaigns now in the last five years, the campaign in North Korea, Sudan, slavery, human trafficking—all led by Christians. Why? Because we fundamentally believe in the human dignity of individuals. Who else has that idea? It's a provocative statement, but it's true. Look into it.

So, first, *human dignity*, which is a Judeo-Christian idea, and second, *the idea of transcendent authority*. I don't think law and government work apart from a transcendent source of authority. When you look at what we have in the West today in free Western liberal democracy, it is a clear result of Reformation doctrines called *sphere sovereignty*, the idea that every sphere of life has its own place. It's a direct result of a book called *Lex, Rex* written by Samuel Rutherford, the Scottish cleric who was sentenced to die for writing it, because it was such a radical idea. It says that the law is king, not the king is law, and the rule of law comes from that. You look at all of the elements of Western liberal democracy, and you can see clearly that they've come out of Christian contributions. Islam has not produced one. Buddhism hasn't produced one. Western liberal democracy is a creation of Christian thinking. Another provocative idea.

Third, *you have to have a motive to build a culture*. There's a wonderful book out—I hope you buy it and read it—called *Victory of Reason: How Christianity Led to Freedom, Capitalism, and Western Success* by Professor Rodney Stark. He used to be at Berkeley, then was at the University of Washington, and now he's at Baylor. It's a powerful book, because he explains how the Christian influence built Western civilization. It contains many, many things you would never normally think about. I wear eyeglasses, and I wouldn't see you very well if I were not wearing them. But eyeglasses were invented by Christians who believed that it was tragic that some people had to be slaves and couldn't work, because they couldn't see. So, they invented eyeglasses as a humanitarian effort to enable people to get jobs. Did you know that? Hydroelectric power came from Christians who said, "Slavery is wrong, and it's wrong for these people to bring the water in on their shoulders." It was a radical departure from the Greeks. These Christians didn't want slaves carrying that water, and so, they developed hydro-electric power to keep these people from having to carry the water.

Fourth, *Christianity provides the moral impulse to care for other people.* Look at the great compassion reforms; look at what we do in Prison Fellowship. Why would you go into prisons? In a utilitarian society, we would do the greatest good for the greatest number and maximize personal happiness. So, who cares about prisoners? "Forget about 'em, let them break rocks, let 'em die." Why should we go into prisons? Christianity is countercultural in the extreme, when it comes to a culture that exalts the self. We're saying that the object and meaning of life is what you can do for others, not what you do for yourself. That is completely contrary to human instincts, and yet that is exactly what Christianity does.

> **Christianity is countercultural in the extreme, when it comes to a culture that exalts the self. We're saying that the object and meaning of life is what you can do for others, not what you do for yourself.**

You start adding these things up, and you realize that we live in a society that has been formed by conceptions of the good life that come from the way God has created us and taught us to live. No other formulation works. And so, Christians say today, "We're accused of being the big, bad Religious Right that wants to impose our views"—but no, we can't impose on anybody.

We recognize what Martin Luther King Jr. said: "Whom you would change, you must first love," and we become instruments of spreading that and offering that and making a great proposal. So, I put before you that great proposal—that life really only has meaning when you understand it in terms of the way God sees it and you won't be happy until you find it. You'll be infinitely restless. Augustine said, "Our heart is restless until it finds rest in thee." It's true. Try it.

Antony Flew, whom I met in England—the philosopher of atheism, eighty-one years old—renounced atheism, because he studied the intelligent design movement and realized that there had to be an Intelligence in the universe. He came to the same conclusion that Einstein did and turned away from his atheism and has suddenly seen a whole new way of understanding life. That is the proposal I make to you. It makes sense only to ourselves when we find that rest that we find "only in thee"—in God—and when we begin to understand life the way we're told to live it, which is the only way to sustain it. That is my proposal.

Q & A

T hank you, Chuck. That was amazing. I think you are probably using
steroids.

As usual, we have time for questions. But remember, as always
at Socrates in the City, keep your questions in the form of a *question*. Very
important.

Q: My question has to do with discussions that I have had with different
friends. It is on the idea that we bring up Islamic countries, and we say the
atrocities that go on, but then they counter with, "Well, Western countries
were involved in all sorts of atrocities in the guise of Christ." The Inquisition
and the Crusades are the two hot points. I was just wondering how you actually touch on those two.

A: The Inquisition went over several centuries. You hear this all the time. You
hear that worse things are done in the name of religion than in the name of
anything else. That is tossed out there, and everybody kind of accepts it. It is
basically false. Stark's book says the Dark Ages weren't dark at all, and he goes
on and explains why they weren't. The Inquisition went on over a period of
three centuries. Many horrible things took place. Nobody would defend it,
nor should defend it. People were killed for heretical beliefs.

But the total number over three centuries was in the hundreds. If you put it in a historical context, it certainly pales in significance compared to the horrors of the twentieth century.

The Crusades and the counter-Crusades, if you go back and read the history about the back-and-forth battles between Islam and the West, they were simply not about religion. It wasn't trying to quell a heresy. It was all about politics.

I spent a lot of time in Ireland with both sides, talking to them. It was never about Catholic versus Protestant. It was about who controlled the Northern Ireland and who provided the jobs. The Crusades were very much that, and they were a blot on Islam and a blot on the West. No one would say it, but there is a fundamental difference, and I don't mean to be picking on Islam, but there is a fundamental difference when Islam launches a crusade to kill Christians and Jews. It is acting in a way that is consistent with its belief system. When Christians do it, they are acting contrary to what they believe. They're clearly wrong. We can be hypocrites, because we acknowledge something is wrong, and therefore if we don't live by it, we're hypocrites. If you don't ever acknowledge anything is wrong, you can never be a hypocrite. So, we are more guilty in the world's eyes because of that, but in terms of numbers, in terms of consequences, I don't think anything even comes close to the horrors that were done in the name of atheism in the twentieth century.

Q: In truth, I am from Hartford, and I've never confused it with Buffalo. In terms of Islam, we have a Western society that is rooted in guilt, which is not remitted and feels very much intimidated by Islam. I want to put before you a question I have come up with, and I wonder how you think its applicability is for the culture, if we were to pose this to Islam: Is Islam strong enough to handle freedom?

A: One would have to say that the jury is still out. I honestly don't know, but theoretically, no. Theoretically, a theocracy cannot be a democracy, almost by definition. The only hope you've got is an Atatürk in every Muslim country, and even that is pretty shaky, because it hasn't had the lasting effect we would like to see.

You see battles going on everywhere. I happen to believe that this administration is right about exporting democracy to the one part of the world where it has been resisted most strenuously, because I don't see another long-term answer. I think, otherwise, we're going to be in terrorist wars for the next thousand years. You've got to remember that Americans have a very short memory. We think of 9/11 as being "a long time ago," and why aren't the troops home? This is the way Americans think. Islam doesn't think in those terms.

Think of it. Muhammad started writing the Koran in 632 A.D., and a hundred years later, Islamic armies were up within a hundred miles of Paris and were defeated at Poitiers. The battles went back and forth. Much of what is later Eastern Europe, much of Spain, southern France, and North Africa were conquered territories. This battle went on until 1683, when the Polish and German infantry turned back the Turks just outside of Vienna. It was a decisive battle that defeated the Ottoman Empire, and that was a thousand years later—from Muhammad.

Interestingly enough—in case you think worldviews don't matter, in case you think ideas don't have consequences—when the Polish and German infantry turned back the Turks in 1683, the day they did it was on the day of the decisive battle—September 11. Don't think bin Laden, who was a well-trained theologian and scholar, was not aware of that. They are telling us it is a long war, and we are sitting around saying, "Why can't we get this thing over with?" My fear is that if we can't promote democracy around the world, we are going to be fighting a long time. That is not a pretty picture.

Q: I'm glad you remembered Charles Martel's contribution to the defense of the West, and anyone who says the French haven't done anything for us lately can cast their eyes back to that. It seems to me there is a crisis of confidence in our culture, and how can we recover our cultural confidence?

A: I believe cultures are changed not by great fiats, by either cultural or political leaders. Cultures are changed over the backyard fence, the charcoal grill, one person at a time, and you have some really negative influences in American culture today. Bad news sells. So, you always hear the negative side of things.

There's what Os Guinness correctly calls a "crisis of authority," because if there is no overarching standard of truth from which you can form a moral consensus about what is right or wrong, you break into ideological warfare. That is a whole other area to get into.

You never can get people to agree on things, and the negative constantly surfaces, because there is so much rancor in political discourse and social discourse. So, you suffer a lack of confidence. None of you in the room, I am sure, follow Wall Street and the market. But it was amazing to me for six months watching all this incredibly positive economic data and all this tremendous economic journalism about "how bad things are."

It has become self-fulfilling. If you keep talking about it being bad long enough, people will believe it. There's a serious crisis in confidence. I think you win it back the same way you have always changed every culture going back through history. That is when the habits of the heart—the attitudes and values and dispositions of people—change, and that is not done from the top down. It is done from the bottom up. That is why thinking people like this could make a difference. I don't think you're going to suddenly change the gatekeepers of society like this. I think you're going to change public attitudes.

Q: I am a chaplain in transportation in New York City and pioneering that at sixty-five, going on sixty-six. I'm concerned that there is a spiritual war going on all over the world and about the role of evangelism and also what is going on in terms of the Christian Church. How do we speak to this? I think so much evangelism comes across as condemnation. I would love to hear your views, because my approach is person to person.

A: The latest poll data shows that when non-Christian people are asked to categorize Christians, the adjective most commonly given is *judgmental*. They're judgmental, and it's sad that Christians give that impression. I like what Bishop Niles once said, "Christianity is one beggar telling another beggar where he found bread." We should not be judging people; we should be loving people. There's a lot of judgmentalism. On the other hand, I think that is also an excuse, a cop-out. "I'm not going to listen to your claims because you guys are so judgmental." That is painting with a pretty broad brush, because I don't think a lot of people are [judgmental].

It really is a reaction moved by the dominant value in American life today. The dominant value in American life is tolerance. Tolerance has been elevated over truth, but it is not the tolerance that we think. It is not what I was taught in school or grew up believing it was, that is, listening respectfully to somebody with whose point of view I vehemently disagree, but I will protect their right to say something that I fundamentally disagree with.

Today, if you say something with which somebody disagrees, you have offended that person, and now suddenly, that is the cardinal vice. We have distorted the definition of tolerance. In *The Good Life*, I quote Dorothy Sayers, who had a magnificent quote on tolerance. She says, "In the world, it is called Tolerance; in Hell it is called despair." We have given up, because there's nothing worth arguing about. So, this paints a very ugly picture of Christians as intolerant and judgmental, and a lot of people have that. We've got to work hard to change it, but you also have to have a society in which presenting a truth claim is not an offense, and truth claims are, by definition, exclusive.

I had lunch in Silicon Valley a few years ago, which I tell about in *The Good Life*. It was a really fun time, because there were a lot of Christian guys there, a lot of entrepreneurs, some non-Christian guys, and the world's number one leading futurologist, who writes newsletters—Paul Saffo. He was sitting on my left, and about halfway through lunch, he turned and got very indignant. He said, "What I resent about you Christians is you think you've got the only way. All religions end up in the same place. You can't say one religion is different than another."

I said to him, "I can't say one religion is necessarily better than the other, but I certainly can say they are different, whether or not you're born into the covenant and are a Jew. And Jesus says, 'No one comes to the Father, except through me.' Every religion makes its own rules about truth claims. They all can't be right. They can all be wrong, but they can't all be right." We got into the most incredible argument, and finally, he said he would not acknowledge that until I took out my pen and dropped it about six times.

I said, "Every time that drops, there's a law, a physical law, and there are also moral laws. I can't say this pen is going to not drop, because it dropped."

Now he was getting red around the neck and

> **"Every religion makes its own rules about truth claims. They all can't be right. They can all be wrong, but they can't all be right." We got into the most incredible argument.**

very upset; then he said, "Well, that is particles passing through particles. Quantum physics."

I said, "Baloney. That is a mass hitting a mass. That's what you are seeing with your eyes."

We finally got to the point where he said, "Well, all right, I will concede that some things are extra-natural."

People pull themselves into a terrible box, and that makes evangelism hard. I think that was your point.

Q: I'd like you to address the issue of what you seem to think is going to be a very long war between the West and Islam. Does the West actually stand a chance if it does not return to its Christian roots and just tries to convert one country after the next—whether it's Iraq or Iran—into a peaceful democracy, without actually having a Christian foundation to that?

A: I don't think we have even a chance, a remote chance, of turning Afghanistan or Iraq into Christian countries. It would be, from my perspective, rationally, the best system, because I think it is superior to any other system. I think you could make that argument. I think it's true. I think there is a natural order, and there's a way God created things. When you live that way, you're going to live comfortably. When you don't, you're going to be spitting against the wind and cutting against the grain of the universe. So, I would rather see that, but I don't think it's going to happen.

The best thing we can do in any of these countries is to create a system of genuine pluralism, where different religious systems can be respected. Now, we don't have that in Afghanistan. That is why—I can't remember his name—the man who converted to Christianity in Pakistan and came back to Afghanistan and was sentenced to die had to get out of the country and went to Italy, because he would have been killed. So, they don't have a genuinely pluralistic system, for all of the American treasure and blood that have been shed.

It's going to be a long, hard process, and all we can hope for is honest, open pluralism and giving free markets a chance. The interesting thing, and this is something that those of you who think deeply about this will see, if you think deeply about it from a religious perspective: Western liberal democracy has exploded in India, in China, in South America. It's exploding even in Africa, in parts of *Africa*, in Russia, *not* in Islamic countries. Why is that? It is a theological question.

If you believe that God dictated his Word, then what he says and what is contained in the Koran is inviolable. If you believe God spoke in an inspired way through humans, which is what the Bible is, then you spend thousands of years trying to understand rationally what it means. You're far less dogmatic.

There's no flexibility and no give in Islam. That's why it has never produced a great culture. There have been periods when it has, mostly copied from the Greeks. Mostly they kept Aristotle and Plato alive during parts of the Dark Ages, certainly, when the barbarians overtook Europe. Those were good years for Islam, but it was nothing original. They have created nothing original in the way of original culture.

Stark makes that point in *The Victory of Reason* very powerfully and explains it theologically. When you understand that, you realize the problem is really a theological question.

Simply Christian: Why Christianity Makes Sense

N. T. WRIGHT

October 27, 2006

Introduction

Good evening, and welcome to Socrates in the City, the thinking person's alternative to doing macramé and decoupage.

My name is Eric Metaxas. It is my pleasure to see so very many of you here this evening, almost as many of you as there are seats.

I have to say that I am genuinely amazed to see New Yorkers like yourselves, if not yourselves, come to a beautiful club to have a glass of wine and hear a brilliant speaker. It just amazes me. It just doesn't add up. I don't know why you are here, but I want to welcome you.

For those of you who have had a glass of wine, it should be taking effect right about now. You should begin feeling sleepy; your eyelids are feeling heavy, heavy. The room is warm; you just want to close them, don't you? You just want to close them, but don't, because it is offensive to the speaker. Don't do that, okay? But you can do that later.

Tonight at Socrates in the City, it is our privilege to hear from Bishop N. T. Wright. Yes, once again, we at Socrates in the City deliver to

Yes, once again, we at Socrates in the City deliver to you a speaker with a British accent. . . . These are authentic accents— every single one of them. Not a phony one that we have detected yet. The thing is our focus groups have told us that five to one, you prefer speakers with a British accent.

you a speaker with a British accent. . . . These are authentic accents—every single one of them. Not a phony one that we have detected yet. The thing is our focus groups have told us that five to one, you prefer speakers with a British accent. We try to bring you what you asked for. Focus groups also tell us that any kind of a title is a plus. For you guys, tonight we found somebody with a title *and* a British accent.

If you end up not really caring for what the good bishop has to say, you take it up with the focus groups. I don't want to hear about it, okay? We just gave you what you said you wanted in the surveys. Is that clear? Don't take it up with me.

Look, we kid around, but Americans are undeniably fascinated with things British. Part of that is because of the richness of British history. We don't have that here; we don't have as much history. We Americans really trace our history no farther back than 1976, when Bruce Jenner won the gold medal in the Olympic decathlon. That is about as far back as we go with our history. Before that, it is all very hazy. We know very little. Vikings. Dinosaurs. We don't know. It's all a haze before Jenner took the gold.

But in Britain, they have such a rich history, and we value that. So, we are impressed by Britain and, of course, by British-accented speakers. We have had Jonathan Aitken and David Aikman, but to be fair, we can also be a little intimidated by the Brits, as I like to call them. Sometimes they are beyond our comfort zone. Who can forget a couple of months ago when Baroness Cox showed up in that magnificent embroidered silk gown? With the wimple and that preposterous starched ruff! Remember that huge starched ruff? Americans aren't used to that. We are much more into jogging suits and comfortable clothing like that.

Remember when Sir John Polkinghorne showed up in the full suit of armor? Some of you were here for that. Putting his beaver up only to speak and to glower at us in that titled British way that I find just so un-American.

So, *that* side of British culture we can do without, thank you very much. To be perfectly honest, inviting British speakers is really something of a crapshoot, isn't it? You just don't know what you're going to get.

And I have to say that I think we're all a bit relieved that the bishop hasn't come in here with his miter and crosier and that whole thing. So, thank you in advance for not wearing that stuff. I always hate to bring up that kind of thing with the speakers in advance, but I have been stung twice before, and I think it's just something I need to mention because it makes us uncomfortable.

So, tonight, of course, we are going to hear from Bishop N. T. Wright, who is speaking on the subject of his latest book, *Simply Christian: Why Christianity Makes Sense.*

Now, in case you didn't know it, our speaker N. T. Wright is the Bishop of Durham. And strangely enough—I'm not making this up—this morning at seven A.M. at something called the New Canaan Society—which is a UFO cult that I am a part of up in Connecticut—I introduced a speaker whose last name is also Wright, same spelling, and who is a pastor. Guess where? Durham, North Carolina. Isn't that creepy? What is God saying? It is freaking me out. But that is true.

So, Bishop Wright, you are the second pastoral figure named Wright from Durham that I have introduced today. That really is about enough. Two are my limit. Doctor's orders. If there's a third, I'm sorry, but I am going to have to excuse myself.

Anyway, the Wright that I introduced this morning had a North Carolina accent, and just as the silliest thing you, Bishop Wright, might say will sound brilliant because of your British accent, everything brilliant he said still sounded like he was just "a-pickin' and a-grinnin'."

That's not fair, but there it is. That is just the way it is. Well, now the book we are going to hear about tonight, *Simply Christian*, is not entirely unlike a book I have written, titled *Everything You Have Always Wanted to Know About God (but Were Afraid to Ask)*, not that my book is equal to the Bishop's extraordinary work. But I believe that with the right marketing and distribution we can give you a run for your money, Bishop. I do, I do.

I wanted to say that I have to plug my second book for the evening. I have just been working on a biography of William Wilberforce, the eighteenth-century abolitionist. When we realized that we would have the privilege of hearing from Bishop Wright this evening and the term *Bishop of Durham* came up, I said, "This rings a bell. Bishop of Durham." So, I searched through my manuscript, which is now being copyedited, and I found, in fact, that I had a little thing in there about the Bishop of Durham, *circa* 1795.

Since nobody really will dare stop me, I am going to read from my own manuscript. What can you do? You're stuck.

But the scene is interesting. In 1795, things were not looking good for abolition. Wilberforce was really and truly struggling. It was just the dark night of the soul. Things were looking bad and people were starting to leave the movement. In the book, I mention how Wilberforce's friend James Stephen came to visit him, all the way from the West Indies, to encourage him and everyone else to buck up. And so, when he finally showed up, he brought his whole family and *three West Indian turtles* with him to London. This is before you had to clear that kind of stuff with customs officials, right?

He decided to give these three West Indian turtles to William Wilberforce as a present. In a couple of years, Wilberforce would be married and have children and a menagerie of animals, but at this point he was single and could barely feed himself, much less take care of three turtles from another hemisphere. And so, quoting from my book here:

"So, Wilberforce gave the three West Indian turtles to his friend the Bishop of Durham, who, in turn, gave them to his cook. The cook, in his turn, gave them to several waiters, who gave them to the bishop's guests at a banquet for fifty-five people, who all enjoyed them thoroughly and who were all—the bishop informed Wilberforce in his thank-you note—supporters of abolition."

So, there you have it. Before we let you speak here, Bishop Wright, I just want to say, if anyone gives you a pet, you really mustn't cook it. It is just not to be done. But that is what your forebear did. Is he your forebear? Can we describe him that way? Of course not.

Anyway, to be serious for a final paragraph. Bishop Wright is one of the world's leading New Testament scholars, and we are thrilled to have him with us today. He was the Dean of Lichfield Cathedral and the Canon Theologian of Westminster Abbey. And he is currently, as we have said, the Bishop of Durham.

He has taught at Cambridge and Oxford universities and has written over thirty books. He has also been on numerous television programs, including *ABC News, Dateline,* and *American Bandstand.* That last one might be a typo; I don't know.

As usual, our speaker will speak for thirty-five or forty minutes on the topic, after which we will have about the same length of time for questions and answers. There should be microphones set up. Do make your way to the microphone for Q & A at that point.

But without further ado, it is my privilege to introduce Bishop N. T. Wright.

Talk

T hank you very much. I don't think I've ever had an introduction quite like that before, and I don't think I'll ever get one quite like that again. All that stuff about Britishness reminded me of something a friend told me not long ago.

My friend and former colleague John Bowater, who is a leading English theologian who used to trot across to America frequently for conferences, told me that one time he looked in his diary [planner] and discovered there was a conference at which he was supposed to give a paper. He had to get on a plane right away and hadn't actually thought about what to say; so, he glanced at his diary to see what he was talking about, and it said, "God in the twenty-first century," or something like that. So, he penned something very quickly, got to the conference, went straight to the platform, did his fifty-minute lecture, and reached his stirring conclusion about God: that, if the doctrine of the Trinity didn't exist, it would be necessary to invent it.

There was thunderous applause, and as he sat down, the person next to him, said, "Very daring, very daring," and he said, "Daring? Why? I thought that was rather orthodox." And the man said, "This is a Unitarian conference." He said, "So, why are they all applauding?" The man said, "They just love your accent."

So, what I lack in clarity of thought I may make up in clarity of British speech.

But, now that I have been for the last three years, rather to my horror, a member of the House of Lords—you didn't sufficiently rub that in, Eric!—I was reminded of the splendid moment some years ago now when Lord Hailsham was Lord Chancellor of England. A lord chancellor wears some very fine robes and the whole legal kit and so on, and often you have parties of visitors and tourists who are being shown around the corridors of the Houses of Parliament. Hailsham came out of his own room in the House of Lords face to face with a party of American tourists. At the same time, a door opened further down the corridor. A member of Parliament, a man called Neal Marten, who was MP from Banbury at the time, emerged from the door, maybe thirty yards down the corridor. Hailsham wanted to attract Neal Marten's attention; so, ignoring the tourists who were facing him, he raised his hand and called, "Neal." And the tourists, of course, all did.

So, I think these are the pitfalls an Englishman has when addressing American audiences. The possibilities for misunderstanding within our common language or not-so-common language are legion and well known and written about elsewhere. And they even come in the American edition of this book, *Simply Christian*, and the British edition, which I have in my hands, and they're written by two different people. This one is written by N. T. Wright, and this one is written by Tom Wright; in England, my publishers think that if it's designed to be a user-friendly book, as opposed to one of those academic tomes, they prefer me to be Tom. But in America, the publishers apparently want me to look a bit more serious; so, they give me my full initials, N. T. Wright. It's the same book. I think I prefer the American cover actually, but there it is. You never quite know what you're publishing.

We live in a very confused world. I've just been lecturing in another place, a little way north of here in Cambridge, Massachusetts, at Harvard University, and I've been talking about some of the confusions that are out there in culture right now. I'm reminded of a splendid op-ed piece, which our UK Chief Rabbi Jonathan Sacks did recently in the London *Times*. Sacks is one of the most articulate, elegant expositors of faith and life in the UK today, along with our archbishop, Rowan Williams.

Anyway, Jonathan Sacks wrote a splendid piece about the children of

Israel walking through the wilderness with God trying to guide them. He used a GPS system as his model for how this was working. What happens when you have a GPS system in your car, or as we call them, "a satellite navigation system," in your car? Sacks said—and I wouldn't have had the temerity to say it, but this is how he put it—"Whoever invented this GPS with a woman's voice telling you that in two hundred yards, you must turn right didn't do so with the average Jewish male in mind, because everybody knows that when this voice says, 'In two hundred yards turn left,' the answer is, 'Who do you think I am? I'm not going to do that; I'm going to turn right.' When you do that, there's a sort of pause. After a while, the voice says in effect, 'This wasn't what we really had in mind. Since we're now here, you probably want to do this and this and this.'"

And he said, "That's what it was like with the children of Israel. They had God in the midst, saying, 'Do this, do this.' 'No,' they said, 'we're going to do that and that instead.'" But God hangs in there, goes along with them.

Is that a model of our culture? Is that what we're like in Western civilization today? Is there still a divine voice in our midst saying, "Do this, do this, do this," and are we paying any attention? Rabbi Sacks said the trouble is you can't actually guarantee that that's the situation. There's another model for what might be going on, and this might be the one that is actually relevant right now.

The other model works like this. Apparently, there is a certain type of ant that, when it is lost, is programmed to follow the ant in front. Now, normally that's a smart thing to do, because somewhere out there, there's a furry little creature that knows where it's going, and somehow you'll get there too. "But," said Sacks, "sometimes you have an entire colony of ants going round and round in an enormous circle. Each is following the one in front. They all die of starvation, because none of them know where they're going and they don't know how to get out of that circle."

So, Jonathan Sacks's article ended with this rather sharp question: Which are we more like? Are we more like the children of Israel, maybe getting it wrong, but maybe still just about listening for a voice? Or are we like those ants just merely following the ant in front, everybody hoping that if we follow where the fashion is going intellectually, societally, culturally, or whatever, then we'll all get somewhere, while, in fact, all we are doing is going round in circles? I began this book with that sort of image in mind.

This book, *Simply Christian*, has three sections. Let me say a word about that.

I actually planned four sections. I got to the end of the third, and the writing time that I budgeted for the book was just about up. So, I phoned the publisher and said, "I've finished three sections, and I actually want to do the fourth one, but I'm not sure when I'm going to do it." He said, "If you've already written three and it's already two hundred pages, that's quite long enough, and actually it looks like a book to me." So, there are other things I would have liked to talk about as well. Maybe they will form the basis of another book.

The first section is called "Echoes of a Voice." I'm not here talking explicitly about satellite navigation systems or about the children of Israel in the wilderness. I'm talking about voices that I believe virtually all human beings, in virtually all cultures, listen for and know, but are puzzled by.

The first of these is a voice that tells us to do justice. You don't have to teach people that there is such a thing as justice. Go to a school playground where four-year-olds are playing together. If you listen to what they say—and this is a point straight out of C. S. Lewis's *Mere Christianity*, to which I happily doff my cap at this point—sooner or later, you'll hear one of these kids say, "That's not fair!"

Has the child been to a seminar on modern theories of justice? No, he hasn't. The child just knows that there is such a thing as fairness and that this child who is beating him up or who has just stolen his ball is not obedient to this thing called justice, or fairness. But, of course, we adults do exactly the same thing; and so do nations and countries and societies. We all know there should be such a thing as *putting things right*: doing justice, getting it all sorted out. But we all find it extraordinarily difficult.

This point came home to me strongly when I lived in Westminster. I lived maybe within a five-iron shot (my golf isn't so good; maybe it was a three-iron shot) of four or five leading judicial establishments: the Houses of Parliament; the Lord Chancellor's office; New Scotland Yard (where all the police hang out); and one or two other places too. Then, just down the river in the City of London, there are enough barristers to man a battleship (although, with all those barristers arguing, the battleship would be going around in circles). And even with all those institutions and all those lawyers, we still can't do justice.

There are all these people—highly paid—working at justice, and yet justice continues to slip through our fingers. We sometimes get it right. We often get it wrong.

The same is true internationally and globally. You don't need me to tell you that the doing of justice on the worldwide scale is a major problem right now. Each time we think, *Right, we now know what to do*, and we go and try to do it, as often as not, we make matters worse.

So, we are faced with an oddity, a puzzle. I describe the call to justice, of which we are all aware, as the "echo of a voice." We sort of hear this voice somewhere saying, "You know in your bones that things ought to be fair; they ought to be sorted out; they ought to be just. What are you doing about it?" And we respond, "Well, yes, we wish we could do something." But, of course, we all put in a secret escape clause. Complete justice could be a trifle inconvenient in my own case. There may be moments when, though I think everyone else should do justice, I'd be happy to sneak around the back and avoid this. So, we are left with a residual oddity in human experience—whatever your religious and cultural background: We all know justice matters and we all know it's very difficult and we all want to make occasional exceptions in our own case.

The second echo of a voice that I've tracked here is "spirituality." Thirty or forty years ago, with secularism rampant, the very word *spirituality* was not a buzzword. When I grew up, people were not talking about spirituality much. They might talk about prayer, usually with the comment that "That's something I used to do when I was a kid, but I don't do it anymore." But "spirituality" wasn't something people talked about as such.

Now, imagine: Imagine a country with lots of springs of water bubbling up everywhere, making everything muddy and messy. Sooner or later, a dictator comes along and paves the whole thing over with concrete and says, "If you want water, we will pipe it to certain outlets. That'll be safe; you can have it there." That was the world I grew up in, the world of secularism that had paved over the rich, bubbling springs of spirituality. And people then said, "We have these outlets called *churches*. If you want some spirituality, you can go there, perhaps." But not many people did. Then, continuing with the image, after a while the springs of water get too energetic. They break open the concrete and spill out all over everywhere, and it's very confusing. And people are so thirsty that they're drinking any water they can get, even if it's muddy and messy.

That is the situation we now have, since the demise of secularism in the face of the New Age spirituality's neo-pantheism. There are all kinds of new religious movements. Go into the average bookstore or look at the mind-body-spirit section or whatever it's called there. You'll find all kinds of weird and wacky and wonderful religions, all except for normal mainstream Christianity. Isn't that funny? People think they want spirituality but they assume they're not going to find it in church. Sadly, they are quite often correct. Shame on our churches.

But the quest for an authentic spirituality, the sense that there are more dimensions to life than what you can put in a test tube or a bank balance—that sense haunts people in many different cultures. But again and again, they don't know quite what to do about it. Perhaps they try to pray. One day it works and the next day it doesn't. Or they read a bit of a holy book: one day it makes sense; the next day they haven't a clue what it's about. And so on.

The quest for an authentic spirituality, the sense that there are more dimensions to life than what you can put in a test tube or a bank balance—that sense haunts people in many different cultures.

So, this, too, is like the echo of a voice, a voice that is calling us to a different dimension of human life. The voice is insistent: "You ought to be listening to this." And we say, "Yes, I know, but I'm not quite sure what to do with it." We all know—unless we shut our ears to this voice—that we are made for multidimensional human living; but we are unsure where to find genuine, rich, lasting spirituality.

The third echo of a voice is "relationships." Basically, we all know we are made for one another, and we all mess it up. We do that in terms of our most close-up intimate relationships—in our families, our marriages, our workplaces: we manage to foul up relationships. But we do it globally as well. We all know that it would be wonderful if we could all get along as a global society. We work at it and we have highly paid diplomats. We have the UN and other agencies. We strain every nerve to get it right, but we still get it wrong. There are still wars and rumors of wars. If you ask almost anyone around the world if that's the way it ought to be, they will say, "No, we ought to be able to do this relationship thing. We ought to be able to get it right." And we can't.

So, this too is a puzzle, a haunting echo of a voice.

The fourth echo is "beauty." I'm going to read you just a little bit from the book. This is the parable that I use at the beginning of the chapter on beauty:

> One day, rummaging through a dusty old attic in a small Austrian town, a collector comes across a faded manuscript containing many pages of music. It's written for the piano. Curious, he takes it to a dealer. The dealer phones a friend who appears a half hour later. When he sees the music, he becomes excited, then puzzled. This looks like the handwriting of Mozart himself. But it isn't a well-known piece. In fact, he's never heard it before. More phone calls. More excitement. More consultations. It really does seem to be Mozart. And though some parts seem distantly familiar, it doesn't correspond to anything already known in his works. . . . But it seems incomplete.

Let me summarize the story as it goes on. There are gaps in the music. Just where it seems to come to a climax, it seems to stop and then pick up again later. Gradually the truth dawns on the excited little group. What they are looking at is indeed by Mozart. It is, indeed, beautiful, but it's the piano part that involves another instrument or perhaps other instruments. By itself, it is frustratingly incomplete. It is a signpost to something that once was there and might still turn up one day.

In case anyone should wonder, I wrote that little piece of fiction just a few months before an enterprising librarian in Philadelphia came upon a Beethoven manuscript that turned out to be the composer's own transcription—of the *Grosse Fuge* for two pianos from one of his final quartets. Life and art imitate one another in another very curious way.

My point is this: That's the position we are in when we are confronted by beauty. We stand before a great painting. (I went to the Met today and thought about this.) When you stand before the most amazing sunset or when you see the beauty of a human face, whether it's a little baby or a lovely wise old person, there is a haunting quality to it, as though it's not just complete in itself.

It's a signpost to a larger truth that is just around the corner, just out of sight. We can't grip it, can't get our hands on it. It's as though we're hearing the echo of a voice, and we'd love to hear whose that voice is and what story it's telling. Part of the joy of beauty is the realization that it is part of a larger whole, most of which appears to be just out of sight. We are drawn forward toward something . . . and left waiting, wondering.

Then, of course, as with justice, spirituality, and relationships, there is a problem. The sunset fades. Beauty vanishes. The lovely face grows hard and cold. Was it all a trick? Were we fooled into thinking there was something there of lasting value and importance?

There are, no doubt, other echoes of other voices that would make the same point. If I were writing the book now, I think I would include "freedom," and do the same kind of analysis. But these four will serve for the moment as ways in to what I am talking about.

You see, I don't think you can *prove* the existence of God. That is to say, I don't think you can set up a framework (call it "post-Enlightenment rationality" or something like that) and then run the "God" experiment through such a framework, waiting to see if "God" passes the test. There are, no doubt, plenty of people who think that's what we're supposed to do: to try to "prove" God's existence against some absolute standard or by some kind of experiment. But what you do in such a case is first to divinize your framework of thought. Any being that actually fit into that framework would not be God, because if there is such a being as God, God is by definition superior to all our frameworks of thought. That just isn't how things work.

So, is there no way that we can conduct the discussion about God? Yes, and I think these "echoes of a voice" are the ways to do it. We do not have "proofs" that are mathematical, rationalistic in nature. What we have are *signposts*: features of our world, elements within more or less universal human experience—things like justice, spirituality, relationships, beauty, freedom, and perhaps many others—which at least raise a puzzle, ask a question, and force us to confront issues. Even those of us who live frantically busy lives, dashing around doing a million things, need to stop for a moment now and then and take stock of all these issues.

So, having set out these "echoes of a voice," I move within the central part of the book to talk about the Christian story. I call it "staring at the sun" for precisely this reason: If you stare at the sun, it dazzles you. Actually, you can't quite *see* the sun; it's too bright. That's what it's like when you start to look at God. If you think you've got him nailed down, you've missed the point.

At least, there was one time—as I say in the book—when, according to the Christian story, they did nail God down. That's one of the most shocking and revelatory moments. It redefines what the word *God* actually means. Consider this. If you stand in the middle of a busy street and begin asking people, "Do you believe in God?" what sort of answers will you get? I don't know what the stats are in America at the moment, but in my country, you might get about a 50 percent *yes* and a 50 percent *no*. But the really interesting question isn't whether you believe in "God" or not, and the really interesting answer isn't from the person who gives you a *yes* or a *no* but who stares right back at you and says, "Which God are you talking about?"

You see, for most people in our culture, the word *God* is univocal. But that is by no means the case. I used to be a college chaplain at Oxford when I was teaching New Testament there. Often, some of the undergraduates who would come would say when they first arrived—some of them were anxious, never having had dealings with an Anglican priest before—"Well, you won't be seeing much of me, because I don't believe in God."

I would routinely say to such people, "Which God is it that you don't believe in?" They would be puzzled by that. They would, often enough, stumble out this business about an old man with a beard sitting on a cloud, looking down, being cross with us, and sending some people to heaven and other people to hell. And I would say, "Well, I've got great news for you. I don't believe in that God either."

I would see a sort of shadow cross their face. Then I would say, "No. I believe in the God revealed in Jesus of Nazareth; and I and my brothers and sisters in the Church discover he is active through this strange force, through the strange wind we call *the Holy Spirit*. If you want to get to know that God, he's very different from the one you just described." That God, I used to suggest, might just be worth investigating further. Some people took me up on that invitation; others didn't.

So, how do we understand God? Here there are two extremes. This is broad-brush theology, but it may help; and actually, this is the running theme that continues throughout the book. It's helpful to consider the two main ways in which people, historically speaking, have understood God.

On the one hand, you have the pantheism: God and the world as basically the same thing. This is, more or less, grown-up paganism. Paganism says that a river is a god, the sky is a god, and the tree is a god; a marriage is a god, war is a god, and everything is a god. Everything's divine—a god or perhaps, often enough, a goddess. That's paganism. And pantheism puts all of those together and says, "Let's be a bit more sophisticated about this. There is a divinity in everything. There is divine power in everything and in everyone so that *you* have divine power within you." This may seem at first to be flattering, but there's bad news: If there's divine power in the tree and the stone and the river as well, it may not be such a big deal after all. But pantheism is one way of accounting for the sense that many people have that there is a strangeness, a strange power—call it *divinity* if you like—within the world and within us as we are. We're not just flatlanders. The world is multidimensional. It throbs with life: divine life, perhaps.

The trouble with pantheism is that there's no answer to the problem of evil. If everything is in some sense divine, how do you explain the existence of evil? And, never mind explaining it, how do you *deal with* the problem of evil? How do you cope? There were many pantheists in the first century, and the normal answer to the question was that if you didn't like the way things were, if you didn't like the hand that life seemed to have dealt you, then the door was open and you were free to leave. Suicide is the pantheistic answer to the problem of evil. Not a very happy thought. It's on the increase today due to that very idea—there's nothing that can be done to make things better; so, you might as well get out now.

Pantheism scrunches God and the world together, but at the other end of the scale theologically, we meet a world in which God is a long way away. The belief called *Deism* suggests that God may conceivably have made the world and might just have intervened in the world from time to time. Notice what the language of "intervention" implies: God is out there, reaching down into the world and then quickly going back to heaven. But for the most part, we are by ourselves; we will have to run the world our own way. (For some people, that's good news: We don't have to bother about God anymore, since he's left us to our own devices; we can get on with things the way we want!) That kind of Deism constitutes a form of dualism in which God and the world are firmly split apart.

That is the basis for a great deal of the Western civilization of the last two hundred years. Actually, the United States of America was sort of built on it. It's in Jefferson; it's in the Constitution. That's why you in America have this radical separation of church and state, of private faith and public life. This, I believe, causes all sorts of problems. (We in the UK have our own problems, but they are different ones!) Most people in our culture, as I say, have lived within that latter view: God and the world a great distance apart.

So, there are those two basic ways of doing the God-and-the-world question: Either you collapse God and the world toward one another, as paganism and pantheism do, or you separate them out, as Deism does. But neither Judaism nor classic Christianity does it like that. Judaism and Christianity have a view of God in the world that is much more interesting and complex—where God and the world, heaven and earth, actually overlap and interlock in interesting ways. Part of the point of the Temple in Jerusalem was that it was the actual place on *terra firma* where heaven and earth overlap. So, when you went into the Temple, it wasn't *as if* you were going into the presence of God. You *were* going into heaven, into the presence of God. So, that's why the Psalms are what they are in the Hebrew Bible. They are the means by which people on earth join the chorus of praise in heaven.

And this idea of heaven and earth overlapping and interlocking, and sometimes being present to one another in ways that we didn't expect, gives a much richer context and matrix of thought for understanding what Judaism was and is or what Christianity was and is than that *either/or* of either pantheism or Deism. So, when I talk about God in this book, it's that richer context that I am trying to explore.

Judaism and Christianity have a view of God in the world that is much more interesting and complex—where God and the world, heaven and earth, actually overlap and interlock in interesting ways.

Then, in the next chapter, I look at the question of Israel. This may seem surprising to some; too many Christians have allowed themselves to think of God, of Jesus, and of the Spirit without reference to Israel. But you cannot understand Jesus Christ without understanding the people of Israel or their story, in other words, without the Old Testament or, if you like, the Hebrew Bible.

So, when it comes to telling and retelling the story of Israel, as I do in this chapter, we discover that the story of Israel has a great deal to do with listening to the voice whose echoes we have been tracking in the opening section. Israel is called to listen to the voice that says, "Do justice." Israel is called to discover the presence of God, which means spirituality—think of the Psalms again but also of those intimate and powerful passages in the prophets and in Job. Israel is called to learn how to live together, how to do human relationships at every level; this is what a lot of the Jewish Torah is about: how to live together. It's what the book of Proverbs is about—how to live together in a wise human society. Israel is called to foster and celebrate beauty, the beauty that we glimpse not the least again in the Temple, the beautiful place in Jerusalem, the joy of the whole earth. Israel is called to cherish and celebrate the vision that grows out of that kind of language, of the ultimate beauty of a new creation, when "God will make all things new" and "the earth will be filled with the glory of God as the waters cover the sea." These are wonderful images answering to those four great longings, those echoes of a voice. And, as I said before, if I were to go beyond what I wrote in the book, we could do the same with the theme of freedom, which is arguably the key in which, whether major or minor, all Israel's music is written.

So, when we turn over the page from the Old Testament, where heaven and earth overlap in these ways, and meet the figure of Jesus in the Gospels, we shouldn't be surprised that out of that Jewish tradition there comes someone who is speaking about God and the world finally getting it together. The slogan "kingdom of God" is about God putting the world to right, taking his power, and reigning. And there, announcing it, is Jesus: passionately concerned with justice and spirituality and relationships and, yes, beauty. "Consider the lilies of the field," he says. Think for a moment of what sort of world we live in and what does his statement tell you about the sort of God who made this world.

The thing about putting together heaven and earth is that there is this thing called the "problem of evil." You will recall that, when we mentioned paganism and pantheism earlier on, we noted that this was the main problem: If God and the world are, as it were, all part of the same thing, you can neither understand evil nor deal with it. It's just part of the show. It's radical, and it's not to be wished away or waved away by saying that it doesn't really matter, that it's only some people who have problems from time to time. No, evil runs through each of us, and through each human society. If God and the world did get it together—and this is endemic in the Jewish tradition in the Old Testament and comes together with a rush in the story of Jesus in the New Testament—then we are bound to find all sorts of things also come to their climax. This is where all the lines, all the tensions, finally converge. Unless we learn to read the gospels this way, we will never understand what they're about.

Here is a short section from the chapter where I discuss how the ultimate clash came about:

> The meaning of the story is found in every detail [of the Passion narratives of the Gospels] as well as in the broad narrative. The pain and tears of all the years were met together on Calvary. The sorrow of heaven joined with the anguish of earth; the forgiving love stored up in God's future was poured out into the present; the voices that echo in a million human hearts crying for justice, longing for spirituality, eager for relationship, yearning for beauty, drew themselves together into a final scream of desolation. Nothing in all the history of paganism comes anywhere near this combination of event in tension and meaning. Nothing in Judaism had prepared for it except in puzzling, shadowy prophecy.
>
> The death of Jesus of Nazareth as the King of the Jews, the bearer of Israel's destiny, the fulfillment of God's promises to his people of old, is either the most stupid, senseless waste and misunderstanding the world has ever seen or it is the fulcrum around which world history turns. And Christianity is based on the belief that it was and is the latter.

The point of the story of Jesus is not that Jesus came to give us some new moral teaching, as though we needed to wise up a bit on our ethics. Well, no doubt, we do, but that's not the point of why Jesus came. Nor did Jesus come to give us a good example. People often say, "Jesus set this wonderful moral example!" As I said before, I'm a pretty hopeless golfer. When I see Tiger Woods hitting a golf ball, it's a fantastic example, but I don't then say, "Now

I know how to do it." It makes me think, *I'll never be able to do it like that.* And if I look at the moral example of Jesus, frankly, that's how I feel.

No, what Jesus came to do was to bring world history to its climax. One of the reasons that we in the Western world have found it so difficult to grasp that idea is that we have lived out of a controlling narrative. In our controlling narrative, world history reached its climax when the European philosophers invented this thing called *the Enlightenment* in the eighteenth century. Many, many people today live by that story, that world history really got to its alpha-and-omega story with the Enlightenment, and we just happen to live out of that a little bit.

So, of course, you can't have two climaxes in world history. If the Enlightenment is right, then Christianity must be wrong. So, the Enlightenment has reduced Christianity to a set of moral truths or a set of doctrinal truths to which you can give moral assent or to a nice way of being spiritual in the present and getting to heaven when you die. That's not the point. Doctrine matters; spirituality matters; ultimate destiny matters; but the point of Jesus is that in and through him world history reached its climax, turned its great corner. This is the moment around which everything else revolves. The point is that with Jesus of Nazareth, a great door swung open in the cosmos, and we are invited to go through it.

That is part of the core meaning of Jesus's resurrection. Let me say a word about that. I have written about the resurrection in the longest book I've produced to date: *The Resurrection of the Son of God*, all 750 pages of it. I sent it to my father, because I send everything I write to my father, and he finished it at a run in about three and a half days. He's an old man; he's retired and has nothing better to do than to read his son's book all day. Poor chap. He phoned me up and said, "I just finished the book. I really started to enjoy it after about page six hundred"—one of the nicest compliments I ever had.

But the point about the Resurrection—it's been so misunderstood in contemporary culture—is that resurrection is not primarily about going to heaven when you die. Oh, of course, Paul says, "My desire is to depart and be with Christ, for that is far better." Resurrection is about what happens *after* that. Resurrection is about the reaffirmation of the goodness of creation, and it's about the beginning, the launching, of God's project of new creation, beginning with Easter.

You see, there's far too much Gnostic escapism around in our culture, as though the real point about religion or faith or Christianity was to leave this wretched old world behind and go to somewhere else. But the good news is much better than that. The good news is that by dealing with the evil of the world on the Cross, Jesus has been able to launch God's project of new creation and has invited us to be not only its beneficiaries but also its agents. How can that be? Not by just hoping that if I get out there and start trying to make the world a better place, it will just happen through my own cleverness and good will and energy. No, plenty of people have tried that, and it has failed again and again. The way things will work is, rather, by invoking the new wind, the new breath, the power of God, which is freely available through God's Spirit.

So, at the end of the section of "Staring at the sun," I have two chapters on the Holy Spirit. The Spirit has been much misunderstood. There isn't time here to say more about this, and I suggest you simply read the chapters for yourselves.

So, to sum up the middle section of the book, when you start to look at this picture staring at the sun and focus your attention on the Christian story about God, then the basic thesis of this book is that as you pay attention to the real story, to who Jesus *really* was and to the purpose of God revealed in those Gospel stories, then those echoes of a voice that you heard before—of justice and spirituality and relationships and beauty—make you start to realize that you know whose voice it is that you were listening to. When you tell this story, you begin to recognize the voice you heard before.

This is quite a scary thought. What are we going to do about it?

Well, the third and final part of the book is called "Reflecting the Image." The point is this: Many people think that being Christian makes you sort of subhuman or semihuman or, at least, less than fully human. Guys out there on the street (people think) are having a wonderful time enjoying human life to the fullest, and we in the church are sort of cramped and constricted. Well, things shouldn't be that way. Being a Christian is supposed to make you *more truly human*, more fully yourself. That means that you are supposed to become somebody who is reflecting the image of God.

Being human, according to Genesis 1, means reflecting the image of God. But what does *that* mean? The idea of the "image" isn't simply about a mirror in which, when God looks down at it, he sees his own reflection coming back up at him. No doubt, it's meant to be that as well. But the main point is that it's supposed to be an *angled* mirror. Humans are made to reflect God out into the world—and at the same time, to reflect the rest of the world back to the Creator in worship and praise.

Let me explain. I'm an ancient historian by training. Once, when I was going through the Ashmolean Museum in Oxford, it struck me that all the great statues of Roman emperors and their families they've got in that museum were found, not in Rome but in Turkey, Greece, Syria, Palestine, Egypt, and North Africa: all over the place, in other words. In Rome, they knew who their emperor was. But out there in the provinces, the emperors put images of themselves so as to say to all the cities and countries over which they ruled, "This is who your boss is."

And the point about Genesis 1 is that the gracious God, who is as unlike a Roman emperor as you could wish him to be, has put into his world an image of himself called *men and women* made in his image to show his world what he is like. Tragically, we humans decided we would prefer to turn it around and reflect the world back to itself and worship and serve the creature rather than the Creator, as Saint Paul puts it. This has caused the image to be fractured and broken, distorting human rule over the world. But the point is that once we listen to those echoes of a voice and once we are renewed and refreshed in listening to the story of Jesus, then we begin to be able to reflect the image once more.

It starts with worship; it must start with worship. For many Christians, being a Christian is something they've done with their heads, something they've figured out with their moral lives, something they've started to enjoy in common with friends, and so on—and then they go to church on Sunday and sing a few hymns. But that's not how it's meant to be. Being a Christian is about gazing at the God in whose image you were made and, in love, reflecting that image out into the world. That means worship: One of the basic laws of spirituality is that you become like what you worship, so that if you worship the God in whose image you were made, you will start to reflect that God into the world.

So, worship is absolutely central. For many Christians, that's a puzzle, because they're bored with church when it's not their culture. For many, "church" isn't their scene; it's not their style. That's a problem we all live with in today's pluriform culture; I fully accept that. But we have to work at it to find ways of expressing our worship and praise to our creator and redeemer. We mustn't give up. This is central.

And in the middle of worship, there grows prayer. As with many other things, you can track the different ways people think about prayer on the grid we set up earlier.

There's option one: the prayer of the pantheist. If God and the world are basically the same thing, then praying is just getting in touch with the "divinity" that's all around us. Well, no doubt, it's better to be in touch with divine forces than to forget that they're there or to try to scream them out. But that's not Christian or Jewish prayer.

Then, there's option two. With the Deist, or dualist, world, prayer means shouting across the void to a distant God who might or might not be listening. It's like the traditional picture of a sailor who's lost and puts a message in a bottle and flings it into the water, hoping that somebody, somewhere, might eventually read it. For a lot of people, that's what prayer is like. But it's not actually what Christian prayer is supposed to be like.

If you read chapters 13 through 17 of John's gospel, you'll discover a wonderful model of Christian prayer. Prayer is supposed to be simultaneously intimate and awesome. That's an odd combination to us, but actually that's how it is. There is an awe in the presence of one's Creator, but there is also an intimacy because the Creator invites us to call him *Father*.

Living with that extraordinary business of awe and intimacy and discovery, as we open ourselves in prayer, means coming closer to Jesus and getting to know this Jesus better. The danger is, of course, that the closer you get to Jesus, the closer you get to the Cross; and you may well find that the pain of the world, as well as the joys of the world, will stretch you and pull you until you feel as though you were being pulled apart. Saint Paul says that's precisely the point: that's what we should expect to happen when the Holy Spirit is at work in someone's heart so that they are being "conformed to the image of God's Son." That is the meaning of fully Chris-

The danger is, of course, that the closer you get to Jesus, the closer you get to the Cross, and you may well find that the pain, as well as the joys of the world, will stretch you and pull you until you feel as though you were being pulled apart.

tian prayer. Part of the Christian calling is to be a person and a community where the pain of the world and the pain of God can come together. Read Romans 8; it's all in there.

So, prayer is the most extraordinary calling, and it echoes and models the truth that, as we have been saying, God and the world are not the same thing; they are not far apart, but they overlap and interlock. We're called to be people who live at that point. This can be very painful; it also can be very joyful.

In the middle of all this, we find the Bible. I've been quoting the Bible, referring to it quite a lot already. Many Christians in your culture have a real problem with the Bible. You may have been beaten over the head with a Bible as a kid.

I know a lot of people who are in the guild of professional biblical scholarship, and for many, the reason they're in biblical studies is because they grew up with the Bible morning, noon, and night. They couldn't get it out of their systems. When they went off to college and studied it, they discovered that it was actually a human artifact written by ordinary people like themselves. Their professors pointed out to them that the Bible appears to be full of puzzles and oddities, and even contradictions. And then we find, once again, the two options. Some people regard the Bible simply as a human artifact that's grown up from within the community. If there's any "divinity" about it, we have to understand it within that pantheistic model. Others, though, think of the Bible in a dualistic fashion: that it's a book which God, who is himself distant from us, has, as it were, sent from that great distance. The Bible has, as it were, floated down to us from this far-off God. That is at the root of much fundamentalism.

I once heard Michael Ramsey, the former archbishop of Canterbury, doing a lecture on this. He said, "There are all these people who think that the Bible came down from heaven in black leather binding, *complete with maps*." That is the classic dualist view, but the Bible is much richer than that. Yes, it is a human artifact, but it is one of those places where the divine and the human overlap and interlock. This is confusing, but we don't solve the confusion by oversimplifying in either of those two ways.

I mentioned my father before, and when I sent him this book—bless him—the next time I saw him, he said, "The book always falls apart at page 148. (He was, of course, using the British edition.) And why is that? "Whenever somebody comes to the house," he said, "I'm always reading them the opening book of this chapter." He was talking about chapter 13 "The Book God Breathed." This is how it goes:

> It's a big book, full of big stories with big characters. They have big ideas (not least about themselves) and big mistakes. It's about God and greed and grace; about life, lust, laughter, and loneliness. It's about birth, beginnings, and betrayal; about siblings, squabbles, and sex; about power and prayer and prison and passion.

And that's only Genesis.

We have forgotten just how amazing the Bible is. I say morning prayer each day with my chaplain, and we naturally read the passages from Scripture we find in the Lectionary. It may be fifteen or twenty verses from the Old Testament, and a further similar passage from the New. We take time to pause and reflect. Sometimes after the service, I find myself thinking that if that passage had been lost and some archaeologist had dug it up in the sands of Egypt—whether it's Isaiah or Kings or Zechariah or whether it's Luke or Revelation or whatever—if somebody had discovered it in our own day and published about it in some archaeological magazine, it would make headlines around the world. People would say it was the most amazing poetry, rich and dense and powerful, and so amazingly ancient. We Christians often take the Bible for granted, but we shouldn't. This material is breathtaking: beautiful, dense, rich, and strong.

We Christians take the Bible off the shelf, read the next bit, vaguely remember something about it, and put it back again. We forget what a treasure we're sitting on. We really need to reinhabit the whole story of the Bible, the whole thing. It's more than just "worth it"; it's absolutely life giving. There are all sorts of things I could say about that, but for that you must look to my other writings since our time is running away.

I then have a chapter on the church. The word *church* is such a turnoff to so many people, but for many people, the word *church* in today's world is an absolute lifeline. Let me give you an example.

One of the things we bishops do is go around doing Confirmation service. I was in Gateshead, which is in the northern end of the diocese, just across the River Tyne from Newcastle. A few weeks ago I was doing a Confirmation there. A string of young adults came forward to be confirmed, and they were being interviewed about why they had come to church and what it meant for them now. One young woman was very nervous and hadn't prepared what she was going to say. But when the rector said, "Would you tell us what it's like now that you are what you are and who you are?" She looked around at the church and said, "It's like having a great, big second family." Then, she looked around at me and said, "Was I supposed to say that?" and I said, "Yes, you were!" Nobody had taught her about what the church was *supposed* to be; she had found it out in practice.

She had discovered the reality of having brothers and sisters who cared for her, who were there for her and with her, supporting her in good times and bad. I thank God for that—an ordinary parish, in an ordinary, not very well-off place, being church. That's what "church" is supposed to be like.

The final chapter in the book is about new creation, starting now. The point of the new creation is this: Being a Christian isn't about just stumbling our way through the world the way it is, maybe making a little bit of difference here and there, but eventually having this spiritual destination (called *heaven*) where we go when we die.

I've said it before, and I'll say it again: heaven is important, but it's not the end of the world. In the Bible we are promised *new heavens and new earth*, and those go together. In Revelation, the last scene of the Bible, the climax is not that we get snatched up from earth to heaven; it's that the New Jerusalem comes down from heaven to earth. This is the ultimate denial of all Gnosticism, all escapist spirituality.

God intends to renew the sad, old earth. God's not finished with it, and what began with Jesus's Resurrection on the third day will be complete when earth and heaven are one and when, in that wonderful prophetic vision from Isaiah 11, "the wolf will live with the lamb . . . and a little child shall lead them," and "the earth shall be full of the knowledge of the LORD as the waters cover the sea."

That's the vision the New Testament inherits. Much of modern western Christianity has screened that stuff out. It doesn't know what to do with it. But the idea of new creation is there; it's right through the New Testament, and it matters. The point is this: That's the context in which we do Christian ethics. Christian ethics is not a bunch of funny old rules that somebody dreamed up, a kind of set of Kantian categorical imperatives, hanging in the

SIMPLY CHRISTIAN: WHY CHRISTIANITY MAKES SENSE — 221

sky, threatening us. Nor is Christian ethics simply a matter of getting in touch with our deepest feelings. That is the world of existentialism and romanticism, not of Christian ethics. That is a version of the first option, the "pantheist" way of looking at the world: All you have to do is to get in touch with your deepest self and that will be "right," or at least "right for you." (As with other aspects of pantheism, the problem then is that there is no critique of evil; supposing your "deepest self" turns out to be a mass-murderer?)

The second option, the Deist or dualist way of thinking, is no better. Many people today think of "Christian ethics" in that framework: A distant God has made up a bunch of odd rules to cramp your style, and he'll be cross with you if you break them. But no: That's not Christian ethics either.

Christian ethics is saying that we live in God's good creation, but that creation is spoiled by radical evil. However, God in Jesus Christ has dealt and is dealing with the radical infection of rebellion and evil—call it *sin*, if you like, as long as you remember that doesn't mean the arbitrary breaking of arbitrary commands. And God is, therefore, launching his new creation, starting with you and me, but not stopping there. If we are to be angled mirrors, reflecting the image of God out into the world, we are called to be *agents of a new creation*. That means serious Christian work for ecology, serious Christian work on reducing and hopefully abolishing global debt, serious Christian work to turn the chemical and scientific community around to say, "Those people who have AIDS need vaccinations, and they need them now, whatever it's going to mean economically." There's serious Christian work at many different levels: locally, on your street and mine; globally, through your politicians and mine.

And let's be clear. When we're doing that kind of work, we're not oiling the wheels of a machine that will one day drop off a cliff. Instead, we are *anticipating*, in the present, the new creation that will be complete in the future. We're not "building the Kingdom of God" by our own efforts. That's what the "old social gospel" was always in danger of claiming, and it leads to arrogance and false expectations. Don't get me wrong. The Kingdom of God will remain a fresh gift of God's good grace. But what we can and must do is to set up signposts for the Kingdom. When the Kingdom comes, those signposts will be seen to have really partaken in the reality toward which they point.

The image that I've often used for this is as follows. Imagine a stonemason working on a great huge cathedral. The architect has got these wonderful plans; the stonemason doesn't understand them; he doesn't really know what the finished building is going to be like. He's just been given this one stone; he's been told he's got to carve this bit of a pattern on it, and he doesn't even know what the next bit of the pattern is going to look like. His task is to be obedient, to carve this stone according to the instructions he's received. It's then up to the architect as to where he chooses to put that into the building.

This is what the Apostle Paul means when he says at the end of First Corinthians 15, that we must get on with our work, because it's not going to be wasted. Everything we do in the present in the power of the Spirit and out of love for God and our neighbor will be, eventually, part of God's new world, even though at the present moment we have no idea how, or what that will look like.

This is what I mean when I say that we are called to be *agents* of new creation, not only its beneficiaries. It's not as though salvation is all about me. Salvation is God's gift, not just to the church but *through* the church.

So, let me, in closing, just read the last paragraph of this book:

> Made for spirituality, we wallow in introspection. Made for joy, we settle for pleasure. Made for justice, we clamor for vengeance. Made for relationship, we insist on our own way. Made for beauty, we are satisfied with sentiment. But new creation has already begun. The sun has begun to rise. Christians are called to leave behind, in the tomb of Jesus, all that belongs to the brokenness and incompleteness of the present world. It is time, in the power of the Spirit, to take up our proper role, our fully human role, as agents, heralds, and stewards of the new day that is dawning. That, quite simply, is what it means to be Christian, to follow Jesus Christ into the new world, God's new world, which he has thrown open before us.

Q & A

___

I f you have a question, leap to a microphone—run. Please keep your questions extremely brief. I am looking for seventeen to twenty syllables. We have staff that counts, and they will cut you off at twenty-one. So, please make your way to the microphone if you have a question. Surely you have a question. Go ahead.

Q: Recently, we started using your book on Romans in our Bible study in our home group.

A: Which one, the big one or the little one?

Q: *Paul for Everyone*. Love it. I have to ask you about this revolutionary concept of your Christian worldview. I agree with it wholeheartedly. I think that as Christians we need to be salt and light in this world in a tangible way. It affects policy and purpose and reaching out in Africa and all these different policies. My one question is, how do you see that happening, because it seems somewhat utopian from the outset? How do you see that?

I think that when you are talking about the prayers of Christ, he is speaking mostly about unity. How do you see all of the different denominations coming to this utopian worldview? How do you see that happening?

A: There are two different questions inside there. One is about "Is it utopian?" and one is about church unity. They do belong closely together. It may seem utopian, especially to those of us who've lived in churches that haven't even grasped the vision, let alone have seen it happening.

Actually, in my lifetime, there have been two extraordinary examples where the church has made a huge and radical difference. The first one is in South Africa. Some of you are old enough to remember how things were in the mid-seventies. Maggie and I were in South Africa in 1975. You never would have dreamed that twenty years later, you would have a black archbishop chairing a commission for truth and reconciliation, hearing the tragic stories, and having a community seeking reconciliation and forgiveness— that was just quite extraordinary. And if you want to know how it happened, you would have to say that God did it, and God did it through the faithful and very dangerous witness of the Church.

The other example, of course, is that when they elected a Polish pope in the late seventies, nobody quite realized that within two or three years that would be giving the Polish people courage to raise the Solidarity flag, which was the crack in the dike of Eastern European Communism and in the next decade completely finished the whole thing off. People have credited other agents, particularly in this country, with the finishing off of Eastern European Communism. But actually, I think it started right there when they elected Pope John Paul II, and yes, life is more complicated than that, but there is power in the old Gospel yet. And that was what was being lived out.

So, you can see it at the macro level, but I want to tell you what I have seen—and have been proud to see, because it wasn't my initiative—on the streets of my own diocese. I live in a very poor diocese, by and large, and the Church is coming to grips with what is happening on the street. There is one wonderful project in South Shields, which has major unemployment in the area. Half of the shops are shut. The bank was shut, because it wasn't getting enough business. The church, an ordinary little church, got together with the other churches for church unity—Anglicans with Romans [Roman Catholics] with Methodists and one or two others. They took over that old bank, and they run it as a literacy-training place, as a credit union, as a place for mothers and toddlers, as a day-care center for old people. And it is enough to make you weep with joy. You come out of the church after the Eucharist, and you can just see the Gospel happening, transforming people's lives on the street. It can happen.

Of course, there are *huge* problems, because it is only ever fitful and partial. Just like our own obedience is only ever fitful and partial. But it can happen, and it does transform people's lives, not just short term. It can actually make a lasting difference to that whole community. So, it does happen.

The thing about church unity is that if we could say to ourselves across the denominations, "This is the stuff we ought to be doing," we would find we could agree about an awful lot of that. We could be solving some of the theological problems as we are drawing up our sleeves and painting people's walls or sorting out old people's homes or whatever it was. I have seen that happen.

Q: You started off by referring to the children of Israel and the GPS satellite navigation system, and I thought that was a remarkable Metaxian coincidence. I am Jewish, and I have been writing about GPS for the last seven years. I think there is a symbolism there, because the GPS system was invented by the Pentagon, and today we see in Europe a Galileo system, which is basically the product, I believe, largely of envy on the part of the Europeans. They have satellite navigation envy.

I think this is a symptom of a profound divorce that is happening between America and Europe. I was just wondering if you had anything to say about that because you have mentioned some things.

A: On the divorce between America and Europe?

Q: Yes, the divorce. The incredible hostility that we see developing. From our side we see it, and I am sure that on your side you see it differently. But I would just be interested to see if you had anything to say about that.

A: I can't speak for the rest of Europe, and actually the European Union is a very, very diverse place. You would get different answers if you went to Berlin or if you went to Paris or if you went to Madrid.

In England, we cherish our friendship with America, and I think there are a great many of us who love coming here. Many of our best friends are American. Are we allowed to use that old line? There is a huge amount of respect and affection and admiration for your energy and all the rest of it. But that doesn't mean that we necessarily agree with all the policies of every single government that you have ever had. Just as in the same way, even when I taught at the Hebrew University once—and I have lots of Jewish friends, I have worked in Jerusalem, I have lived there—that doesn't mean that I am signed up to approving all the policies of the Jewish [Israeli] government and all the things they do. And if I disapprove, that doesn't make me anti-Jewish, just as if I disapprove of what any one president—let's not name any names at the moment—that doesn't make me anti-American.

The trouble is sometimes some presidents and some Congresses and Senates have pursued policies that English people simply can't understand. Studying the divergences in the two cultures enables us to understand why it is that some Americans are driven by controlling narratives which we in Europe simply don't have.

Robert Jewett wrote about this in *The Myth of the American Superhero*. We in England just don't have that particular myth. We look at it and see that that is how people work in America. When people act out what to them is a normal controlling narrative, it seems very strange to us, and so on. So, there are all sorts of things going on there.

Q: I think it was just this past Sunday that *The New York Times* reviewed Richard Dawkins's new book *The God Delusion*.

A: What did they say about it?

Q: I skimmed it, but I think they thought it was a bit excessive, which is probably not the first time he has been found excessive. But in a broader sense, I was wondering if you might have any rejoinder or any resources to deal with that whole question, that whole point of view that says, "It is all in the mind, human beings are programmed to look for patterns, to look for purpose, to invent it when it is not there; mysticism is just synapses firing and certain parts of your brain backing up."

A: I haven't finished reading Dawkins's book. I brought it on this trip with me, and I am about halfway through. I've just read, while on the road, two recent reviews that have been published in England. One is by Terry Eagleton, who is an old Marxist literary critic from way back when; he doesn't mince his words.

Q: I saw that one.

A: Dawkins's book is absolutely rubbish. It is in the *London Review of Books* and is available on the fulcrum web site at www.fulcrum-anglican.org.uk. Anyway, Eagleton's is a remarkable review. Also, there's one by my friend and colleague David Atkinson, the Bishop of Thetford, who is a scientist turned theologian. And he is much more cautious in what he says, but he basically points out the weaknesses in the model.

Dawkins picks the wrong people to argue against. He picks the ultra-creationists, he picks the fundamentalists, and among the theologians, he picks the ones that are actually the easiest targets for him. He doesn't do any interaction with people like John Polkinghorne, like Arthur Peacocke. He quotes them and says, "These people are routinely held up as scientists who are also Christians. Well, I have been to conferences with those guys. I have listened to them carefully and frankly I don't know what they are talking about and that is the end."

Well, excuse me; are we going to have any engagement with this? I am not a scientist. I make no pretense at that. I never studied science at school even, except in the most rudimentary fashion. So, I never got into that. But I was disappointed by Dawkins's book, because it says, "Here is a challenge for all those who think they are thinking Christians," but I'm halfway through the book, and there is nothing to get your teeth into yet. It is all polemic, all rant. There are, of course, wise people out there writing more serious books than that. But interestingly, the old debate comes back to where C. S. Lewis left it fifty years ago, when he was meeting the same sort of stuff.

Lewis's answer went like this: If you say that religion and belief in God are all actually just the way we are programmed so that it's just like a nervous twitch that you shouldn't take notice of, then you also have to say that the idea that we are thus programmed is itself a product of that same system of blind chance. That doesn't actually get you very far, but it merely points back at the person who is saying it and says, "So, why are we even bothering to listen to you? Why don't we all just hang out and do what comes naturally?" And really, nobody wants to live like that.

In the middle of it, there are these four echoes of voices, which most human beings hear and which, I think, still demand attention. Dawkins and others can try to reduce them, but I don't think they are so easily quieted.

Q: You talked a lot about relationships with the Jewish people and God, et cetera. Where do the Palestinians fit into your equation?

A: Great question. Very closely, I happen to believe, and as I say, I lived there, and I have friends on both sides of the Green Line and keep up as best I can with what is going on there. At the moment in America, there is this massive move of some on the Religious Right to say that ethnic and geographical Israel is the fulfillment of prophecies in Zechariah and Daniel and Ezekiel, and so on. *Christian Zionism* is what it's called.

I remember being fascinated by that view when I was a graduate student thirty-plus years ago. Eventually, after I studied the New Testament, expecting to find confirmation of that view, my study of Paul, in particular, led me to think that that was not, in fact, the right way to go. In the New Testament— Romans 8, again, is the classic example of this—*the whole world is now God's holy land.* Something about what God did in and through Jesus compels us to conclude that the Holy Land in the Old Testament was an advance metaphor for God's claim on the whole creation. It was a kind of signpost. With the Acts of the Apostles we have moved into that new moment, that new reality toward which the old signpost was pointing.

Within that, Paul then immediately turns around in Romans 9 and says, "Where does that leave us with the Jewish people?" He wrestles with that question, and I have followed that wrestling and tried to be obedient to it. But when we then discover a claim, made not only by Jews but also by some Christians, that the land inalienably still belongs to the ethnically Jewish people and that therefore they have some kind of inalienable right to do whatever is going to suit them vis-à-vis the Palestinians, I say, purely in terms of that echo of the voice that says, "Do justice," we cannot simply stand by and shrug our shoulders.

Interestingly, the Palestinian Liberation theologian Naim Ateek wrote a book nearly twenty years ago now called *Justice and Only Justice*, which is a quote from Deuteronomy [16:20]. One of the rabbis expounding that line "Justice and only justice shall you seek" says, "Why does God say the word *justice* twice?" And this rabbi says, "Because there must be justice for Israel and for her neighbors."

That is the point that Naim draws out. Yes, there must be justice for Israel. There must be a safe place. The Jewish people must be secure. We have learned that lesson to the *n*th degree, I hope and pray. But that justice must never be at the expense of doing violence and horrible injustice to their neighbors all around. I know, of course, that it's not as easy as that. There is massive fault on both sides, and a long history—as there is in South Africa, of course!—of scandalous deeds and complex wickedness. All I can do here is to give a short answer to a long and complicated question, but that is where I would start.

Q: Dr. Wright, you always seem to make very compelling arguments in defending the Gospel. I would love to know what is the most difficult argument you have faced from a critic who is an unbeliever—whether it is historical, philosophical, scientific—whatever it might be. What is the hardest argument you have had to struggle with?

A: It is hard to pick, because they're always coming. But I think there are dimensions to the problem of evil that go so deep they challenge me to say, "Did Jesus really deal with that on the Cross?"

I have a friend who is a scientist and writes about the Darwin wars—the kind of intra-Darwinism infighting that is going on. He says that the thing he finds the hardest is that when he looks at the created order, it turns out that some remarkably high proportion of creatures that exist on the planet are parasites that live inside other creatures and are eating away at them from the inside. He said, "If the good God made the world, I can't see how he would have done it like that."

Now, I have not studied that stuff, but it seems to me there are problems of that sort that do need to be wrestled with. And you might say, if you like, that is the result of the Fall. That is exactly explaining one unknown by another comparative unknown.

We can't actually solve the problem of evil. If you find that you have produced an argument that says, "Ah, there we are. We have finally understood why evil exists. So, that is all right; we can go home and relax," then you have not taken it seriously enough, because evil is absurd. I don't just mean "absurd" as in "funny." I mean that evil goes against the grain of the universe. It is a nasty, dark force that goes down within each of us, as I said, and cuts through each human society. If you think you have escaped or your society has escaped (because we are modern western democrats!) or your family has escaped it, then you really are living in cloud-cuckoo land.

So, arguments about the problem of evil are always going to be tough, and the Christian answer has always been and must always be to come back to the foot of the Cross. Think about the way the Gospel story is told so as to draw all the forces of evil together onto Christ on the Cross. That is always going to be the toughest.

Q: I agree with you that as agents of the Kingdom, we should be signposting, as it were. It seems to me that those signposts ought to be accurate. You said something about the U.S. being formed around this Enlightenment idea. Perhaps a variation of the first question posed to you is, how do we as Christians put our finger along the seam between ideologies, the world, and this clear biblical narrative that should be animating our signposting? It seems to me that it is not just as simple as "Go read the Bible." Could you speak to that? How do we put our finger along this seam and make sure we are not conflating ideas being on the right side of that?

A: I love that idea of the finger on the seam. The problem is the seam seems to be shifting all the time. As I said, I have just been lecturing the last week and a half on the interplay between Gnosis and empire and modernity in our culture, each of which impinges on the other and each of which can be addressed from within the Christian Gospel. But most people in our culture don't actually articulate the problem in that way at all.

So, we are moving around half in the dark. Most people, certainly in my country, have no idea where the large narratives are that are driving them to think and act in particular ways. The problem then comes when, if they try to address the world with a Christian gospel, they are addressing only little bits of the world. No doubt, I am guilty of that as well.

But then it becomes less cultural and more purely personal. The trouble is that there is no such thing as a person outside of culture. We all live with cultural imperatives resonating through our skulls all the time, and those are the things that need addressing with the Gospel. Those are the things that need converting. So, it is a very, very difficult task, and it takes a constant vigilance.

This is why it has to be a whole-church thing. It can't be one person doing it. Some of us are called to be cultural critics as well as biblical scholars, but most people haven't got the time to do that, and yet here you are in one of the most vibrant cultural cities the world has ever known. There must be quite a few people in this room who actually do have their finger, much more than I do, on what is going on in theater, in cinema, in art, in music, in all sorts of ways of high culture and low culture.

Please, reflect on that. Reflect Christianly on it. Ask yourself the key questions. The thing is don't be dualistic about it. Paul says in Philippians 4, whatever is true, lovely, honorable, of good report—think about these things. And there is lots of that stuff out there, irrespective of the artist or the musician in question, and we can celebrate the art or the music. Just as with the Enlightenment. I celebrate a great deal that was good about the Enlightenment. I am sometimes seen as anti-Enlightenment, but I am not. The Enlightenment brought great blessings as well as great problems.

Postmodernity is a necessary answer to the Enlightenment, but it too leaves us deeply unsatisfied. The Christian's task is always to go through the other side, to take the best that there has been, to thank God for it and celebrate it and build on it, but to do so constantly looking, constantly vigilant. There is no one answer I can give you that we can then put in our pockets for the next generation. It's a wonderfully exciting task, and I commend it to you.

Postmodernity is a necessary answer to the Enlightenment, but it too leaves us deeply unsatisfied.

Q: Do you believe that the Apocrypha have a use?

A: The Apocrypha certainly have a use. (The Apocrypha, for those who don't know, are the books that are sometimes printed between the Old and New Testaments—the book of the Maccabees and the Wisdom of Solomon, and so forth.) The apocryphal books shed a flood of light on what it meant to be a first-century Jew. The more I read that stuff, the more I think, *We are really in touch with what it was like for those people.* Some of those books, in particular the Wisdom of Solomon, give us direct access to how people were thinking about the concept of wisdom, the concept of life and death, the concept of empire, in a way that then opens up like a flower. When you then come to read the New Testament, it makes the sense it makes as coming from, and being addressed to, that world.

Paul looks as if he knew the Wisdom of Solomon, at least was in dialogue with it, at least engaging with it. So, yes, the Apocrypha are enormously important. Most Christians don't study first-century Judaism nearly enough. Get hold of the *Penguin Classic* of Josephus. Get hold of an English edition of the Dead Sea Scrolls. Just read that stuff, because you will then be able to avoid the massive anachronisms into which we otherwise routinely fall.

Q: In the Gospel of Thomas that just came out?

A: New Testament Apocrypha, that is a very different thing.

Q: That was actually my question.

A: Ah, I'm sorry. I had thought you meant the Apocrypha as normally described. He gets two questions for the price of one. The word *Apocrypha*, without further qualification, is normally reserved for the *Old* Testament apocryphal books; it was only as a kind of secondary development that people began to speak of some post-New Testament writings as, in some sense, a *New* Testament apocrypha. Within that latter category, there are several books called *Gospels* that didn't make it into the New Testament. There has been a major fad in New Testament scholarship over the last decade or two—especially, actually almost uniquely, in America—which has said: "These were the really exciting Gospels, and they got squelched by the boring Christians who preferred their solid, stable Matthew, Mark, Luke, and John."

This is an enormously important question. It's vital that we understand why that proposal is wrong. I happen to have another little book that was just published called *Judas and the Gospel of Jesus* by Baker [the book's publisher], and that is a response to the (so-called) Gospel of Judas, which was just published at Easter.

There is no time to say it all, but let me say this as a foretaste: In the second century, the people who are being thrown to the lions and burned at the stake were not reading Thomas and Judas and Philip and Peter and the Gospel of Mary Magdalene. They were reading Matthew, Mark, Luke, and John, because they are the books that say, "Jesus is Lord, and Caesar isn't," whereas Thomas and Company are agnostic, dualist, escapist, and have a Jesus who is all about escaping this world. So, *why would it matter if God's Kingdom should come and his will be done on earth as in heaven?*

Matthew, Mark, Luke, and John, I am afraid, are the really radical ones, not the flaky Gnostic stuff. (If you want to understand one of the strands that run very deep in western culture, you should try to understand Gnosticism. And if you want to understand how as Christians we should address our western culture, you need to understand why the four gospels in the Bible are what they are and how they offer a completely different, and far more radical, message than anything you find in those so-called "Gnostic gospels." The message of Jesus—the "Simply Christian" message, if you like—is that through the work of Jesus, climaxing in his death and resurrection, God's sovereign, saving rule is arriving on earth as in heaven. That is the genuine thing. Don't be fooled by the cheap but radically different lookalike substitutes. The Gnostic gospels offer you an escapist vision of a private spirituality, an otherworldly salvation. They don't actually tell you good *news*; they only offer *advice*. But the gospel of Jesus is good *news* about something that has *happened* and as a result of which the world is a different place. That's what Christian faith is all about.

The Twilight of Atheism: The Rise and Fall of Disbelief in the Modern World

ALISTER MCGRATH

November 21, 2006

Introduction

S hall we start? Look, I don't want to be here any more than you do.

Good evening, I'm Eric Metaxas, and I welcome you to Socrates in the City, the thinking person's alternative to watching the *Flavor of Love** on the E! channel.

Flavor Flav was going to be here tonight, but, of course, he's a no-show. Flavor Flav sends his regrets.

Happily, we have the lovely Sue Song to play the piano for us, to tickle the ivories with her hip-hop favorites. So, thank you, Sue Song.

It is a great joy to see so many of you here the week of Thanksgiving. I was sure about forty people would show up. I guess I was wrong. Actually, we want to be exact. If you are here tonight, would you please raise your hand? I just want to get a quick count. That is almost twenty. Anyway, thank you for almost being here.

We really are very, very excited about having Dr. Alister McGrath with us tonight, but I am almost more excited to bring you yet another unimpeachably straight line of British-accented speakers. It is almost extraordinary how we have been able to pull that off, going all the way back to Baroness Cox.

In the interests of full disclosure, Dr. McGrath was born and raised in

---

* A short-lived reality TV program featuring the semi-intentionally-jocular rapper known as Flavor Flav.

Syosset, Long Island, and now divides his time between the Trump Towers and Mineola (also Ronkonkoma, I believe).* So, the reality is that the accent is going to be fake tonight, but it is actually said to be quite good, not like Dick Van Dyke's accent in *Mary Poppins*, which is atrocious. At least I thought so—a very fake kind of Cockney.

Tonight you are going to get the real thing—an exquisite, fake British accent. I don't know about you, but I am really looking forward to hearing it. During rehearsals today, Dr. McGrath just would not give me even a taste of his British accent. He said he wanted to save his voice for the performance.

I always get a little nervous. I just need to hear something that will put me at ease. I need a real British accent; you know, just give me a little something like "'Ello, guvnah." Just something so I know it's British and not from New Zealand. I didn't get so much as an "'Ello, guvnah" from him. So, keep your fingers crossed. I get nervous.

If it is a really great accent, then perhaps later on, Dr. McGrath may be persuaded to sing "I've Got a Lovely Bunch of Coconuts."†

A word on Socrates in the City. If you don't know who we are or what we do at Socrates in the City, would you please stand up? I'm not going to embarrass you; I just want to know if you would maybe stand up and sing something, just a few bars of something. Don't be shy.

Seriously, how many of you have never been to a Socrates before, and this is your first one? So, quite a few of you. All right, and how many of you think this is probably going to be your last time? Great, because we need the space.

Let me tell you, if you don't know what Socrates in the City is, Socrates rather famously said, "The unexamined life is not worth living." I think he just broke up with his girlfriend and was being a little bit philosophical. He was kind of bumming out. So, he got to really thinking. He said, "The unexamined life is not worth living," and I think that a group of folks—some of my friends and I—thought it would be like a cultural service, like a soup kitchen for the mind, to create some kind of a venue in New York City where we dared to ask the big, bold questions.

---

* Mineola and Ronkonkoma are located in Long Island, New York.
† The late talk-show host Merv Griffin got his start in show business as a singer, first hitting the charts with this song sung in a false British accent.

The big questions are not asked much in places like Manhattan or even on programs like *Jimmy Kimmel*. They just don't go there.

Previous Socrates in the City events have dealt with, for example, whether there is life after death, whether God exists—kind of a big question—and whether we can prove it. We've asked, "How can a good God allow suffering?" We have talked about the concept of evil. There's a light summery topic for you. We asked whether a scientist can believe in God, and of course, we had a scientist right there who talked about that. We have also asked, "How is the NASDAQ doing today?" That snuck in there; that is *not* one of the big questions.

We did start in the fall of 2000, and we have been fund-raising ever since. Just something we like to do. Have you ever noticed that whenever you ask some wealthy folks to give to something like this, they say *no*? But if they have any kind of conscience, they want to give you a little piece of advice about how you can raise funds with somebody *other than themselves*. Or how you can be more successful, and it is always to start small: "You want to grow this thing right; don't throw money at it the way I did with the house and yacht and stuff. Grow it small, you know, and just see." You know what I am talking about?

So, we took that advice. We didn't start out meeting in places like this, because we couldn't afford to meet in places like this, and we still can't afford it. But we did start small in different kinds of places. I remember the first year we were playing little honky-tonk clubs in Alabama. That is just where we were at the time. We were just going to see how that went. I remember there was chicken wire around the stage. Every place seemed to reek of beer and broken dreams. It was kind of sad.

I will never forget the look on Sir John Polkinghorne's face at one of those places. He claimed never to have heard the term *juke joint* and didn't know what a "two-drink minimum" was. He kept saying, "Oh my, oh my." I guess he didn't

> I will never forget the look on Sir John Polkinghorne's face at one of those places. He claimed never to have heard the term *juke joint* and didn't know what a "two-drink minimum" was. He kept saying, "Oh my, oh my." I guess he didn't understand the chicken wire, because they don't have that at the Royal Society.

understand the chicken wire, because they don't have that at the Royal Society.

I remember when he began to speak on some of the same subjects for which he would later that year win the coveted Templeton Prize, he suddenly understood very well what the chicken wire was for. Yes, his talk didn't go over so well. They thought he was putting on airs, evidently. They started throwing some things. Anyway, it was very regretful what happened.

No, but seriously, we have come a very long way since those humble juke joints in Alabama. Today, we are privileged, as you can see, to have almost no chicken wire in the room and an audience that seems to require none.

But we are going to keep our eyes on you. "Trust, but verify," I like to say. Of course, our caliber of speakers has not budged. We have just continued to be spectacular from Polkinghorne onward. That is a pretty good place to start, wouldn't you think? I think so. Of course, we are thrilled tonight to have with us, in this rather upscale juke joint called the Union League Club, the extraordinary Dr. Alister McGrath, from whom you will be hearing in just a moment.

Dr. McGrath is a professor of historical theology at Oxford University and president of the Oxford Center for Christian Apologetics. He is also the author of numerous books, including *The Twilight of Atheism: The Rise and Fall of Disbelief in the Modern World.* He will be talking on that subject this evening, and immediately after, he will be signing copies of his book right here. We would like to encourage you to avail yourself of that, and I would be happy to sign the book as well. Just trying to do my part.

Dr. McGrath earned his PhD in molecular biophysics, as so many of us have. But what particularly distinguishes Dr. McGrath from the rest of us run-of-the-mill molecular biophysicists is that he is also a world-renowned theologian. That combo, of course, is a bit rare. In intellectual circles that is what is called a *twofer*. Am I getting that right—twofer? I don't know.

He is also the author of many, many other books, including *Dawkins' God*, which, I believe, we have at our book table here and which deals with the presumably nonexistent God of Richard Dawkins, the atheist whose descent into twilight we shall soon hear about in a British accent, I think. I am hoping, I am hoping.

Dr. McGrath is also the author of the controversial *If I Had Done It. If I*

Had Done It.* Is that subjunctive? *If I Had Done It* has the subtitle *Indeed If I Had, What a Frightful Thing It Might Have Been* (pronounced *bean*).

And the lighthearted sequel to *If I Had Done It* is the bestselling *Hada Woulda Shoulda*. Anyway, these are all marvelous books, and all of the other books Dr. McGrath has written are also available at our book table, and most of them will be promoted with a Fox TV special next week during sweeps. If not, you can probably catch it on YouTube in a month.

I think I'd better get out of here. Our speaker, in this case, Dr. McGrath, will speak for thirty-five or forty minutes, at which point we will have thirty-five or forty minutes of Q & A. We really enjoy that time. Think hard about what your questions are and frame them in such a way as not to exceed twelve or thirteen syllables. We are going to hold you to that. If you're a friend of mine, then fourteen. Now, without further ado, it's our privilege to have Dr. Alister McGrath with us. Welcome, Dr. McGrath.

---

* This was the title of a highly controversial book written by O. J. Simpson. The publisher, HarperCollins, eventually decided to pull the book, and the Fox special never aired.

Talk

Well, Eric, thank you very much for those kind words. Welcome.
I hope you like the accent. I've been rehearsing it all my life. If
anyone would have told me years ago that I would be coming
here to this immensely exciting place in New York to talk about the twilight
of atheism, I think I would have been really very surprised.

Now, you see, I grew up in Northern Ireland. For those of you who don't
know Northern Ireland, to outsiders it's a kind of backward place; so, my
apologies to anyone else who comes from Northern Ireland. The great intellectual excitement of my youth was the annual donkey derby. So, coming to
New York for someone like this would really be moving upscale in a very big
way, and that would be very exciting.

Also, it would surprise me for another reason, which is that when I was in
high school, I was an atheist, and, I have to say, quite an aggressive atheist as
well. So, the idea that I would be coming to talk about my own Christian faith
and also reflect on the future of atheism would really have come to be a great
surprise to me.

As you all know, atheists come in different kinds. There's a kind of very nice
atheist who says, "I don't believe in God, but I'm so glad you do." Then there's the
rather more aggressive sort who really want to use language like "God delusion,"
all kinds of things like that to imply that really, it's such a pity that the psychiatric
hospital is so full these days, because let's create room for a few more.

I was in that second category. You know, I was very much of the view as a younger person that religion was malevolent, was evil, was destructive, and more than that, it was on its way out—that during my lifetime religion would simply fade away into complete insignificance, and that would be a good thing.

Certainly, you can see why I believed this. I grew up in Northern Ireland, which back in the 1960s—and still even, I think, today—was noted for its religious violence. It just seemed to me obvious that religion causes violence. *Get rid of religion; get rid of violence. What's the problem? Let's do it.* That was the kind of attitude I had as a young man.

I'm sure you've all heard the story of the Englishman who visited Northern Ireland and went to Belfast. He went out late one Saturday night and was confronted by a group of young men with baseball bats, and they asked him a question: "Are you a Protestant, or are you a Roman Catholic?"

He paused and thought, because he realized his own personal future might actually depend rather a lot on the answer he gave, and he gave quite a good answer. He said, "I'm an atheist," and there was a slight pause. "Are you a Protestant atheist, or are you . . . ?"

So, you can see things were very bad. Certainly, it seemed to be obvious that atheism made sense. Also at the time, I was majoring in natural sciences because I knew that my career would be in natural sciences. Again, it seemed obvious to me that the sciences don't just inculcate atheism, they necessitate it. A good scientist is an atheist. Science simply disproves the existence of God, and that is the end of the matter. There is no further discussion to be had.

Now, I was sixteen or seventeen at the time. Maybe I could be forgiven for that. Nevertheless, this was the way I thought and the way that many still think of this whole question. I went to Oxford to study chemistry and went on to do research and various things, and I found that my attitudes changed in quite a big way. I'll talk about that more later in this lecture, but one of the points that I want to make at a very early stage in this lecture is actually that I moved from atheism to Christianity and found the natural sciences actually were implicated in that transition, because the more I began to understand the sciences, the more it helped me to understand that science didn't actually prove or disprove religious beliefs with anything like the certainty I had thought. There was much more conceptual room for belief, for God, than I had ever imagined.

And as Richard Dawkins would say, for example, the only viable alternative is turning from religious belief to atheism, as in his own case, many others and I would say there are alternatives which are well worth thinking about.

So, let's begin to talk about atheism. Atheism has always been around. It was there for example in ancient Greece, but, of course, it became really significant in the West in the eighteenth century. Now, I would suggest that we can identify a period of almost exactly two hundred years when atheism moved from being a fringe movement to really dominating the center of Western culture.

You could frame this with two events. One event was the French Revolution of 1789—more than that, the fall of the Bastille, which was seen as a symbol of tyranny, and in many ways, the French Revolution can be seen as about atheism being a liberator. If we abandon belief in God, we are no longer shackled to the past. We can break out of this, we can do new things, we can do exciting things, the future is bright, it's godless, and it's free. Certainly, those very powerful sentiments have had a very big impact on Western culture.

But in 1989, two hundred years later, something else happened, as you all know: The Berlin Wall fell. The Berlin Wall had become a symbol of oppression. When it fell, people danced on its ruins. Why? Because by that stage, atheism, at least in Eastern Europe, had begun to be seen as oppressive. The same atheism that once had been seen as a liberator ushering in a new phase of freedom, hope, and optimism in Western culture seemed to many people, instead, to have brought in a new oppression.

So, in this talk, I want to try to look at some themes that emerged from atheism. What I'm going to do, if I may, is look at the main lines of argument that atheism has found so persuasive over that period and begin to engage with them.

This has become a major issue in Western culture since 9/11, because for many cultural observers—not all, but many—9/11 is all about religion inspiring acts of violence. You'll find writings by Sam Harris, Daniel Dennett, and by Richard Dawkins, all of which take as their inspiration 9/11. They argue very powerfully, very rhetorically, that atheism is needed more today than ever before, because if there were atheism, there would be no more 9/11s. And it's a very powerful line of argument.

What I want to do in this lecture is to just begin to raise some issues in relation to those main lines of argument and see where they take us. Let's begin to look at these; I'll interact from time to time with Harris, with Dennett, with Dawkins, especially in his book *The God Delusion*, and try to ask, "Where are things going in modern atheism?"

Let me begin, if I may, by asking a very simple question. If you take Daniel Dennett's book *Breaking the Spell*, Richard Dawkins's book *The God Delusion*, and Sam Harris's rather short recent book *Letter to a Christian Nation*, they come up to about nine hundred pages. Why is it necessary to write nine hundred pages showing that atheism is right when religion is meant to have disappeared altogether from Western culture by now, because many of you here this evening will remember the ethos of the 1960s. I can remember it: "Religion is on its way out."

You remember the *Time* magazine cover: "Is God Dead?" Very dramatic stuff: all this language about the future secularization of our culture, that religion was simply being marginalized, that it was playing no role in private life or, indeed, public-square life from the end of the century onward. And it just hasn't worked out. Indeed, Michael Shermer, president of the Skeptics Society, wrote a book four years ago in which he said that "never in America's history has God been so significant in public life."

So, obviously there's a real issue there. Nobody likes a failed prophecy, and clearly that's what we have in this situation. Why has religion made such a comeback?

Well, the answer we find in these writers can be summarized along a number of lines. I'll try to indicate what they are. Number one, because people want to believe in God, and they lead such sad and unimaginative lives that they really need *something* to give them dignity, to give them meaning, to give a sense of locatedness and position. So, they invent God; God is a delusion, which they willfully or sometimes accidentally take on board.

Now, again, you'll find the argument in Richard Dawkins's book *The God Delusion*, but really it goes all the way back to the 1830s, to Ludwig Feuerbach.

Many of you will know his argument: There is no God. Therefore, the fact that people do believe in God requires to be explained. Since there isn't a God, we have to explain why people should invent one, and they invent a God, because they project their longings onto some kind of imaginary, transcendent screen, and they call the result *God*.

And again, it's a very influential argument. It's also, you may have noticed, slightly circular: *There is no God; therefore, we have to kind of assume believing in God means that there's some kind of mental misfiring going on.*

But listen to the argument very carefully. People want to believe in God. Well, actually, a lot of Christian theologians would agree with that. Think of Augustine or C. S. Lewis; take the famous prayer from Augustine: "You have made us for yourself, and our heart is restless until it finds its rest in you." For Christians, people are hardwired to believe in God. That's just the way things are. That's just the way we are.

Back to Feuerbach. Feuerbach's argument is this: People want there to be a God, and therefore, this means that God cannot exist. You can see there is some force to what he's saying. It's agreed that nothing need exist because I want it to. It would be wonderful if I had a pile of a hundred-dollar bills or if I could speak with an accent like Eric's. Wouldn't it be wonderful? It's just not going to happen. I can wish all I want, but does it follow that because I want something, it can't be there?

As you hear, my voice is going rather croaky. I might say, "Wouldn't it be wonderful if I could find a glass of water?" Oh, my goodness! What do we have here? [*Points to a glass of water*]

The point I'm trying to make is this: Wishing something to be so and it being so are not actually inconsistent whatsoever. There really is a kind of logical flaw there that we need to look at.

Again, many people have made a further point that Feuerbach's argument, if it proves anything, actually proves that atheism is in the same category as religious faith. Why do people not believe in God? Because they want that to be the case. If

> Feuerbach's argument, if it proves anything, actually proves that atheism is in the same category as religious faith. Why do people not believe in God? Because they want that to be the case. If there is no God, then we can do what we like.

there is no God, then we can do what we like. There's no higher authority; we are our own masters. We can be autonomous.

Think of Czeslaw Milosz's very wonderful article "The Discreet Charm of Nihilism," in which he says the new opium of the people is the idea that there is no God, because if there is no God, we are accountable to nobody; we can do what we like, and nobody is going to stop us.

Again, you can argue that atheism itself can be explained away on this basis. I'm not sure how far that takes us. Let's move on and look at another major theme that we find in contemporary atheist critiques of religion.

Let's go for the big one, which, I think, is an important one, namely that religion leads to violence. I think that's a very plausible criticism. As I was growing up in Northern Ireland, it just seemed so obviously true.

We have to begin, I think, by saying that there is no doubt that religion can and has been involved in eliciting acts of violence. That's something that needs to be put on a table. That's something that needs to be addressed. It's real, and it's important.

But I think there is a deeper question that needs to be asked. Every movement has its pathological side. Is this actually typical of religion, or is it to be seen more as an unfortunate tendency in some sections of the movement? It's a very important point, because certainly, if you think of the history of the twentieth century, you begin to realize that when atheism moved from being on the fringes of culture to being a truly very significant power in its own right, for example, in the Soviet Union, it actually seemed to replicate the worst vices of religion.

Again, Richard Dawkins, in his book *The God Delusion*, says that atheists would never, and have never, committed acts of violence or oppression in the name of atheism. This is a personal creedal statement, I think, which is masquerading as history. Those of you who know the history of the Soviet Union will know that between about 1918 and 1941, something like 90 percent of Russian churches were dynamited, and about 90 percent of Soviet priests were simply eliminated.

There's a serious issue here. Why was this done? Because religion was seen to be an enemy, something that needed to be eliminated. So, I want to try to put on the table the fact that atheism, too, has generated its own form of violence, but actually I want to put a much more important question on the table as well: Is this really about religion and atheism, or is it actually a question about human nature? In other words, is there something about human nature which means there is something inside us that is inspired to great positive actions but might also be sucked down to do some dreadful things as well?

That's certainly what Nietzsche said about human nature as well. There seems to be some tension in that we long to do the good, but we end up doing bad things as well.

Let me give you an example.

When I was studying chemistry, one of my set textbooks was called *Fieser's Reagents for Organic Synthesis*. It was hundreds of pages long. I got to know Professor Fieser very well on many late nights in the college library. It was a very, very good book, and as I learned more about Professor Fieser, who was professor of chemistry at Harvard, I discovered some incredible things about him. He synthesized an incredible variety of chemicals that are significant medically: the blood's anticoagulating factor, various forms of steroid. If any of you are hemophiliacs or know hemophiliacs, this man would have been of importance to you.

So, Fieser is noted for many, many good things, but also for one invention that isn't talked about very much. Because in the year 1942, the U.S. Army came to Professor Fieser and explained to him they were having a slight problem. They were trying to neutralize Japanese troop formations on various islands in the Pacific, and they couldn't do it. They needed something that would be effective against troops, especially troops who were dug in, and Professor Fieser invented napalm. Napalm was designed to kill.

What am I to make of this? I could say, "Science is evil, because of Professor Fieser, and we ought to excoriate him and the natural sciences because of that." I wouldn't do that at all. I think that all the evidence would show that he was a man of great aspirations, but maybe he ended up doing something that he might have looked back on and later regretted.

Actually, I think that most of us are like that. We find ourselves lifted upward but also at times pulled down. So, I'm not sure this simplistic mantra "Religion leads to violence" is really quite as simple as we are led to believe.

Some of you may have read Robert Pape's very interesting book on suicide bombings [*Dying to Win*] in which he looks at every known case, and his conclusion is very interesting. He argues that when you look at every case, the religion is neither a necessary nor a sufficient condition for this phenomenon. What seems to matter is a people group who feel that they are being oppressed by a much bigger nation. They have no regular military resources at their disposal whatsoever, and therefore, they are driven to use themselves as weapons and to try to take as many people with them in order to resist this occupying force. Now, again, politically, that may well be right, but it does remind us that the role of religion in these things isn't anything as straightforward as some more simplistic analyses might suggest.

But you might say, "That might be right, but nevertheless, if there were no religion in the world, then this world would surely be a place that is much less prone to violence." Let's try thinking about that for a while, because it seems to me to be a very important argument—certainly one that I would have resonated with as a younger man.

Those of you who are sociologists will know that human beings are very, very good at inventing social distinctions—in other words, ways of distinguishing in-groups and out-groups. Religion is one of them; so is race; so is tribal identity; so is economic status. And the list goes on. The real issue is that religion is in there along with a long list of other things that can become major causes of division and lead to violence, but it's not the only one, by any means.

> The real issue is that religion is in there along with a long list of other things that can become major causes of division and lead to violence, but it's not the only one, by any means.

One of the things I think we need to be aware of is that human beings are very good at—I have to use a technical, rather clumsy word here—they're very good at *transcendentalizing* things. In other words, you take something that is not actually divine at all, but you make it something that is of supreme authority which cannot be challenged and defines a people group and in the end becomes a cause of social division.

To give you an example, think back to the French Revolution, to the year 1793 when the Reign of Terror was underway and things were really getting quite nasty. It was the atheist phase of the French Revolution. Madame Roland was brought to the guillotine in the Place de la Révolution to be executed on trumped-up charges. She had become politically inconvenient. As she was led to the guillotine, she pointed to a statue of liberty and said, "Liberty, what crimes are committed in your name!"

You see the point: If there's no God, well, we elevate something else to fill that gap. We take something, and we ramp it up so that it has almost quasi-divine status. In this case, it will be liberty; in other cases, it might be integrity; it might be political correctness; whatever it is, you can see how it happens. And again, it just seems to be part of the way that we are as people.

I think we need to work very hard to eliminate violence of all sorts, certainly, including religious violence. Of course, I am very, very keen on these dialogues that are trying to do something about that. But I don't think eliminating religion is going to make things better, and I think trying to eliminate religion is actually going to cause such violence, because of the importance that people actually attach to their religious identity.

Let's move on. A major theme that we find in a lot of recent atheist writing is "Science disproves God, and there is an inexorable tension between natural sciences and Christianity—all religions, above all, Christianity—and science and religion are locked in a battle to the death, which only one can win, and it is going to be science."

I regret to say that you find that view in the writings of Richard Dawkins. I say that, because I simply don't believe it's true. It's not true historically, and I don't think it's true as a present-day reality at all. The historians of science will tell us that the reality looks rather different. In fact, Ronald Numbers at the University of Wisconsin says that one of the prime myths of popular historiography is that science and religion are locked in mortal combat. He says it's just not like that. At times, they've been intensely collaborative; at times, there have been real tensions, but it's always a complex, nuanced picture, and this idea of a perennial warfare between science and religion really belongs to the 1890s.

So, let's just try to focus on the questions that are being raised here. "Science disproves God." Again, you've all heard that mantra. It's a very significant popular feeling, but I'm afraid it doesn't necessarily mean that it's right. In my own case, I moved from atheism to Christian faith, catalyzed by my growing interest in the sciences and my knowledge of the philosophy of science. Just think of some recent books that have been published. In 2006, you've seen books by Daniel Dennett, Richard Dawkins, and Sam Harris, all arguing for a link between science and atheism. Maybe not so well known, but they should be, are Owen Gingerich's book *God's Universe*—he's an astronomer at Harvard; Francis Collins's very interesting book *The Language of God*—he directs the Human Genome Project; and Paul Davies's intriguing book *The Goldilocks Enigma*, about the fine-tuning of the universe. Why Goldilocks? Remember the story: porridge—some too hot, some too cold, and some just right. *The Goldilocks Enigma* is all about the universe being just right for the emergence of life.

Interestingly, Gingerich and Collins argue that science makes the most sense seen from a Christian perspective. Paul Davies doesn't say that. He says there is something in there or out there that inclines us to believe in a God, but not necessarily a Christian God. Again, you can see the point. These are all significant scientists pointing in the opposite direction.

It seems to me the situation is simply that we can interpret the natural world in an atheist way; we can interpret the natural world in a Christian way or we can interpret the natural world in an agnostic way. A good case could be made for each, but it is not necessitated by nature itself. Or to put that in very simple English, all of these viewpoints are perfectly okay, but nature itself does not force us to choose this one, rather than that one.

Indeed, as you probably know, the evidence suggests that most scientists get their beliefs about God from somewhere else and then take them and use them in their scientific work. Some recent surveys suggest—and not entirely accurately—about 40 percent of scientists do believe in God; 20 percent don't, and 20 percent aren't sure. What sort of God is being talked about? Interestingly, the question asked was "Do you believe in a God who could be expected to answer prayer?" So, it's a very specific notion of God. It seems to me that the question is much more complex than some of these rather simple discussions might suggest.

Stephen J. Gould, who died recently of lung cancer, had some very interesting things to say. In his book *Rocks of Ages*, he argues that science simply cannot, by the legitimate application of its methods, decide the God question one way or the other. I think most scientists would think that is the case. Now, again, Richard Dawkins does not think that that is the case. He argues that real scientists ought to be atheists, and, therefore, I regret to say, challenges the scientific credentials of people like Freeman Dyson for daring to take an interest in religion and occasionally saying something nice about it.

If I could express a real concern here . . . You know, I love the sciences. I think they are wonderful, but, if you say, as Dawkins does, that science entails atheism, which everyone knows isn't the case, then actually what you are going to do is persuade a large body of religious people that science is off-limits, and I don't think that's right. I think that the position of science in our culture is so precarious that if you actually imply that it's antireligious, then it's going to lose its support at a moment in history when it needs all the support it can get. And, therefore, I want to say that Richard Dawkins is doing science a disservice by portraying it in this way.

But let's look at another argument that we often hear, which is that in some way, religion is pathological. In other words, it is bad for people. It causes them to do some silly things—to go on guilt trips and things like that. That is a serious issue. I think all of us will know people who, we feel, in some way have been damaged by religion.

But it is extremely important to draw a distinction between what is normal and what is pathological. Again, Freud's great stereotype, I think, still lingers, that in some way all religion is pathological. But I'm not really sure that's helpful, and I'm certainly sure that's not right.

Since about 1990, there's been a huge amount of empirical research trying to ask, "What impact does religion have on people's well-being?" Again, you need to be aware that this is an ongoing research field and that there are all kinds of problems involved in the research. For example, what counts as being religious? What counts as well-being? The answer generally is longevity and speedy recovery from illness. Let's agree that there are all kinds of difficulty here, but the work has been done and continues to be done.

In a very important survey of 2001, Harvey J. Cohen and Harold G. Koenig looked at a hundred evidence-based studies—not one hundred people, but one hundred peer-reviewed studies. Here is what they found: 79 percent of these studies showed at least one positive correlation between religious involvement and well-being. Then, twenty either showed no pattern or a mixed pattern—a little bit good, a little bit bad, but nothing conclusive. And one showed a negative correlation between religious involvement and well-being. Now, we must not overstate this point. This does not prove there is a God, and as the research is still ongoing, we mustn't say, "That's how things are; that's the end of it," because clearly the work is still being done. There are two points to make here.

Number one, if people like Richard Dawkins and Sam Harris were right, shouldn't those figures actually have been the other way around? Shouldn't they have shown that, in some way, religious involvement actually was having a negative impact on people's well-being, because of psychological damage? But that is not seen.

And secondly, a major issue here in the United States: If a person's religious commitment and spirituality are implicated in well-being and are implicated in speedy recovery, doesn't that have implications for public health-care policy in this nation? Again, a very sensitive, but very interesting, issue to raise.

Let me move on very briefly to one major area in which atheists have had a lot to say. It has to do with the idea of faith. Again, if we take Richard Dawkins, we find the characteristic position being something like this: "The sciences are based on rigorous evidence-based thinking; they *prove* their conclusions. On the other hand, religious belief is simply about running away from any kind of intellectual engagement. It's about disengagement and believing, despite the evidence or in the teeth of the evidence."

Again, you will find that in Dawkins's writing from 1976 until the present day. It's a very widespread position within much atheist writing, and it is well worth thinking about.

In 2004, I published a book called *Dawkins' GOD*, looking at Dawkins's religious views, and since then, I find myself going around England, giving lectures exactly on that topic. What I do is say, "Here is what Richard Dawkins says, here are his arguments, and here are my responses for those arguments." After one lecture I was confronted by a very angry young man who came up to me; wagging his finger at me, he said, "You have destroyed my faith. You know, I believed passionately in atheism because of Dawkins's writings, and you have destroyed my faith by showing his arguments do not hold water."

As I reflected on this, two thoughts went through my mind: Number one, *Well, if he did base his faith on Richard Dawkins, then maybe this was to be expected.* Secondly, and much more importantly, *How much faith matters to people,* because it actually means you construct a worldview, you base your ethics, your understanding of who you are—your understanding of what life's all about—on a set of beliefs that actually cannot be proven.

Some of you may have read Terry Eagleton's very interesting review of Dawkins's *The God Delusion* in the *London Review of Books,* and one of the points he makes—and again, it's an intriguing point that you may like to think about—is that all of us are perfectly used to holding certain beliefs as true or even reliable, even though we cannot prove them to be absolutely true. That's just the way life is, Terry Eagleton says, and therefore, we ought to expect that the best we can hope to show is there are good reasons for thinking that these beliefs are true, even if we cannot prove them with absolute certainty.

Just think of a hypothetical experiment. I want you to imagine that you have a leading atheist philosopher sharing this platform with me, and both this philosopher and I are challenged to prove our beliefs. I would try very hard to give you the reasons why I believe in God, and I'm sure I would do it reasonably well. However, I would not be able to prove my case with knock-down certainty, but neither would my opponent. The whole argument—whether there is a God, whether there isn't—is stalemated and has been so for many years. Intriguingly, that brings us to the position that the person who says there is a God and the person who says there is no God are actually taking their positions as a matter of faith. So, it's an intriguing possibility to think about that.

What do we say about this? I think there are two things I want to say. One is that I believe passionately that religious belief does need to be challenged: *Why do you believe this? Can you give us reasons for thinking this makes sense?* I think that's right. It's about being held accountable in the public arena, and I'm very, very happy to do that. I think it's very necessary and very important.

The second is that there are many Christian writers who already do this, and I'm slightly surprised when I read Harris, Dawkins, and Dennett, who seem to have managed to have gotten to this point in their lives without actually having encountered people like Richard Swinburne, Alvin Plantinga, Nicholas Wolterstorff, C. S. Lewis even, and Thomas Aquinas, all of whom, I think, give good indications of what the intellectual basis of faith might be.

But there's a much more important point here, which I want to just make as I bring this lecture to an end. And it's this: Might there be limits to the natural sciences? Again, very often, the question of whether we can prove God's existence is very often treated as a scientific question, whereas clearly, it is a much broader issue.

Now, if you take an atheist philosopher like Bertrand Russell, Russell will argue that the only knowledge we can have is scientific knowledge—that what the sciences cannot show cannot be truly known.

But let me offer a counter-perspective. Sir Peter Medawar won the Nobel Prize for medicine in the 1960s for his work in immunobiology, and in a book intriguingly entitled *The Limits of Science*, published in 1986, Medawar argued like this: When it comes to explaining the material world, there are no limits to science. If it can't explain them now, it will be able to explain them in the future.

But then he says there are metaphysical questions. He gives some examples: "What is the point to life? Why are we here?" He makes the point that these are real questions that matter to people. His argument is that science actually cannot give convincing answers to those questions. If they can be answered, they have to be answered on other grounds, and that seems, to me, to be a very important point.

For example, a quotation from Richard Dawkins's *A Devil's Chaplain*, published in 2003: "Science has no means of determining what is right and what is wrong." Now, on that point, I think he's right. Here would be the question I would want to ask in response: One of the biggest questions confronting the human race is what is the good and how do we live the good life? So if the scientists cannot tell us what is good, are we left without any guidance at all as to how we live the good life? I don't think we are. I think we are able to say that science cannot help us here. That's no criticism of science. It's simply saying that it's not very good in this field, and in this field, we need some help from other sources. It just seems to me that it opens up some very important questions about the limits of science, the sources of our knowledge, and questions like that.

But I must bring this lecture to an end. I

want to raise the possibility that atheism may be going through a difficult phase at the moment. Again, you might say, "There are always atheist books appearing, and surely this suggests that it's going through a renaissance."

Having read those books, I want to just make a suggestion: I see a lot of assertion, a lot of rhetoric, but I am quite sure I don't see the knockdown arguments that would really persuade me that atheism is on an upward cusp about to make a major comeback. Indeed, when I read, in particular, Harris's book and Dawkins's book, I did a kind of reverse-engineering job, trying to ask, "What kind of reader is envisaged by these works?" My own feeling is that these are probably meant to reassure that everything is okay within that worldview. Then again, I may be wrong on that.

If atheism is going through a difficult time, is that the end of the matter? Well, I don't think it is. Let me make one historical observation, which I then want to apply to the present-day situation. Historically, atheism has always been at its strongest—and also its most plausible—when religion is seen to be far too powerful and possibly dangerous. What if that kind of perspective begins to become plausible again in North America? So, paradoxically, the future of atheism might actually lie with religious people who, if they were to do some very silly or very dangerous things, might persuade the American public that maybe the time has come to reexamine atheism and see if it has something to say in that situation.

I have spoken for far too long; I have raised a whole series of very contentious issues, and I'm very happy to engage in a dialogue about any of them or, indeed, answer any questions that I didn't deal with in this talk that you'd like to explore.

Thank you very much, indeed, for being so patient.

Q & A

Q: Thank you, Dr. McGrath, for a fascinating talk. Two questions. I will phrase them very quickly. First, about twenty years ago, I was at Yale at a conference with Alvin Plantinga and Sir John Eccles. Sir John Eccles, who was a neurophysiologist and a man of faith, said that for him the greatest question, the greatest argument, against the existence of God was the scientific materialist assertion that we don't actually have free will, that what we think of as our souls, our consciousness, is simply the result of deterministic events in the brain. In other words, dominoes knocking over other dominoes as a result of purely causal, mechanistic events that can be explained materialistically.

Eccles tried to get around that using quantum physics. He argued that at the level of the neurology of the brain and the firing of the neurons in the brain, that was quantum indeterminate; in other words, indeterminacy intervened there, and mechanistic determinism could not explain that. However, it has been twenty years since then, and I am wondering if the research has answered that question.

Second quick one . . . Sorry, that is a slam dunk. Isn't atheism—from a Darwinian point of view—a counter-adaptive strategy, because atheists don't have kids and they are going to disappear anyway?

A: We will have to think about that second one. The first is a very good question. I haven't talked about *The God Delusion* by Dawkins all that much, but certainly in one of the sections, he talks about being psychologically predisposed toward religion. He does give a recognizable variant of what you just described as an explanation for this. In some way, we are neurologically pre-programmed to believe in God. Again, I find the argument puzzling. I think there are two elements to my puzzlement.

The first is that the clarification of psychological mechanisms is part of a picture, but it is only *part* of a picture. For example, I could say, "What a nice picture it is," and point toward it, and you could give a very good neurological account of what motivated me to look in that direction, to extend my arm, how all the muscles were coordinated in doing so. But that is only the explanation of actually how I did that; it does not account for the thought that was actually elicited by looking at that picture.

So, the key point in any psychological explanation is that of multiple causality. There are many interacting causes. So, one can't simply say there is one cause: *The firing of neurons is it.* It is clearly more complex than that. The second point is that there are many schools of thought about whether there is a God, about whether there is not a God. I would say they make very interesting points that need to be assessed. I am not entirely persuaded by those that say those different schools of thought are to be explained mechanistically, deterministically, randomly, simply by the firing of neurons.

It seems to me that the clarification of the mechanism may be important, but it does not eliminate the fact that there are still rational arguments that need to be deployed in evaluating different positions. It seems to me that actually on that point, although we have clarified much about the mechanisms, the arguments remain on the table and have been surprisingly little disturbed by the advances you describe.

Q: Although from the standpoint of history and epistemology, I don't actually subscribe to much of what you said, my question will not be about polemical potshots against atheism, which is my interpretation of your very articulate talk. My question is, instead, about your chosen faith. You describe yourself as a Christian, and I am curious why do you embrace Christianity, in particular, as opposed to Deism or any of the other Scripture-revealed religions or the infinite number of many other religions that have existed through time?

A: I think that is a very fair question, and certainly there are many worldviews that might be described as "religious" and some not. There are many different kinds of atheism. I think very often atheism is reactive and, therefore, is defined as "the kind of God you don't believe in," as well, of course, as Deism, as Christianity, Buddhism, and Islam, and so on. So, I think all of us who choose any world religion have to give an account as to why we chose that, rather than this.

In my own case, certainly, I am a Christian and have chosen that, I hope, not on the basis of polemical potshots at atheism, but more so from a considered evaluation of all the options—and from a considered reflection that this seems the best. I will try to give you a response to this in the short time I have at my disposal.

One of the key questions is this. The way in which one judges any worldview, I think, is partly in terms of its internal consistency, partly on account of its evidential foundations, but also because of its capacity to make sense of things. In other words, I am asking, "How much explanatory potential does this worldview have?" In the case of atheism, the very big issue is "How much light does it cast on religious belief?" which is a very significant phenomenon. In my case, I take the view—this is open to challenge; I am very, very clear about this—that Christianity offers the best big picture, making sense of things.

Again, if I may quote from C. S. Lewis—whom I very often find a useful discussion partner in this point—in a very interesting essay on theology and poetry, he wrote these words: "I believe in Christianity as I believe that the sun has risen: not simply because I see it, but because by it I see everything else." The point that he was trying to make was that there was an explanatory fecundity, an explanatory richness that really made a lot of sense of things. So, again, because I haven't very much time to answer it, but again I want to stress that it is a very good question, my response would be that I am a Christian because I believe, to use the language of Gilbert Harman's famous essay, it offers the best explanation, best evidence, but also the best explanatory capacity. That, I think, is something that I would have to debate and prove rather than simply assert. So, although it may seem that I am asserting it, I am simply trying to explain why this, rather than something else. I would be very happy to explain it further afterward, if we had time to do so. So, thank you for that.

Q: I enjoy a challenge. So, I ask you to take the other side and tell me how atheists explain the phenomenon of Jesus. You have, no doubt, heard "One Solitary Life"—he only preached for three years. He was crucified; he had nothing going for him. And yet, now we have Christianity off the back of a three-year ministry. How do they explain that that could be possible, unless it were true?

A: That's a very interesting question, and what you are asking is that I step into the way I used to think and try to give a response. Again, I would have to say that to be fair to atheism, the response I will give would not be as good as if an atheist were to give it. So, I need to be very clear about this, but again, let me try to say what, for example, Richard Dawkins would say on the basis of a discussion of cargo cults in his book *The God Delusion*.

What Dawkins would say is, "Actually, human beings are very gullible, and they are predisposed to believe things on the basis of insubstantial evidence." He would, therefore, I suspect, argue that there would be a whole series of convergent issues here. One would be that there was some kind of possible mass hysteria or hallucination or some kind of social pressure to believe in Jesus, which was sustained by a group dynamic that can be at least partially explained by social psychology. Again, he would have to be here to actually defend that.

> The reason that Christianity is still here today is that it is seen to be intellectually resilient and spiritually nourishing. Although not all believe in it, a sufficient number do, indicating there really is something that needs to be taken with immense seriousness.

My own response would be that, certainly, one must take such challenges very, very seriously. Nonetheless, the reason that Christianity is still here today is that it is seen to be intellectually resilient and spiritually nourishing. Although not all believe in it, a sufficient number do, indicating there really is something that needs to be taken with immense seriousness.

I think that my difficulty with many of the atheist critiques of Christ that I have read is that they very often have to present him in a very, very inadequate way to actually make him fit the theory. Again, for example, if you read Dawkins's book *The God Delusion*, which is simply very much on my mind at the moment, he spends two and a half pages talking about Jesus, and he argues that Jesus has "dodgy [shaky] family values." After all, he was rude to his mother.

Dawkins also makes a very curious point at some length, which is that Jesus encourages the formation of in-groups that exclude Gentiles and those who are on the margins of society. I find that quite difficult, because as I read the parable of the Good Samaritan, I see Jesus doing quite the opposite— actually going out of his way to reach beyond the margins of traditional Judaism to include women, to include Gentiles, to even include children.

Again, I have to say that I find that section of his book *The God Delusion* really very, very unsatisfactory. I find it difficult really to empathize completely with atheism on this point. One of my favorite German theologians is Jürgen Moltmann, who tells the story of becoming a Christian of all places in a prisoner of war camp in England. He says that he just found something so compelling about Jesus. Although he didn't personally believe in God, he began to believe in God, because Jesus did. See what I am saying? That really was a starting point for his spiritual pilgrimage.

Again, your question needs a much more detailed answer. I just sketched the beginnings of one, but thank you very much for that very intriguing question.

Q: Well, thank you, but you have failed to convince me.

A: We can talk afterward, thank you.

Q: Could you perhaps expand on your final point about how American Christians may encourage atheists to reconsider the worldview of atheism? Could you give a few examples of what you mean?

A: I think if we look at the rise of atheism in eighteenth-century Europe, France is a very good example, but of course, you begin to see the same thing happening subsequently in Germany and England. There is this perception that Christianity occupies a position of social status that has privilege, that has power, and that it is potentially quite dangerous, because it allows you to bring transcendental arguments to justify actions that might not seem defensible on other grounds. In other words, it has far too much power, and that power is potentially arbitrary and dangerous.

And therefore, the argument that was the only way to deal with this was, in effect, not to critique religion's power, but rather to critique religion itself. In other words, the best way of neutralizing the influence of religion is by deconstructing its intellectual foundations in the first place. Now, again, the question I raise at the end of this is what happens if, for example, here in the United States, a sufficient critical mass of people begin to feel that actually Christianity has had a dangerous impact on public policy, and therefore, atheism begins to gain public credibility as a belief system—because people feel that religion is not being exercised responsibly?

The only way of dealing with that, therefore, is to discredit religion. That is a scenario I ask you to consider. It may never happen, but I just want to raise the possibility that religious people do need to be very self-critical so that this point does not actually happen. In effect, it lies within the power of those who are Christians to make sure their faith is always exercised responsibly so that the public pressure for challenging the intellectual foundations of faith does not actually become significant, because religion is seen to be exercised responsibly.

Again, I make a similar point in relation to religious violence. It's there, but we can do something about it. There is possibility of reform; it's not abolition that we need—it's reform. That is why I'm just suggesting that, while I personally think atheism is not in a very healthy state at the moment, I don't think Christians should become complacent. There is always this need to self-examine and ask, "Are we really living out the Christian life in the best possible way?" or "Do we need to rethink at a couple of points?" Thank you.

> **There is always this need to self-examine and ask, "Are we really living out the Christian life in the best possible way?" or "Do we need to rethink at a couple of points?"**

Q: You obviously have a very unique perspective as a biophysicist and a theologian. You seem to believe that religion and science can have some kind of fruitful interaction. Can you offer some insight into what dialogue there is between the creation accounts in the first few chapters of Genesis and current scientific opinion on that, and maybe even just outline an approach to Genesis that leads to some kind of fruitful dialogue?

A: I am very glad to talk about that. We need, I think, to remember that the whole idea of creation is not limited to the first chapters of Genesis. It's at every level of the Old Testament, and very often Christians focus down on those first chapters of Genesis as if that is it. In fact, that is a relatively small part of a much bigger Christian witness to the whole idea of creation. It seems to me that there are some very important issues here. One of them, obviously, is how you interpret those opening chapters: Are they to be taken as literal history? Are they to be taken as a rather poetical description of the ultimate dependence of the world upon God? How are we to do that? Certainly, that is an extremely important debate that should take place in Christian theology.

As you all know, a very significant debate is whether the book of Genesis, in some way, renders incomprehensible the idea of evolution. Certainly, some North American Christians argue that. Others would say, "No, the language there about the Earth bringing things forth actually is a way of beginning to think about the emergence of things from within a natural process."

I think the most interesting question that emerges from this is this: If we do believe in some form of creation—that is to say that in some way, the nature of God is reflected in the way the world is—then that actually gives a motivation for scientific research. There has been enormously important evidence in cultural history that—if you go back to 1560, and read, for example, John Calvin, Calvin gives two examples. He talks about philosophers and astronomers, and he says that these people have the opportunity of studying the wisdom of God much more closely than he can, because they are able to study the works of God, meaning creation: "I hence gained a deepened appreciation of God's wisdom."

And certainly for many natural scientists, that is an extremely important religious motivation for scientific research. It is all about looking at what God has done and getting an enhanced appreciation of the wisdom of God by an engagement with nature. That is still here in our culture, and I certainly think we need to keep on encouraging that. Thank you.

Eric Metaxas: This will have to be our last question.

Q: Are you sure?

Eric Metaxas: That was the last question.

Q: You're kidding me.

Eric Metaxas: All right, I'll give you one more question.

Q: At the beginning of the twentieth century in Vienna philosophy school, when Wittgenstein was first studying philosophy at the university, most of his peers, out of intellectual honesty, committed suicide. Wittgenstein moved forward, as you know, and died in the fifties, whenever it was. He was being baptized into the Catholic faith and said to one of his colleagues who asked him why he was doing that, "Because of hope." Is there any hope in the atheistic movement, and how do they communicate hope? It is a very moving and purposeful question for me.

Is there any hope in the atheistic movement, and how do they communicate hope?

A: Yes, that's a very good question. You are certainly very right about the early Vienna Circle. You think of Rudolf Carnap and others, for example. There is this very, very strong sense that we are limited to what we can see, what we can observe; we can't go beyond that. Again, if you look at how they responded to the emerging political crisis in Austria around that time, there was nothing transcendent, and they were simply limited to what they could see. For that reason, as you quite rightly say, many of them were reduced to despair. Now, Wittgenstein branched off in a rather different direction.

The early Vienna Circle actually had a huge problem with the sciences. Most scientists would simply say, "Look, there is what we can observe, but then what we observe actually points to other things that we can't observe." In other words, we see this, this, and this, and that leads us to suggest that there may be something else that we can't observe at present but we need to postulate in order to make sense of things.

Again, for example, if you think of the discovery of the electron, that was originally simply because, "Look, we can't see this, but we need to invoke this to make sense of what we do." In many ways, Christian theology is doing the very same thing. It's saying, "Look, we see this and this and this, and we ask, 'What is the best way of making sense of this?'" The very classic answer is "There is this God, and this God actually helps to make sense of things."

Moving on to the theme of hope. That is such an important theme. I think that there have been enough false hopes in the history of humanity to make us very, very wary of this. Indeed, when some people use the word *hope*, people immediately become suspicious. They think it's about running away from reality. If what you see is what you get, there is no room for hope. The history of the world frequently reduced us to despair! But suppose there is a deeper picture, something that goes beyond what you see on the surface. Atheism limits itself to a surface reading of things. Faith goes deeper, and sees a bigger picture. And it is this bigger picture that allows us to speak of hope. Atheism just sees a meaningless world, devoid of purpose, as Richard Dawkins so often emphasizes. But faith goes deeper, and sees purpose and meaning beneath the surface. This sort of hope is not about running away from reality. It's about going deeper than a purely surface reading of things. It's a hope that is deeply grounded in the way things really are!

The Case for Civility— and Why Our Future Depends on It

OS GUINNESS

February 13, 2008

Introduction

I am Eric Metaxas, and I just want you to know that I am very sorry about the weather. Sometimes I think that if Giuliani maybe had a third term as mayor, he would have licked the weather problem. Do you ever get that idea?

Socrates in the City. If you don't know what it is, the best I can tell you is that Socrates said, "The unexamined life is not worth living." And I'm sure that New York is a city where people tend not to examine their lives too closely. We're all very busy. So, a number of us thought it would be nice to have a forum where we could ask the big questions—the huge questions about "life, God, and other small topics," as we sometimes put it.

We have been doing that for about eight years now, and we still don't have a clue about what is going on. But eventually we are going to get answers, somehow. That's my vow to you.

We have had an extraordinary array of speakers over the years, and if you go on our web site you can see all of them. I think I can say that with the exception of Chuck Colson and Jonathan Aitken, none of our speakers has been incarcerated. That is true.

We have probably had about twenty-five speakers, and only two have been incarcerated. So, anyway. I think that is pretty good.

There are still seats up front, in case anybody really wants to hear anything that Os or I have to say. Well, anyway, that is true. Only two people have been incarcerated. But probably—I don't know if you can say this—I think the least incarcerated of all would be Os Guinness. If you know Os, you could say that. He has just not had much trouble with the law over the years, and I think it has a lot to do with the fact that cops are intimidated by the British accent. It has been working for Os for many years, and it's absolutely phony; I know that. He does it very, very well. Even British people are fooled by it.

Anyway, tonight Os's talk is called "The Case for Civility—and Why Our Future Depends on It." That is also the title of Os's new book, which, if you think about it, is a mind-blowing coincidence. I mean, what are the odds?

Now, I don't think it would take much for me to convince you that civility is a timely subject right now, one that deserves our attention. And I really don't know about you, but as far as I am concerned, people who are uncivil are stupid jerks who should be shot.

Some of you might think that by saying that, I myself was uncivil just then. And as far as I'm concerned, you're a stupid jerk who should also be shot.

It's just an opinion.

No matter how you look at it, the issue of civility is obviously a problem in our culture. I don't know if you saw the news this afternoon. Michelle Obama threw a shoe at Hillary. Did you see that? That is what things have come down to. It actually hit Hillary but didn't do any damage. It was a tiny shoe. It belonged to Dennis Kucinich. He had thrown it at Senator Obama during one of the debates, and that is how the Obama camp got hold of the shoe. I think Kucinich originally got it at a leprechaun swap meet.

Look, the point is that throwing shoes is no way to elect a president. So, this has to stop. I hope we can agree on that. Can we agree on that? Okay.

I am always extremely excited to have my dear friend Os Guinness here at Socrates in the City. As many of you know, I came up with the idea for Socrates in the City with Os Guinness. We came up with it together. Actually, it was so long ago that I don't really know when it was. It might have been the early seventies, because I remember we were riding our choppers through the Badlands of South Dakota. I don't know if you remember that, Os. Remember we were debating Kierkegaard? Kierkegaard was actually on a third chopper between us, and we were debating him at the time.

You probably think I am so dumb that I don't realize that it's not possible that Kierkegaard was driving a chopper in the early seventies. I know he wasn't driving it. He was riding on the back of it. There was some guy named Moose who was driving it, and Moose really didn't say that much.

It is a sad commentary that I would say that about Os Guinness. But it is true we were hanging out in the early seventies. We were different people then. I remember we were poor and young. We actually were so poor that we shared a pair of mutton-chop side-whiskers between us. Do you remember that, Os?

What did you ever do with those mutton-chop whiskers, Os? I think he shaved them off to get that job, like in 1980. Remember that? Yes, you sold out.

Anyway, this was long before we were into this whole civility nonsense thing, right? Anyway, obviously that is a joke, but the fact is that Os and I did come up with the idea for Socrates in the City together. And Os, to me, has always represented the ideal Socrates speaker, because he's a great thinker and also a great writer, but also a great speaker.

Which is important, since this is a speaking event. Have you noticed? And today, of course, we know that Os got to be a great thinker and a great speaker, in part by taking anabolic steroids. And he's going to be talking to Congress about that next week.

But seriously, folks, let me tell you a little bit about my dear friend Os Guinness. Os lives with his wife, Jenny, in the Washington, DC, area, and Jenny has never been to a Socrates in the City before, but she is here tonight. Welcome, Jenny. Jenny does not have a phony British accent, you will notice if you talk to her. She has a very phony *American* accent.

Os, please don't leave. Os is the great-great-grandson of Arthur Guinness, the Dublin brewer. That's true. Os was born during World War II in China, where his parents were medical missionaries, and he was a witness to the climax of the Chinese revolution in 1949. He was expelled with many other foreigners in 1951 and returned to Europe, where he was educated in England.

Os completed his undergraduate degree at the University of London and his Doctor of Philosophy in the social sciences from Oriel College, Oxford. He has written or edited more than twenty books. Before Os came to the U.S. in 1984, he was a freelance reporter with the BBC. He has been a guest scholar at the Woodrow Wilson International Center for Scholars and a guest scholar and a visiting fellow at the Brookings Institution from 1991 until just earlier this last year. He was a senior fellow at the Trinity Forum and a frequent speaker and seminar leader at political and business conferences in both the United States and Europe. He has lectured at many, many universities, including Oxford, Cambridge, Harvard, and Stanford. Never Yale, though. Right?

He knows how to hurt me.

Os has also spoken at the White House, Capitol Hill, and many other public-policy arenas around Washington, DC. As a European visitor to the United States and an admirer but detached observer of American culture, Os stands in the long tradition of outside voices that have contributed much to America's ongoing discussion about the state of the union. You will see that from a number of his books, but it is really a particular pleasure for me to introduce my dear friend Os Guinness.

Talk

Thank you. I leave you to work out from all that fun what was true and what was false, though it was all inimitably Eric. But I would just add gently, Eric, there really is no such thing as a "British accent." There are English accents, there are Scottish accents, there are Irish accents, and there are Welsh accents, but there is no British accent as such.

I was once speaking on the same platform as the celebrated Tony Campolo. When it was his turn to speak, he said, "Now, listen, this man with his English accent speaks for about twenty minutes before you realize that he isn't saying anything at all." He paused and then said, "With my Philadelphia accent, I have to speak for about twenty minutes before you realize that I am saying something."

Last week I was at a large Washington gathering, and as people were coming out after a speech that was remarkably off the point, a congressman came up to me and said: "I fear America is in decline, but many of our national leaders are in denial. Who today is raising the biggest issues in this campaign?" Now, whether or not you agree with the congressman, I want to raise one of America's big issues tonight. You could argue that there are about a dozen or so issues that will be standing or falling issues for the United States in the next generation. Unless they are tackled and resolved, this country will decline. I am not saying that decline is necessary or automatic, but certain things have to be tackled and resolved if renewal is to be possible. Tonight, I want to pick up just one of them: how do we live with our deepest differences, especially when those differences are religious and ideological?

It would have been a safe but sad bet at any moment over the last twenty-five years, that someone, somewhere in the world, was being killed in the name of religion. Our screens have been filled with the Sunni and the Shiites murdering each other. We cross over to Kashmir; it would be the Muslims and the Hindus. Drop down to Sri Lanka, and it would be the Hindus and the Buddhists. Go back only a little while to Ulster, and it would be the Catholics and the Protestants. As we look back at the last years of the twentieth century, we can see a humanitarian nightmare—a witches' brew of ancient hatreds and sectarian violence that preceded the religiously based terrorism.

This is where our atheist friends, such as Richard Dawkins, Sam Harris, and Christopher Hitchens, jump in together and proclaim loudly how this confirms that "religion poisons everything." But in the debate that has followed their books, they have been forced to face the fact that more people were killed by secularist regimes, with secularist leaders, in the name of secularist ideologies, than in all the religious persecutions and oppressions in the West put together. In other words, it's not just religion but secularism too that is part of the problem. Secularism, after all, is a faith too.

If one hundred million were killed in war in the twentieth century and another hundred million under political repression, it is a sad fact that yet another hundred million were killed through ethnic and sectarian violence. As we ponder this appalling situation and reflect on the most murderous century the world has ever seen, some very simple lessons come to the fore.

The first lesson is that the challenge of living with our deep differences is now a truly global problem.

The first lesson is that the challenge of living with our deep differences is now a truly global problem. The issue may sound abstract, compared, say, with nuclear proliferation or HIV/AIDS or other urgent problems. But the fact is that just as many people will die because of this issue as will die from other problems. So, how do we live with our deep differences? In the globalized age, for obvious reasons such as travel, the media, and the massive movements of people in the world, it is commonly said that "everyone is now everywhere."

That is a little exaggerated, but compared with the past it is certainly true.

We find ourselves in a world where living with our deep differences has become a profound challenge. And we realize immediately that we are not just talking about our private, little worldviews that people keep to themselves at home. We are talking about entire worldviews and entire ways of life elbow to elbow with other entire worldviews and ways of life, all within the same society, and often within the same school or workplace.

The second lesson of the last century is that we're seeing the aggravation of the problem because of the emergence of the beginnings of a "global public square." The United States is part of the Western tradition that goes back to the Greeks and their notion of the *agora*—the public square, the physical place where people could meet together to discuss, debate, and decide issues of common public concern. The Romans called it the *forum*.

As things developed over the centuries since Athens, the notion of the public square developed from being physical to being metaphorical too. The "public square" became a metaphor for any forum where issues of public life were discussed. So, while it might start with the Houses of Parliament, the French Assembly, and the United States Congress, it has gone beyond the formal to the informal, and included such other forums as the op-ed pages of the newspaper and neighborhood discussions in coffee bars.

Today in the global era, the "public square' is morphing again. Having expanded from the physical to the metaphorical, it is now expanding through the Internet to the virtual. One feature of the global public square in the age of the Internet is very simple. Even when we are not deliberately or consciously speaking to the world, we can be heard by the world, and the world can speak back.

I first noticed this trend some years ago when the late Jerry Falwell made some rude remarks about Muhammad in a private setting in Lynchburg, Virginia, and a week later, riots broke out in the Middle East. Rude remarks in Lynchburg, riots in the Middle East.

Of course, since then we have also witnessed such viral responses as the *fatwas* against the novelist Salman Rushdie, the controversies over the Danish cartoons, the responses to Pope Benedict XVI's speech at the University of Regensburg. Tonight I could make some inadvertent remark that is considered "blasphemous," and tomorrow there could be some rent-a-crowd response somewhere in the world.

That is our world in the age of the World Wide Web and the Internet.

So, the challenge of living with our deep differences has now transferred from the local public square, as we have understood it in the West, to a grand public square that now, potentially, is worldwide. It is true that this notion of a "global public square" is extremely rudimentary, but it is real and it will grow.

The third lesson, as we look back over the end of the last century, is closer to home. James Madison described the United States as having discovered the "true remedy" for dealing with this problem of religion and public life, of living with our deep differences.

The framers called America the *novus ordo seclorum*, the "new order of the ages." As you know well from the history, the framers understood that they were tackling something quintessentially modern, and later historians called this country "the first new nation," referring to the fact that the American republic was a grand political answer to many of the rising challenges of the modern age.

Not surprisingly, the rest of the world continued in its traditional ways, and was therefore uninterested in the novelty of "the American experiment." Today, however, almost all of the modern world is convulsed by challenges, such as immigration and living with deep differences. So, for better or worse, the American way is more relevant than ever before. But at just the moment when the world looks across the oceans to see what it can learn from the self-professed "city on a hill," with its "true remedy," the United States is not doing so well itself. For nearly fifty years, the American culture wars, with religion as their holy war front, have made nonsense of American claims to represent any new order worth emulating.

And in all sorts of areas, you can see how contentious this issue is.

I will argue that resolving this issue is absolutely pivotal to the American republic. But it is also absolutely crucial for anyone of any faith who takes his or her faith seriously and wants to live by it with integrity. So many of us, whether citizens or followers of any faith, have a deep stake in understanding and resolving this issue. It truly is a standing or falling issue for each of us.

Let me set out the contours of the issue. And let me make clear that what I will argue for is a minority position at the moment, in the sense that it lacks national leadership at the highest national level. Let me also say that the vision proposed here runs counter to the thinking of the Christian right and many Christians. Many of us, including other people in New York, like [the late] Richard John Neuhaus, believe this is the way forward. But such disagreement in thinking means that each of you has to think it through for yourself.

Besides, you all know that I am an Englishman. So, why should you listen to me? You have got to think it through for yourselves. That is to say, as American citizens and as individual believers, you have to think through what you believe is a constructive resolution of this issue in public life.

Start back in history. Think for a moment how we in this country are the heirs of the three great Western settlements of religion in public life. There are, of course, many other settlements, because each nation, with its own history, its own culture, has done it in a slightly different way, but the three most influential settlements are the French, the English, and the American. In each case, you have a formative event that casts a long shadow down the centuries, but each of them is under severe stress in the advanced modern conditions of the global era and thus needs to be renegotiated today.

At one extreme, you have the French, and clearly the formative year, as so often in French things, was 1789, the year of the French Revolution. And you capture the whole French rationale of the French approach in the cry of Diderot, the encyclopedist, which is picked up by the Jacobin revolutionaries: "We must strangle the last king with the guts of the last priest."

Now, unpack that slogan, and you can understand the French position perfectly. In 1789, there was a state church. The church and the state were in deep collusion; both were corrupt and oppressive; so, the revolution was against both the church and the state.

The mind-set that came out of that was called *laicite*: If you're in favor of faith, you must be reactionary; and if you're in favor of freedom, you must be secular, because secularism was the way forward for freedom. You can see this mentality in the French today; it lies behind the French refusal to give, say, Muslims head scarves in schools, or in their opposition to allow any historical reference to the Christian faith in the preamble to the constitution of the European Union. The French attempt to write out any reference to the Christian faith, which has fifteen hundred years of influence in European history, in the words of the European constitution represents a very strict secularism that today presents itself in the extreme in the light of the collapse of Communism, which once was the most strict secularism in the Western system.

As so often, England is in the middle. The key year was 1688—the Glorious Revolution. Unlike the French, the English settlement kept the state church, the Church of England, partly as a bulwark against the Catholic "menace" in France. And to be fair, the English state church was neither as corrupt nor as oppressive as the French church. So, there has never been any militant anticlericalism, never any massive hostility. There was never any Saint Bartholomew's Day Massacre, as you saw with the Huguenots in France.

But it was still a state church, and it was not fully voluntary. So, over the course of the centuries, it has faded away until today, as many people say, the Church of England is rather like a national utility. We have coal, we have electricity, we have gas, we have nuclear energy, and we have the Church of England. It is a national utility, as the cynics say, for the "hatching, matching, and dispatching" (birthing, marrying, and burying) of the citizens. The Church of England has been likened to the "beautiful west front of a Gothic cathedral. Beautiful, but not very influential."

A critical part of this great experiment in ordered liberty was the role of freedom of conscience, or religious liberty, and it is important to see why the founders understood that religious liberty and civil liberty were both twin pillars of the foundations of this country. In contrast today, religious liberty is discounted or dismissed today in ways that are ignorant of its contribution as seen by the founders or later history.

At the other end of the settlement spectrum is the United States. The key year here was 1791 (just down the road in New York), when the First Amendment was added to the Constitution. As you know, the first sixteen words of the First Amendment are the absolutely unique part of the Constitution, rather than the "separation of powers." The religious liberty clauses are also among the most decisive parts of the Constitution. Montesquieu had argued for the separation of powers far earlier, and the Swiss republic had practiced it even earlier still, but the First Amendment broke decisively with fifteen hundred years of European ways of relating religion and public life.

For the first time in European experience, religion was made voluntary. But also importantly, and in strong contrast to the French, the separation of church and state did not mean the separation of religion and public life. The result was not *laicite* but a flourishing of religion—not despite disestablishment, but because of it. And the rest, as you know, is history.

A critical part of this great experiment in

ordered liberty was the role of freedom of conscience, or religious liberty, and it is important to see why the founders understood that religious liberty and civil liberty were both twin pillars of the foundations of this country. In contrast today, religious liberty is discounted or dismissed today in ways that are ignorant of its contribution as seen by the founders or later history.

First, religious liberty was held by the founders to be "the first liberty." On the one hand, it was logically the first of the three great political liberties. Freedom of assembly was prized and protected, but in fact freedom of assembly does not stand alone—it assumes and requires freedom of speech. Freedom is not just a matter of getting together, but of getting together for a common purpose, beginning with the freedom to speak freely to each other.

But in the same way, freedom of speech, which for many Americans is the first liberty today, assumes and requires freedom of conscience. You don't simply want to speak out about the weather and the latest news and gossip. You want to talk freely about convictions that matter to you supremely because you are bound to them by the dictates of conscience.

That has been forgotten recently. For many people today, religious liberty is merely "liberty for the religious." It is constitutionally redundant, like an appendix in the human body, at a time when free speech and the free press are what really matter.

But for the founders, religious liberty was also first historically. It was only when religious liberty was guaranteed and so long as religious liberty was guaranteed that the other liberties were also protected. It was in this sense that the great Jewish lawyer Leo Pfeffer argued more recently that religious liberty is the pattern and pacesetter of the political freedoms.

Second, the First Amendment's protection of religious liberty underlies the spiritual and social vitality of this country. Now, again, in many circles, that would be an odd statement today. If you ask many people, "Why is America so dynamic? Why are Americans so entrepreneurial?" the answer given would be: free market capitalism, level playing fields, free competition, and so on. But if you think about it, capitalism came into this country—it was earlier in Europe—several decades after the First Amendment. The effect of the First Amendment, however, was actually directly parallel to the effect of free-market competition.

What business people talk of as de-monopolization is actually the equivalent of what the First Amendment achieves in disestablishment. Religious liberty with equality for all provides the equivalent of a competitive level playing field in a free-market. And you can see, almost from the beginning, the explosion of a spiritual, social entrepreneurialism that is a result of the First Amendment and the way it touched things, such as the early nineteenth-century educational movement—all the little booster colleges being found across America and the explosion of charitable outreach.

It has been said that the first half of the nineteenth century in Europe and America witnessed the greatest explosion of giving and caring in all human history— rivaling that of the age of Francis of Assisi, or of Basil of Caesarea in the fourth century. No other civilizations had produced anything like it, and most of it was directly rooted in the faith communities reaching out in that way.

And the third great effect was obviously in the reform movements: an explosion of reforms, not just abolition, but supremely abolition and many, many others, all of them lying in that entrepreneurial vitality released by the First Amendment.

This is why I am wary of the current government support for "faith based initiatives." In the early nineteenth century, the faith communities flourished and made their mark precisely when they were independent from any state support at all. In other words, they were at their best when they had to rely on their own beliefs—and on their own believers, their own generosity, their own sacrifice, and their own dedication.

The danger is that when any faith community puts its nose into Uncle Sam's trough, two things tend to happen. One is that they grow dependent on government money and favor, rather than on their own faith. The other is that they undergo a slow, steady, secularization as government rules and regulations undercut the directly spiritual dimensions of their work. Government funded ministries that deal with addictions, for example, cannot use prayer and supernatural healing—which, of course, undercuts the very distinctiveness of the ministry.

The third great legacy of the First Amendment was remarkable, though never perfect. It created the conditions for social harmony. Now, we have to say immediately that America's record has never been perfect in terms of religious liberty. Roman Catholics know well what the Know Nothing movement meant—the vicious prejudice of even great Americans like Samuel Morse. In the same way, many Jews have faced terrible discrimination. Without a doubt, there were egregious violations, but at the same time, I find that many secular liberals cite these exceptions and overlook the fact that the Founders got religious liberty most nearly right from the beginning—and long before Americans got race or the place of women right.

So, while never perfect, the American settlement was much better than that of any other modern nation in the world with such diversity. You might say that it brought together two things rarely brought together in history, and very difficult to bring together today: On the one hand, strong religious convictions and on the other, strong political civility.

That is very easy to say, but hard to do, though many of you so take it for granted that you yawn when you hear a foreigner like me say it. But just think for a moment of the situation elsewhere in the world—contrast is always the mother of clarity. Take Western Europe. For most of the years after World War Two, until the explosion of immigrants coming in from the British Commonwealth, North Africa, and the Middle East, Europe showed a remarkable civility about religion. The one exception was Northern Ireland.

But all of you who know Europe would say, "That's no big deal. There was next to no religion in Europe to be uncivil about." For example, compare the region of America where the Scandinavians have settled with Scandinavia itself. Church-going in Minnesota was around seventy percent, which was higher than the American average, but in Sweden itself it was three percent. If only three percent go to church, they are not likely to fight about religion in public life.

Needless to say, the Middle East and other parts of the world demonstrate the opposite problem—passionate religious convictions, but no civility, no liberty, and no life.

In strong contrast, the United States, for all the imperfections in its record, represents a shining example of social harmony. Of course, the current culture warring means that we are not there today; so, the next step is to analyze the factors that are bedeviling the present situation and threatening to undermine the framers' original settlement.

The first factor, which by itself would not be a problem, is the explosion of pluralism. In the eighteenth century, the middle colonies were probably the most diverse place on the earth. Pennsylvania, for example, had scores and scores of little sects, but they were mostly Protestant. There were Dutch, Scottish, Germans, Swiss, you name it, but almost all Protestant. Then came the Catholics, and then came the Jews. And then in the early nineteenth century, the so-called "made in America" religions were born, such as Mormonism and Jehovah's Witnesses.

Right down to the late fifties, there was an incredible pluralism in this country, but it was loosely biblical. Not with a capital *B*, but in a sense that almost all religious groups traced their ancestry back to the Bible. Whatever one thinks of Mormonism, it does not come from the Qu'ran, or the *Pali Canon* or the *Bhagavad Gita*. It comes, however distant and distorted, from the Bible.

Then, as in so many areas of American culture, the 1960s triggered an extraordinary transformation. On the one hand, there was a huge growth of secularists, who went from something like two to nine, ten or eleven percent, representing the biggest change in the religious map in the twentieth century—which, of course, was highly significant because it happened mostly in the educated classes. On the other hand, there has been an explosion of all the world's religions since then—Buddhists coming in numbers after the Vietnam War and the influx of Muslims and so on. Today, we have adherents of all the world's religions somewhere in this country, most probably in California.

The second factor, slightly lesser in importance but worth noting was an expanding statism. In 1791, there was actually no church and state. There were churches in the plural and states in the plural. But there was no question about the relationship between the two—the churches, or, if you like, the faith communities—were close and powerful, spiritually and socially in people's lives, and the state was far away.

Not so today. Two and a third centuries later, the roles have been reversed. The state is close and powerful in our lives—for example, April 15—and many churches have less decisive authority in their members' lives than their membership in a rotary club or a golf club. This is important because some of the worst recent decisions about religious liberty in the last twenty-five years have been made in the name of the state. If you ask many religious liberty religious activists which was the worst decision of all, many will cite the Smith case.

The details do not matter, but what is interesting is that the Smith case was argued by the most conservative justice, who was also the most devout Christian believer on the Supreme Court—but it was argued in the name of the state.

The third factor is the one that bedevils the other two: an emerging separationism. Some conservative Christians argue that the separation of church and state was not in the Constitution. In the last election, Congresswoman Kathleen Harris even claimed that it was "a myth" and "a lie." Now, that would be a huge surprise to most Americans in most of your history. True, the phrase "separation of church and state" is not in the Constitution, but the idea emphatically is. None of the founders, who often had very different ideas about the relationship of faith and faith in public life, would have disagreed with that.

You only need read Alexis de Tocqueville. Traveling through America in 1831, he says that he did not find anyone in the country who disagreed with the separation of church and state. Surprisingly, even his own fellow believers, Roman Catholics, who in France would have supported a state church, saw it here as the secret of American freedom.

As a matter of fact, almost no one disagreed with the separation of church and state until in the 1940s when there was a shift in understanding what it meant. The separationists who argued the Everson case in 1947 included not only atheists and Jews, but also some Southern Baptists. In fact, the Justice who argued the opinion was a devout Southern Baptist who saw strict separation as a way of keeping Roman Catholics out of public life (sadly, he had also been a member of the Ku Klux Klan).

This "strict separation," or separationism, was definitely something new, and heralded the more recent argument that religion should be inviolably private and the public square inviolably secular. Proponents of the view often quote Thomas Jefferson as the author of the phrase "wall of separation," but it actually goes back to Roger Williams. More importantly, neither Williams nor Jefferson gave this the same meaning that the strict separationists of today give it.

Mr. J, as he is still known in Charlottesville, used the phrase "wall of separation" writing to Danbury Baptists on a Friday in 1801, but the very next Sunday he went to the largest church service in America—under the roof of the Capitol! And every single Sunday he was in Washington, he went there and even contributed to the collections. He also invited Episcopalians and Baptists into the White House, the Treasury, and other Executive Branch buildings. His wall of separation, in short, was far from strict and straight. It was a utilitarian notion that was as wavy as his famous serpentine walls at Monticello and Charlottesville.

Yet despite its weak foundations in history, the separationist position remains strong because it has become the default position of the secularist opponents of religion, which in turn makes it one of the extremes in the culture wars.

There are three models for relating religion and public life on offer today, and it is your privilege as citizens to choose and to argue for your choice. In my view, and again you will remember that I am only a visitor, two of these options form the extremes and third is the wise way forward. At the same time, the two extremes are both nationally led and generously funded, with strong batteries of lawyers facing down equally strong batteries of lawyers. The third position, by contrast, has no national champion at the highest level, and it may appear weak to some because it relies on more than law and litigation

At one extreme, there is the model of what I call the *sacred public square*, a vision of public life where one faith or another is given either an established or a preferred place—for example, the view behind the Religious Right arguing for official Christian prayer in the public schools. The obvious objection to this position is that in a world as diverse as ours is today, to privilege any faith in that way is neither just nor workable, and will therefore be the source of endless controversies.

I would go further, and argue that the Religious Right has helped to bring down against itself the most powerful backlash against religion in all American history. Europe is the most secular continent in the world, and there is no question that Europe's dire secularity today is partly a direct response to yesterday's corrupt state churches. Just think of the Jacobin cry about strangling the last king with the guts of the last priest.

Through the genius of the First Amendment, this country has never had that problem. There was no established church to oppose, and the United States has usually displayed a congenial and hospitable attitude towards all religions.

But ever since the early 1960s, and especially since the rise of the Religious Right in the mid-1970s, and the endless culture warring over the issue since then, you can see a steadily mounting American equivalent of the European repudiation of religion, especially in educated circles.

At first, the backlash was over issues of relating religion and politics, such as Kevin Phillips' *American Theocracy*, which charges that Christians are American theocrats, or even fascists, as Christopher Hedges and others have argued.

Now, of course, the attack has reached a crescendo with the New Atheists, and the problem is no longer religion and politics, but religion of any sort. Christopher Hitchens writes of "how religion poisons everything." Islamist extremism has obviously played its part too, but a major source of the secularist anger is their perception of Christian extremism. If this attitude hardens into concrete, it will be fateful for the future of this country.

At the other extreme is what Richard Neuhaus earlier called *the naked public square*. This is the vision of those who are motivated partly by separationism, the process, and partly by secularism, the philosophy. Led by thinkers such as John Rawls at Harvard, their argument is that the public square is a neutral arena of competing self-interests, where matters of faith, virtue, and character have no place.

Such a vision of the naked public square is even less just and less workable than the sacred public square, if only for the simple reason that most Americans are profoundly religious, whatever their faith. So liberals who exclude religious voices in public have found themselves in profoundly illiberal positions. They are asking citizens to enter public life by shedding the very thing that makes them who they are, helps them to see the world as they do, and to choose right from wrong and justice from injustice. But no human being is truly neutral, and certainly not the secularist, which means that under such demands secularists smuggle their own faith into the public square under the guise of neutrality.

The alternative to these two extremes is the vision of a *civil public square*. Unfortunately, civility has become a wimp word. People confuse it with niceness or Victorian manners or Japanese tea party etiquette. But civility is really all about citizenship and its duties and responsibilities. As such, it is both a republican virtue (with a small *r*) and a democratic necessity (with a small *d*).

What do I mean by a "civil public square"? A civil public square is where people of all faiths—and for our secularist friends we have to add "no faith," although in fact they have a faith, too—are free to enter engaged public life on the basis of their faith. That is religious liberty. But here is the big *but*—but to enter within a framework of what is agreed to be just and free for everyone else, too. So, a right for a Christian is automatically a right for a Jew or an atheist or a Mormon or a Hindu or a person of any faith the country over. In fact, the test of religious liberty is that it is protected even for the smallest faith community and the most unpopular.

In other words, a right for one person is automatically a right for another person, and a responsibility for both. Now, that vision has many implications, including the fact that citizens have to learn to debate our differences robustly but with civility.

This vision of a civil public square is new to many people, and not surprisingly it is surrounded with misunderstandings. First, some people—Christians and Jews, as well as atheists—are suspicious because they confuse a civil public square with a civil religion. Civil religion was a term introduced by Jean Jacques Rousseau to describe what holds a nation together in the absence of an established state religion. Whatever provides the moral legitimacy and binding cohesion to a nation is so important that eventually it is elevated to the point where it is worshipped.

Needless to say, atheists are suspicious because civil religion is a form of religion smuggled back into public life in patriotic colors. But Jews and Christians should be equally opposed to civil religion because it is a form of idolatry. If we worship what binds us together as a people, we are in essence worshipping ourselves, which is another form of idolatry. In the biblical view, there is one God, there is no God but God, and God is most against his own gifts when we put them in place of him. Patriotism is a magnificent gift, for which we are profoundly grateful, but nationalism, as history clearly shows, easily becomes idolatrous and dangerous.

The second misunderstanding is more common. People view civility as a search for a lowest-common-denominator unity, and therefore think it must be pursued through such means as interfaith dialogue. In my view, there is a small but limited place for interfaith dialogue, but at the end of the day, the plain fact is that the differences between the different faiths are ultimate and irreducible. There will always be differences, and those differences always make a difference, not only to individuals but to whole societies.

So, Christians and Muslims can engage in dialogue, but no Muslim will ever bow and say that Jesus Christ is Lord and remain a faithful Muslim, and no faithful follower of Jesus will ever compromise a belief that Jesus is Lord and God and not just an extraordinary moral teacher. There are differences that no amount of love, dialogue, and civility will ever bridge.

Rather, the vision of a civil public square creates a framework within which we are each free to believe what we believe, based on the dictates of conscience, but we are also taught the so-called *3 Rs* of civility (rights, responsibilities, and respect), so that we can deal civilly with the differences of others. In other words, these 3 *Rs* are "articles of peace" rather than "articles of faith."

I picture the scene like the Queensberry rules in boxing. Regardless of what you think of boxing, there is no question its history has been brutal. The Romans, who were not exactly squeamish about blood, loved their gladiatorial games but banned boxing. And as late as the mid-nineteenth century, many a bare-knuckled prize-fight ended in the death of one of the fighters. Boxing became a sport in the modern sense when the Marquess of Queensberry lent his name to the rules that changed boxing.

Boxers now fight in a ring, within rules, and under a referee. But while they may touch gloves at the beginning, and they don't punch below the belt if they don't want to be disqualified, they still fight, and there are winners and losers.

That is a good picture of democratic civility. There are deep differences of all kinds that are contesting each other in public life, and one party or another or one issue or another will always emerge as the winner. William Wilberforce, for instance, fought nearly twenty rounds in Parliament, year after year after year, losing each round as it were until the year when he won and abolished slavery in the British Empire with a clear knock-out.

Put differently, Christians have erred in the culture wars but not because it is wrong to contest issues such as human life and the importance of the family. What has been wrong is the sub-Christian manner in which Christians have fought—for example, fear-mongering when Jesus told his followers to "have no fear" or demonizing and stereotyping their enemies when Jesus commanded his followers to love their enemies.

The third common misunderstanding can be heard from fundamentalists, whether religious or secularist. Richard Dawkins, for example, is famous for his self-professed intolerance. He does not just refuse to tolerate what he views as extremism; he refuses to tolerate moderates who tolerate extremists. If "faith-heads" are in the grip of a delusion, as Dawkins argues, then governments have every right to step in and stop parents from "indoctrinating" their children. Religious fundamentalists often show the same intolerance in reverse.

Now, the word *tolerance* is a slippery term. It became a term of choice in the seventeenth century after the horrors of the wars of religion, and there is no question that tolerance is infinitely better than the alternative—intolerance. But there is a basic problem with tolerance. It is essentially condescending and patronizing. It is a matter of the strong tolerating the weak, the majority tolerating the minority, the government tolerating the citizens, and so on. Unlike freedom of conscience, it is not absolute and inviolable.

How is civility different from a false form of tolerance? Let me put it this way. *The right to believe anything does not mean that anything anyone believes is right.* The first half of that sentence is a matter of freedom of conscience, whereas the second is a matter of nonsense. The right to believe anything is absolute. That is what is enshrined in freedom of conscience, but that does not mean that everything one believes is right. What someone believes may be muddle-headed, it may be socially disastrous, or it may even be evil in its consequences. What civility means is that when we disagree, we do so within a civil framework.

> What someone believes may be muddle-headed, it may be socially disastrous, or it may even be evil in its consequences. What civility means is that when we disagree, we do so within a civil framework.

So, what would it take to work toward a solution? First, a successful resolution requires courageous leadership. At the present moment there is simply no leadership on this issue at the highest national level, and all the best thinking is at levels that are culturally insignificant.

Most political leaders in the last generation have shamelessly used the culture warring in the interest of their own party. When I was working on the Williamsburg Charter, one of President

Reagan's cabinet secretaries said to me, "You will only get to the President over my dead body, because the culture wars are in the interest of the Republicans."

"Mr. Secretary," I said. "Sometimes, the culture wars flow in the direction of the Republicans, and sometimes the Democrats. But they are not in the long-term interests of America, and that is surely more important."

So far, we have had no national leader who has been prepared to stand above the fray and say, in effect, "A pox on both of your houses. Here is a better way for the United States as well as for citizens of all beliefs."

Second, a successful resolution requires vision. I have stated some of these things only cursorily tonight. But the vision has to be argued tirelessly in a way that captures the moral imagination, to inspire people to rise up and break with the tired and fruitless ways of culture-warring that have dominated public life for half a century. Is no one tired of this? Does no one have the courage to stand for a better way?

Third, a successful resolution requires a practical application to the troubled spots—the two main ones being public policy debates and public education. For the last fifty years, the United States has suffered not only a general crisis in the public schools but also a lamentable crisis in citizenship education. It is only when all these first principles are the "habits of the heart" for fifth graders, eighth graders, and eleventh graders that freedom and civility will flourish in America again.

You are American citizens. I am only an outside admirer. I have just finished a magnificent new biography of Alexis de Tocqueville, and I was deeply struck by one of his observations. As you know, he was a great admirer of the American Revolution, and by the same token a disappointed lover of the French Revolution. Toward the end of his life, Tocqueville remarked, "With a revolution, as with a novel, the hardest part to invent is the ending."

For all their flaws, your founders wrote a brilliant first chapter of the American story, and there have been some distinguished and courageous chapters written since then. The challenge to your generation is to pick up your pen and

The challenge to your generation is . . . to summon up your wisdom, courage, and resolve to call your fellow-citizens back to the first principles of this great republic, and so to see that the great torch of freedom is blazing more brightly in your hand than it was when handed on to you.

write a chapter worthy of all that has been written so far—in other words, to summon up your wisdom, courage, and resolve to call your fellow-citizens back to the first principles of this great republic, and so to see that the great torch of freedom is blazing more brightly in your hand than it was when handed on to you. Thank you.

Q & A

Thank you so much, Os. We have a little bit of time for Q&A, and I think we're going to open up some of these windows here. It's hot, isn't it?

We had somebody on that. Maybe their shift is over now. Whoever is supposed to open the windows, if they can do that now, they won't be interrupting anything. Everyone is asleep. It's really hot. Let's do that so we have a few more minutes of questions from the audience.

Q: I thank you very much for those excellent remarks. My question is about Europe. Its atheism—I think you intimated—is a relative atheism. It is still significantly different from that of the United States. I would also characterize it as an atheism from apathy, rather than from militancy. It wasn't driven by the Dawkinses, old or new. My question to you, assuming you accept that premise, is "Is Europe's gradual evolution into relative atheism a positive or a negative trend for the well-being of European society, and why?"

A: I would challenge the idea that Europe is moving toward greater atheism. Actually, there are a lot of qualifications. For instance, if you look at the leadership generation, they are unquestionably secularist. But just as the secularity was a reaction against corrupt religion in previous centuries, you can see the younger generation now reacting to the emptiness of secularism. True, they are often dabbling in a variety of New Age movements of spirituality, but the religious sensibilities are waking.

As regards the older generation, one social scientist talks of them "believing without belonging"—for example, Lord Rees, the Astronomer Royal, who does not believe, but attends church regularly.

The best statements on winning back Europe come from Pope Benedict, but I am among Evangelicals calling for a third mission to Europe. The first mission, of course, was the conversion of the Roman Empire, and the second was the conversion of the barbarian kingdoms. So, our task is to commit ourselves to a third mission to Europe and the West over the next century.

Thus, I say to my fellow-Europeans, "We are now on the verge of a third mission to Europe," and we can take it because Europe is not as secular as it looks, and there are powerful movements under way that show how it might be reversed.

Q: What is a good short question to ask our candidates in this election that gets at this issue of civility?

A: I'll leave you as citizens to answer that one. Obviously, there are far more things to think about than just the culture wars. Other factors behind the incivility would include sound bites on television, the entertainment style of the media, the hate- and fear-driven nature of things like direct mail, and the anonymity of the screen names on many blogs. All such factors need to be in the picture if the analysis is to be accurate. In other words, we need to examine all the technological factors, which are aggravating the problem.

Take the issue we have looked at in the present campaign. The Democrats realized they were sunk if they didn't appeal to religious people. You can see before the election many of the Democratic candidates went out of their way to show that they understood faith.

Ironically, there was even a time when the two Democratic candidates were actually closer to faith than some of the leading Republican candidates, which threw things in the mixer.

So, you have got to work out this yourself. I said in the introduction that there are a dozen or so issues that need to be raised and resolved, and this one is one of the most important. Whatever way you can, insist that these are raised in public life. If I had any influence, I would certainly raise this one. Some leader has got to tackle it, resolve it, and set out a way forward for everyone, or America will decline.

Q: Hello, this is my first time here. So, hopefully it is all right if I ask a question. You brought up John Rawls and his view of the public square, and his project was inherently about bringing the people to the public square around the idea of reason and everyone being reasonable, which is why he wanted everyone to leave religion private. It strikes me that perhaps your project is extremely similar, but you want everyone to come to the public square under the banner of civility, and perhaps the people coming to the public square have very uncivil stories. So, how is your project different from his, and what do you do with people who need to come to the table, but perhaps are not very civilized or perhaps their stories are not very civilized?

A: John Rawls's notion of "publicly accessible reason" is actually an Enlightenment myth, which is common to many secular liberals, but not shared by most people. My basic disagreement is that I believe that people of all faiths should be free to enter and engage public life and *not* leave their faiths behind. But I certainly agree with some of his points.

For example, when a Christian enters the public square and talks about an issue such as abortion or same-sex marriage, it is both inappropriate and ineffective merely to cite Christian authorities ("The Bible says," and so on). Adherents of other faiths do not read the Bible, and they do not accept its authority. The problem with such arguments is not that they are "constitutionally impermissible," but that they are unpersuasive—they are bad apologetics!

What I am arguing is that people of faith have the freedom to enter and engage the public square, but they have to make publicly persuasive arguments and not simply state Christian positions. That, of course, takes a grasp of the principles of Christian persuasion, or apologetics.

So, I agree with Rawls that we have to make publicly persuasive arguments. But his idea that there is a common rationality to which we should all agree is a myth, and his insistence that we should leave our faith behind when we enter the public square is an example of the illiberalism of contemporary liberals from which they need enlightening.

The Language of God:
A Believer Looks at the Human Genome

FRANCIS S. COLLINS, MD, PHD

―――――

December 3, 2008

[This presentation was made during a time that Dr. Collins was a private citizen. Subsequent to that, he was appointed by President Barack Obama as the Director of the National Institutes of Health. The views presented here are Dr. Collins's own, and do not represent any official position of the U.S. government.]

Introduction

Ladies and gentlemen, forgive me for interrupting your conversations. Ladies and gentlemen, I have to interrupt you again to tell you that our speaker is stuck in traffic. Just kidding. Yes, I just made that up.

I am Eric Metaxas, and our speaker is here. He has got to leave in ten minutes. So, we have got to get this going. Before I tell you about Dr. Francis Collins—this is no joke—there is a second black purse, an unclaimed black purse. I have not yet gone through it. John Hackney, does this belong to you?

If anybody would like to claim this . . . I'm amazed that I'm holding up a lost black purse and nobody is claiming this. Anyway, if you bump into anyone who lost a black purse, point him or her to the podium, but wait until Dr. Collins is done. It would be embarrassing to claim it during his speech.

Now, Dr. Collins has a lot to say, and I do not want to cut into his time. On the other hand, if I do cut into his time, what's he going to do? You know, even with all his degrees and awards and everything, there's really nothing that he can do. That is what an education is worth in this culture.

There are some Socrates in the City speakers that need no introduction. Very, very few, yes, that need no introduction, and I would put it to you that Dr. Collins is one of those Socrates in the City speakers. He really does not need much of an introduction, but for those of you who don't read the papers, let me just say that for his role in leading the Human Genome Project—and let me clarify. It's *genome*, *g-e-n-o-m-e*, not *gnome*! Some of my friends said, "Oh, that's pseudoscience," and I said, "Not *gnome*; it's *genome*!" That's the kind of people I hang out with.

Yes, Leslie, that's right. Anyway, genome. By the end of the evening this will all come together. Genome project.

For his role in leading the Human Genome Project, Dr. Collins has been feted at the White House by two presidents, not simultaneously, alas, but by two presidents, Clinton and Bush, no less. He has also gotten the Presidential Medal of Freedom. But let's be honest. Who hasn't gotten one of those? But in this case, it was very splashy, and it was in all the papers and whatever. He wanted me to say that. It was important to him.

For Dr. Collins, evidently, it was a special experience, and he got to meet the president. He also has appeared on the cover of *Time* magazine. There are probably not thirty of us here tonight that have appeared on the cover of *Time*. That is pretty special, right?

In 2003, his was the Biography of the Year on the A&E network. It was voted the number one biography of the year, and he beat out Valerie Bertinelli by *one* vote. Is that amazing? Unbelievable. *One* vote. Incredible. I think she was in the middle of divorcing Eddie Van Halen. It was a big year for her, but he *still* beat her out. This was the man who could do that in that year. The year when everybody was talking, "Bertinelli, Bertinelli," he beat her out by one vote. I'm in awe of that. . . .

Of course, Dr. Collins also has been on *The Charlie Rose Show*, but who hasn't been on *Charlie Rose*? Again, it was a particularly wonderful performance there, and he has been on *The Colbert Report*. Yes, into the lion's den. How sad that they applaud that and not Charlie Rose. You see, that is why we do Socrates in the City. We have to educate them, Collins.

Dr. Collins has just left the head of the National Center for Human Genome Research but continues to be a very, very big shot in the highest government circles. No kidding. This is true—yesterday I got an e-mail from

Dr. Collins saying that at five thirty today he needed a private room. Can I say this, or will I get taken out by snipers or something?

He said he needed a private room at five thirty in the club, because he has to have a special conversation with the Obama transition team. Actually, we thought it was a joke. It took me a second to realize it was no joke. As I read the e-mail again and again, there didn't seem to be any sense of irony or anything. I said, "I think this is real, Justin." Where's Justin? I'm not making this up, right?

So, anyway, at five thirty, we had to take him to a special room so he could have a special phone call with the Obama transition team. I saw him in there talking on the phone. But I have to say this is where it gets kind of sad, because everybody wants to cling to power, and I happen to know that his cell phone is broken. It is *not working*. For him to go through this exercise to convince just a handful of us who are already impressed with Dr. Collins that he is still important, even though he stepped down, I said, "Wow, that's just a picture of human pride, is it not? So sad."

But hey, who isn't like that? I'm like that. We're no different. But it was quite an acting job—all that pacing and stuff, and I know that the phone was dead. So sad, so sad.

I know it's probably okay that I shared that, right? Anyway, obviously, I love this guy; otherwise I wouldn't rake him over the coals like this. The way that I came to hear Dr. Collins talk about what he is going to talk about tonight was at Socrates in the City in San Francisco. It was about a year ago. We've branched out to San Francisco. That night I heard him speak, and I said, "We absolutely must figure out a way to bring Dr. Collins to New York."

So, ladies and gentlemen, tonight I am very, very pleased to give you Dr. Francis Collins.

Talk

Thank you. Well, in the two minutes I have left . . . Eric, are you speaking anywhere in the next few months that I could introduce you? Just let me know. I've already made a few notes. I think that would be a lot of fun for me, if not for you. That was—what can I say?—memorable. That's what it was; it was memorable.

It is a great pleasure to be here with most of you this evening in this really remarkable venue. And Eric, I'm not insulted. You insulted your wife much more than me. So, I'm not worried at all. No, no, all in good fun. What an amazing gathering this is here at the University Club in New York City, and what a privilege it is for me to have a chance to speak to you about a topic that I think is much on people's minds, especially these days when there are a lot of shrill voices talking about whether faith has become irrelevant.

We're going to talk about science, because I'm a scientist and a physician, and I'm also going to talk about faith, because I'm a believer. That surprises people because they assume those two categories don't really get along very well right now. In fact, looking at some of the things that are out on the airwaves or on the bookshelves, you might think there was a bit of a battle going on. I don't think that battle is necessary. I don't think that battle is as difficult as it's being portrayed, but let me try to explain to you why I say that.

Let's be clear here: We're following the Socratic model, which is to follow the argument wherever it leads to see what the facts are that might help us with this question about whether the scientific and the spiritual worldviews are, in fact, incompatible or whether they can be harmonized.

Let me start with genetics. If you've been passing by newsstands—it's been all over the place—*Time* magazine is talking about "Genetics: The Future Is Now" and *Newsweek* is talking about the genome. The genome is our instruction book, marvelous stuff. Another cover of *Time* magazine trumpets "Solving the Mysteries of DNA." That one was published at the time of the fiftieth anniversary of the discovery of DNA, which also happened to be a seminal moment for the understanding of our instruction book—at the same time we had finished reading out all of the letters of the human DNA code, which I will describe in a moment.

These magazine covers tend to have two things in common. One is the double helix of DNA; the other is naked people. Now, what about that? I think that means that editors of magazines have figured out that DNA does not sell, and apparently—surprise, surprise—they know what does.

So, what is the genome anyway? The genome is made of DNA, and it really is an instruction book—that's a pretty good metaphor. It is the way in which all of those instructions you need are packaged, so that going from a single cell, which you all once were, to a pretty fancy organism could come to pass. You have to have the instructions to make that possible. The genome is a pretty elaborate instruction book written in a rather strange and simple language that just has four letters in its alphabet.

All of the DNA of an organism is its genome. The information is encoded within a double helix for which Watson and Crick figured out the structure of back in 1953, when I was three years old. Basically, the way DNA carries information is by the series of chemical bases that are abbreviated *A*, *C*, *G*, and *T*. It's the order of those letters, those chemical bases, that carries out the information that then gets passed from parent to child down through the generations.

Suppose you had to guess, assuming you didn't know the answer, how many of those letters of the instruction book it would take to specify the biological properties of a human being? What number would you guess? It can't be infinite. You have to have this information inside each cell of your body. Every time the cell divides, it's got to copy the whole thing; so, you wouldn't want it to be larger than it had to be, at least, not by much.

The answer is about three billion. Now, three billion is a big number.

Even in Washington, it's a big number, although some might debate that. It's hard to think about that number and the fact that you have that inside each cell of your body. If we decided right now, because this is a special evening and this is Socrates in the City, that we should read the human genome, what do you think? Sure, we can do that. I'll start over here, and you can start reading *A, C, G, T, T, G, C, T*, and so on, and when you get tired, you can pass it to the next person and we'll just keep going until we're done.

You wouldn't mind that, right? That would be memorable. But you might not survive, because for seven days a week, twenty-four hours a day, we would be at this task for thirty-one years, and then we'd finally be done. You have that information inside each cell of your body, which is just a phenomenal thing to contemplate, and you got that from your parents.

The genome is the most fundamental clue to understanding human biology; it's the instruction book. The exciting thing to tell you is that we have now—in fact, through a focused effort involving some twenty laboratories and six countries over the course of several years—a project that I had the privilege of leading—we have read out all of those letters and have derived the complete DNA sequence of Homo sapiens in April 2003.

The team of 2,500 scientists with whom I had the privilege of working made the decision all along the way that this was such fundamental information, such basic pre-competitive information, that it ought to be made available to everyone—and so, it was updated on the Internet every twenty-four hours. That information has empowered this newest generation of biologists and geneticists to begin to figure out what it all means. That's a hard problem because we are just beginning readers even now, trying to read this instruction book. It is very hard to sort out, but we've made some real progress. A major area of focus right now, for those of us who are interested in the medical applications of human genetics—which is most of us and that's why we got into this—is to try to understand those slightly scary-looking, ticking time bombs that are lurking within an individual's DNA and place each of us at risk for something.

If you came here tonight thinking you were the perfect genetic specimen—and there are some good candidates in the room on a superficial level—I'm sorry. Even Eric Metaxas does not have a perfect genome. I'm sorry; I know that's a shock. [*Eric's voice from the background: "My mother's here."*] The bad stuff came from your father, I'm sure.

So, we'd like to understand these individual DNA glitches to the extent that we could use that information to try to understand how each of us may be at risk for some future illness that we could prevent if we knew what was lurking there. We practice prevention now, not very effectively, kind of in a one-size-fits-all approach, but we're not one-size-fits-all people. We're all individuals with different collections of these genetic risk factors. Wouldn't it be nice to be able to apply that in an evidence-based method and be able to focus what you need to do for your particular risks, instead of just trying to do what everybody else is doing in a generic way? We're coming along with that.

Until a couple of years ago, while we had been very successful in finding genetic factors in highly heritable conditions—diseases like cystic fibrosis—we had been really quite stymied trying to discover those factors for things like diabetes or the common cancers or heart disease, the conditions that fill up our hospitals and clinics and afflict so many of us and our families. All that has changed.

In 2005, for the first time, we had a sufficiently comprehensive catalog of human DNA variations to be able to scan the whole genome and say, "Where is the ticking time bomb for a particular disease?" The first success on chromosome 1 over there—which you can't quite read—was for a disease called age-related macular degeneration, a common cause of blindness in the elderly. I'm sure there are people in this room who have family members with that problem. That disease had been a complete mystery and didn't seem like it was likely to be very inheritable. It doesn't come along until you're seventy or eighty years old. But what do you know—a discovery was made of a gene, called *complement factor H*, that nobody would have guessed had anything to do with this disease. There it was, and it almost immediately pointed us to some very exciting new ideas about prevention and treatment. So, we began to think: *This is going to work*.

Now, that was 2005. Since then, the progress in discovering genetic risk factors for common diseases has been breathtaking. Hardly a single issue of the most prominent journals—*Nature*, *Science*, and *Cell*—comes out without a few more of these discoveries popping up by the hard work of people who are taking the tools from the Human Genome Project and shining a bright light into areas that were previously very much obscured—telling us things about the causes, prevention, and, ultimately, cure of diseases we desperately need to know. Now we finally have the power to see what's there.

This is very exciting because it promises the opportunity to revolutionize medicine. This approach can apply to individualized prevention. It also allows us to practice better pharmacology and something called pharmacogenomics—the concept here being that our individual reactions to drugs that we may be given for a particular illness are not all the same. Some people may get a good response; some people may get a toxic effect. Some people may get no response at all. What's that all about? A lot of that variability is due to differences in our DNA. If we knew about that well enough to make a prediction, we could choose the right drug at the right time, at the right dose, for the right person, instead of just doing the one-size-fits-all approach, which doesn't always work as well as we would want it to.

Ultimately, these discoveries, like that gene for macular degeneration I mentioned, point us to new ideas about treatment, therapeutics that we never would have guessed at otherwise. In my view, that may be the biggest payoff of all, but it is also the one that takes the longest time, because you have to go from that early lightbulb experience to an idea about how to develop a drug and then go through animal testing and ultimately clinical trials. That is a long, slow, and expensive process. We as a nation need to be prepared that this is not going to happen overnight, but we have the best chance we've ever had to make huge differences in the diseases that are so much a problem for us and our families.

So, I have reason to be pretty excited about all of this, because I do think that we have crossed a bridge into new territory where we have the chance in a much more fundamental and comprehensive way to understand how life works—and how sometimes disease occurs because of one of these glitches. Most importantly, we are learning what we might do about that. This is truly an exciting era.

Let me come now to the second theme—the worldview represented by faith. I ask you to consider the scientific and the spiritual worldviews and contemplate whether it is necessary to make a choice between them. Or is it possible for a thoughtful, mature individual to find a way to embrace both of these?

If you asked me that question when I was twenty-one, I would have said, "No way." At that time, I was a graduate student, studying physical chemistry. I thought that all that mattered could be described by the laws of physics and chemistry and mathematics, and I had no use for anything of a spiritual sort. I had not been raised in a family where faith was considered particularly important, and I had grown further and further away from any consideration of the spiritual aspect of life. Then I changed my scientific path and decided to go to medical school: there were exciting things happening in human biology, and I wanted to be part of that. But I discovered that studying medicine was not just about equations; it was also about people, people who were facing severe challenges, some of them facing death. I was surprised to discover that some of them seemed to be at peace about that, resting upon their faith in confidence that what they were facing was not so terrible after all.

I looked at myself and realized I would not feel that way. I would be terrified. I would be angry. I would be anything but at peace. Then, one day, one of my patients, after telling me about her faith, which I felt sort of uncomfortable hearing about, turned to me and said in a very simple way, "Doctor, what do you believe?"

I realized that my atheism had never really been based upon a real consideration of the evidence for and against the existence of God. To make a decision about something important without consideration of the evidence was not a good thing for a scientist. And so, over the course of a couple of years, I embarked upon an effort to try to understand what believers believe and why they believe it. Most critically, I wanted to determine if belief was really something that somebody like me, who imagined myself completely driven by reason, could, in fact, embrace as well. Over those two years, I discovered that I had missed out on a profoundly compelling series of arguments which indicate that atheism is, in fact, the least rational of all choices. Instead, I learned that belief in God is, in fact, supported not only by spiritual and theological arguments but also even by some pointers in nature.

Now, that was a surprise. I realized that naturalism—my worldview—had limits. Yes, science was a natural and reliable way to understand how the natural world works, but science provides no answers to some very powerful, important questions, such as "Why am I here?" and "What does love mean?" I'm not talking about *eros* here. I'm talking about love between friends and love you feel

> **I realized that naturalism—my worldview—had limits. Yes, science was a natural and reliable way to understand how the natural world works, but science provides no answers to some very powerful, important questions, such as "Why am I here?" and "What does love mean?"**

for people you've never met because they are people whose concerns are your concerns. Other questions loomed large: "What happens after I die?" and "Is there a God?" That's the big one. Is it not immediately apparent that science can't help you with those questions? So, if you're going to be an atheist, you basically have to decide those are irrelevant. If you are a scientist who also finds those questions important, you have to find some other approach to them that lies outside of naturalism.

To my surprise, I began to realize there were pointers to the existence of something outside of nature that came from nature itself. First of all: There is something instead of nothing. There's no reason why that should be. Then there's the Big Bang, the fact that the universe had a beginning about 13.7 billion years ago in an unimaginable flash where the universe—at that time smaller than a golf ball—exploded and has been blowing itself apart ever since as the galaxies receded from each other and continue to do so today. Our laws of physics and mathematics can't really deal with what happened before that. They break down. So, doesn't that cry out for an explanation?

Have we observed nature to create itself? I don't think so. That seems almost, by definition, to imply a Creator who must be outside of nature and, frankly, must be outside of time and space. Otherwise, you have not solved the problem of who created the Creator. As soon as you admit to the idea that the Creator has to be outside of time, then that so-called infinite-regress problem goes away.

Another clue from nature: Physicist Eugene Wigner's phrase "the unreasonable effectiveness of mathematics"—I was a student of physical chemistry—I used those equations with the full confidence that they describe the behavior of matter and energy. It never occurred to me to wonder why they would work, and why should they? Why should gravity follow an inverse square law? There's no reason that should be the case, but it's true. This begins to make you think that a Creator who's outside of time and space is also a pretty darn good mathematician. And apparently also a pretty good physicist; there is this amazing observation, just coming to light in the last thirty years, that the constants which determine the way in which matter and energy behave— things like the gravitational constant—have been precisely tuned to take on values that are necessary in order for any meaningful complexity to exist in the universe—much less, life.

If you take the gravitational constant and allow it to be just slightly weaker than it currently is, then, after the Big Bang, everything flies apart, and there's never any coalescence of galaxies, stars, planets. If the gravitational constant were a little stronger, just by a tiny bit, one part in a billion, then things come together a little too soon. The Big Bang is followed by a Big Crunch before we humans ever show up. That's one of fifteen—fifteen—physical constants, which, if you tweak their values by a tiny fraction, I mean a very tiny fraction, means that the whole thing doesn't work anymore.

Faced with that evidence, I think one is either forced to say there must be a multitude of parallel universes with different values of these constants, which we can never observe, or this was intentional. Now, which of those options requires more faith? I had trouble accepting this multi-universe hypothesis, and so it began to seem more compelling to imagine that this was not an accident. Einstein apparently felt the same way. But then the larger question emerged: "Okay, if there is a God, does God care about *me*? Or is God one of those Deist concepts that started the universe going and lost interest shortly thereafter?"

I read C. S. Lewis's book *Mere Christianity*. The first chapter has an amazing title called "Right and Wrong as a Clue to the Meaning of the Universe." If you haven't read *Mere Christianity* and you're interested in tonight's discussion, that would be the first book you should look at. It changed my life. The argument Lewis is making is a familiar one down through the centuries, but it was unfamiliar to me. If you were looking for evidence in yourself of the existence of a Creator who cared about human beings and what you found was this inexplicable part of human nature, this knowledge of right and wrong—a constant across cultures and down through history, although we interpret it differently—wouldn't that be an interesting thing to find, written in our own hearts, evidence of a Creator God who cares about human beings and who must be good and holy and is calling us to do the same? I was compelled by that argument at age twenty-six. I am compelled by it today.

Now, you may say, "This morality thing is just a product of evolution. In fact, human beings have been forced by natural selection to be nice to each other, because that helps us all survive." You would be right in certain instances, such as if you're being nice to your own family, because they share your DNA, or you're being nice to people who might be nice to you next week.

You would have some reciprocal benefit. But what do you do about those most radical acts of altruism in which people reach out to someone they've never met, not even of their own group, and do something that potentially puts their own life at risk?

We're in New York tonight. A little more than a year ago, Wesley Autrey, an African-American construction worker, watched as a young white man standing next to him on the subway platform went into an epileptic seizure and fell onto the tracks in front of an oncoming train. Wesley, standing there with his two little girls, asked a passerby to hold their hands and leaped onto the tracks, realizing as he did so that there wasn't time to pull the young man to safety. So, he covered that young man with his own body, wedging both of them between the tracks as the train rolled over them. Miraculously, with only a tiny fraction of an inch clearance, they both survived.

Now, are you not inspired by that? Is that not an example of what we consider human nobility ought to be? Of course, it often isn't, but we all look at this story and say, "That's what we should do when called into action." When we see an Oskar Schindler risking his own life to save Jews from the Holocaust, we admire that. We think that's what we're called to do. When we see a Mother Teresa giving of herself to the dead and dying in Calcutta, we are moved. When we see Jesus teaching about the Good Samaritan, who reached out to one who was hurt and not of his own tribe, whom others had passed by, we feel that was an important lesson. And we resonate with that lesson, don't we?

That kind of radical altruism is a scandal to evolutionary mechanisms, but it is an absolutely compelling pointer toward something within us that seems to be calling us to be better than we would be in our own natural state. It seems to me that this may be a connection to a Creator God who cares about us as individuals, not just as processes of creation of no particular subsequent interest.

All I have said to you here is what many have said better. Immanuel Kant, the noted philosopher, wrote: "Two things fill me with constantly increasing admiration and awe; the longer and more the earnestly I reflect on them, the starry heavens without and the moral law within." I'm there.

At age twenty-seven, I became a believer and a follower of Christ. "Okay," you may say, "that all sounds fine." But "you're a believer and a geneticist. Isn't there a problem here? Doesn't your head explode? After all, you're the guy who studies DNA. Don't you realize that DNA teaches us something about our relationship to other animals, which is absolutely impossible for a Christian believer to accept? Isn't evolution incompatible with faith?"

Many have asked that question. I will tell you right now I have never seen a problem here, but many have. Someone who posed that question to me in front of several million viewers is Stephen Colbert, when he interviewed me in 2009 on his program *The Colbert Report*.

In fact, the Colbert interview was filmed about two blocks from here, and I think that was the whitest my knuckles have ever been. So, okay, Stephen, what's the problem here? What really is the evidence for the theory of evolution?

Let me just spend a couple of minutes on this because it's such a stumbling block for so many people, and yet it need not be so. Do we, in fact, have evidence, now almost one hundred and fifty years after the publication of *The Origin of Species*, for this notion of descent from a common ancestor affected by random changes and acted upon by natural selection to have resulted in significant events over long periods of time? Does it include humans? Because this is clearly a place where people begin to have some difficulty. Darwin's theory is very counterintuitive. It is not the sort of thing that you would have come up with, but what's the evidence?

Let us first compare genomes. We've done our own genomes. Guess what? We've done a bunch of others—the mouse, the chimpanzee, the dog, the honeybee (good heavens), the sea urchin, the macaw—even the platypus has had its genome completed and about thirty others as well. So, what happens if you take those DNA sequences and put them into a computer and ask the computer to tell you what happened here? The computer draws a tree that looks like an evolutionary tree, right down to the details of how various animals are placed onto that diagram, including humans—up there at the top—and matches quite precisely to what had already been inferred by anatomy and by the fossil record. That doesn't mean it's right, but it is certainly interesting and fairly compelling that it comes down with the same answer.

You could also say, and certainly I've had people who are troubled by this say, "Well, you know, God in the process of creating all of those different species used the same motifs over and over so it wouldn't be surprising their

DNA sequences would be similar just on that basis." That does not prove common descent, but there are other issues.

When you start looking at the details, that position becomes very difficult to sustain. The human chromosome 2 is an interesting one. If you compare human and chimpanzee chromosomes, they look a lot alike, except there's one difference. We humans have a big chromosome 2, the next-to-largest ones, and chimps don't have that. They have two smaller ones.

By the way the gorilla looks like the chimp—we're the outlier here. You can imagine that somewhere way back there was a fusion of those chromosomes in the line that led to us. That would be an interesting hypothesis.

Now that we have the complete DNA sequence, we can test that. We can test that in a specific way, because it turns out that at the tips of all human and chimp and every other mammal chromosomes are specific sequences called *telomeres* which don't happen anywhere else. Guess what? In the human, they do happen in one other place—in the middle of chromosome 2. Our chromosome 2 has remnants of telomere sequences in exactly the place you would have predicted, based on that hypothesis of an ancestral fusion. You find this "DNA fossil" showing that's exactly what had happened.

Now, unless you postulate that God placed that telomere sequence there to test our faith, then you are in a tough spot to say that we humans are not part of this amazing tapestry of life.

Let me give you another example. Why did those sailors get scurvy? What is the deal about us and vitamin C? Why do we need this vitamin? Because many other mammals don't. I can tell you why. Consider the gene *GULO*, which stands for *gulonolactone oxidase*. The human, mouse, and cow versions of this gene are all in the same relative place in their genomes, flanked by other genes that perform similar functions. But guess what: the human GULO gene has a huge deletion at the front end of it that renders it completely nonfunctional. That is the gene you need to make the enzyme that synthesizes ascorbic acid, vitamin C.

The sailors got scurvy because they, like all of us, have a nonfunctional *GULO*. But isn't it interesting that there's a remnant of it there? It's lost its original abilities to do anything, but you can still find this DNA signature left over from that deletion event. It's exactly in the place in between the two other genes that common descent would predict. It's very hard to look at that and not conclude that we humans are, in fact, part of this process of common descent. I could give you many other examples as well.

I think it's fair to say—and this is largely data coming from the study of DNA, not so much from the fossil record—that Darwin was right, that common ancestry is correct. A gradual change over time, being operated on by natural selection, has resulted in an amazing diversity of individual species—and also in Homo sapiens.

But if evolution is true, does that leave any room for God? There are certainly many people who would argue you have to make a choice here, that you have to resist evolution if you're a believer because it basically forces you into an atheistic perspective. That, my friends, is really not the truth. Let me explain how I think that is a misunderstanding, even by those who are very much experts in this field.

You may have seen books by Richard Dawkins, a distinguished expositor of evolutionary theory, an incredibly gifted writer who has written about evolution going back to the 1970s with his famous book *The Selfish Gene*. Dawkins has explained the nonintuitive aspect of this in ways that, I think, compelled many people to understand finally what Darwin was talking about. Dawkins, however, has arrived in a different place now later in his career and is putting most of his effort into promoting the evolutionary naturalistic perspective and arguing that it requires atheism. His book *The God Delusion*—one of those rare books that requires no subtitle—is an atheist manifesto. But don't you immediately see the problem here? Dawkins is trying to argue the nonexistence of God based on scientific grounds.

If God has any meaning (unless you're a pantheist), then God is at least, in part, outside of nature. Science has no ability to comment about things that are outside of nature. It's a categorical error to try to do so, and to use scientific argument to say *yes* or *no* to the existence of God is not a productive pathway; yet it is the main thesis of Dawkins's book. Chesterton said it well: "Atheism is the most daring of all dogmas . . . for it is the assertion of a universal negative." It requires a supreme and unmerited degree of confidence to say, "I know there is no God." Suppose the knowledge of God's existence just happens to be outside of what you know at the moment.

Ultimately, at the end of the debate I did with him for *Time* magazine, Dawkins did say, "Well, you know, I can't rule out the possibility that there might be something grand, incomprehensibly complex that our human minds could not possibly get their minds about that might be outside of nature." Well, okay, he got it—a convert, right there. He's not subsequently repeated that statement on a regular basis. I think Dawkins's problem frankly is that he has not taken the time to understand what mature believers believe. So, he caricatures faith and then finds it easy to disassemble.

If I'm so confident there's not a problem here, how, in fact, can evolution and faith be reconciled?

So, let me conclude with what I see as a totally comfortable synthesis. It is a synthesis that most of the 40 percent of scientists who are believers have arrived at. Many of them are thinking they were the first to think of it, but actually it's a fairly traditional pathway to put this all together.

And here it is:

Almighty God, who is not limited in space or time, created our universe 13.7 billion years ago with its parameters precisely tuned to allow the development of complexity—not by accident but by intention—over long periods of time. God's plan included the mechanism of evolution to create this marvelous diversity of living things on our planet. Most especially that plan included Homo sapiens, human beings. After evolution had prepared a sufficiently advanced "house," if you can call it that—the human brain, which was necessary for complicated things like spirituality to have a biological foundation—then God gifted humanity—and this is what Adam and Eve's story is all about—with the knowledge of good and evil [that's the moral law], with free will, and with an immortal soul. And Homo sapiens became Homo *divinus*.

We humans used our free will to break that moral law, leading to our estrangement from God. For me as a Christian, Jesus Christ is the solution to that estrangement that otherwise prevents me from having a relationship with God.

This framework is often referred to as *theistic evolution*, but it's an unfortunate term that turns a lot of people off. It sounds as if evolution is driving this. It's the noun, after all, and *theistic* the adjective—who knows what that means anyway? So, here's a suggested alternative. What I'm really talking about is life and God, *bios* and *logos* in the Greek. We're talking Socrates in the City here. So, it's all right to use Greek here, right? *Bios*—life—through *Logos*—the Word: "In the beginning was the Word," the first chapter of John, "and the Word spoke us into being." More simply, we could merge this into

BioLogos, if you will—God speaking life into being. In that synthesis, yes, DNA can be thought of metaphorically as the language of God.

There are objections to this synthesis, of course. We may be talking about them in a minute in the Q & A. Didn't evolution take an awfully long time? Well, yes, from our perspective. Remember that God is outside of time; it might have been in a blink of an eye for God. Isn't evolution a purely random process? Doesn't that take God out of it? Well, not if God preloaded the whole enterprise. Again, being outside of time with full knowledge of the outcome—or perhaps God inhabits the process in ways that we can't interpret or perceive.

Isn't evolution a purely random process? Doesn't that take God out of it? Well, not if God preloaded the whole enterprise.

The "intelligent design" movement would say, "We might possibly accept common descent, but don't tell us that evolution could produce these marvelous nanomachines that we have inside of our cells or that bacteria have, like the flagellum. Those require some sort of special intervention." And that is the position that Intelligent Design has taken.

Unfortunately, this is not a productive pathway because, in fact, many of those so-called "irreducibly complex" structures like the flagellum are turning out to have arisen by way of multiple intermediate steps that evolution could well have produced. One, therefore, does not have to postulate a supernatural intervention. Frankly, Intelligent Design is not only turning out to be bad science, it's not very good theology either—postulating that God had to step in and fix the process that had had so many flaws that it required numerous supernatural interventions to get the whole thing to work.

Of course, especially for people who have grown up in a faith tradition that has taught them that the interpretation of Genesis must be one of literal twenty-four-hour days, science seems to conflict with that. Well, is that interpretation required by the words of Genesis 1 and 2? If you haven't recently looked at Genesis 1 and 2, have a look tonight; you will see there are two stories of creation, and they don't quite agree. In the first story, the plants appear before humans, and the second story, humans appear before plants. Now, surely that was to indicate to us that we're not to interpret this in an absolutely literal way, or already before you get halfway through Genesis 2, you've got a big problem.

My favorite theologian wrote about this sixteen hundred years ago, when he could hardly be accused of making apology for Darwin. That was Saint Augustine. Augustine was absolutely obsessed, it seems, with the whole issue of how to interpret Genesis. He wrote no less than four books about it and summed all of that up in this marvelous paragraph about Genesis, which I wish was read more frequently: "In matters that are so obscure and far beyond our vision, we find in Holy Scripture passages which can be interpreted in very different ways without prejudice to the faith we have received. In such cases, we should not rush in headlong and so firmly take our stand on one side that if further progress in the search for truth justly undermines this position, we too fall with it."

I fear that the tension that has now come to the fore, especially in America, between those who see it as the truth of evolution based on science, and those who see it as the truth of Scriptures based on the reading of the Bible, has lost sight of Augustine's principle that God's truth can't contradict God's truth. Like many others before me, I believe God gave us two books. One is the book of God's Word—that's the Bible—and the other is the book of God's works, which is nature. I think God gave us intelligence and curiosity and expected us to use those to go and learn about the details of God's creation and to celebrate what we discovered as a glimpse of God's mind—and even as an opportunity to worship. I wrote about this in a book called *The Language of God*, but others have written about it eloquently too. (I'm relieved to see that it's not only the atheists who are writing strongly worded books about science and faith.) Some beautiful books are being written by people like my friend Darrell Falk, who wrote *Coming to Peace with Science*; my friend Karl Giberson offering a book called *Saving Darwin*; Owen Gingerich, astronomer at Harvard, writing an awesome book called *God's Universe*; and recently, David Myers at Hope College in his *A Friendly Letter to Skeptics and Atheists*, pointing out that the arguments coming from Richard Dawkins and Christopher Hitchens and Sam Harris and Daniel Dennett—the four horse-

> I think God gave us intelligence and curiosity and expected us to use those to go and learn about the details of God's creation and to celebrate what we discovered as a glimpse of God's mind—and even as an opportunity to worship.

men of the atheist apocalypse—need not necessarily be embraced on the basis of reason. They are, in fact, violating the usual rules of reason.

Since *The Language of God* was published two years ago, I have made an effort to offer answers to the most frequently asked questions that have been posed to me in hundreds of e-mails and letters. In another couple of months, that will be up on a web site at www.biologos.org, and I hope people who are looking for a debate about science and faith will find that site and engage it in a way that should be interesting.

Now, I conclude. I hope that perhaps some of those same fundamental questions may be posed by all of you. Thank you very much.

Q & A

_____

Thank you, Dr. Collins. We have dessert and coffee. You need coffee after a dull talk, right? It will pick you right back up. Hang in there. It gets better. No, seriously, we are so grateful, Dr. Collins. We are grateful, very grateful to you. We are very grateful to you for coming here. Thank you.

We have about twenty minutes for Q & A. I know some of you have good questions. I know some of you are good friends of mine, and I'm not going to let you talk tonight. You have to really have a good question. We have just a few minutes for some questions. I'm going to walk over to you with a microphone.

Q: The question is that when you started out your presentation, you said you disseminated the information across the Internet. My question to you is, did you put in some defensive mechanisms [to protect the intellectual property]?

A: There was a really important meeting in 1996, just as we were beginning the process of scaling up to sequence the human DNA. All of the leaders of the laboratories that were going to do the work got together and made a decision about this issue. Our concern was that the human genome was information that was going to be very hard to make sense out of. There really wasn't any justification for keeping it out of view for even more than a day. If the goal here was to benefit humankind and if it seemed to us to be such basic information that intellectual property applications wouldn't actually turn out to be beneficial, but actually the reverse, then we should just give it away. That was the decision, and we stuck to it.

I think historians—when they look back—will see that as a pretty important moment. It is a view now that has actually spread in the genomics community to all kinds of other data sets where the ethics now is to release your data even before publication so that other people can begin to use it.

Eric Metaxas: That was good enough. We need the next one to be a multiple choice or true or false. Dick, you had a question here? Are you ready?

Q: A very simple question. Science got you to God, but how did you go from God to Christianity?

A: That is a great question. As I mentioned, I was not raised in a home where religion was practiced as a serious activity. So, I had a pretty blank slate to write on. As I have tried to describe, I went through the arguments that led me to accept the idea of a creator God who cared about people. Then I had to figure out what God is like. I did look at the world's religions, trying to understand their foundations, and realized a lot of what they had to say is overlapping. There are great similarities in terms of the principles and the things we are all called to do on the basis of these religions, but there are also differences.

This investigation of comparative religion came at a time when I was feeling particularly worried about the way my own exploration of faith was going—because just as I began to realize that God was a reality, I was also realizing how far short I fell of what God was calling me to do. I would try to change that by living up to the standards of the moral law, and I would fail over and over again.

This is when I learned about Jesus. The person of Jesus Christ is different from every other figure I had encountered in world religions. He not only claimed to know about God but to be God. And he died on the Cross in a substitutionary way. That strange sacrifice became exactly what I had been looking for—a pathway to allow me to approach God, despite all my imperfections.

So, after resisting this conclusion, because this was not the outcome I expected, ultimately I could no longer resist. At the age of twenty-seven, I became a Christian.

Q: One of the most studied genomes is the yeast DNA. That is one of the most simplistic, in a sense, when you compare it to the human genome. Shouldn't scientists actually argue that it would be more interesting to make us more simple in a sense so that there are fewer problems that can occur in our DNA? Yeast can survive the worst temperatures out there. It will out-survive us as a human race. So, I am just wondering what your thoughts are on the simplicity of the yeast genome compared to the human genome.

A: Yeast is a wonderful model, and we certainly learned a huge amount about biology from studying yeast, but they're not too good at second-order differential equations, and they haven't sequenced their own genomes. So, I think we still have some reasons to be proud of ourselves. Maybe the yeast is actually having a meeting just like this, and we are not aware of it.

Eric Metaxas: And they're putting *us* down. Yes, they're saying we are *too* complex.

Collins: I am sure they don't have an Eric Metaxas in the yeast gathering. No, there is no way.

Eric Metaxas: Thank you. We have a question here.

Q: My question is, as a scientist working on the Human Genome Project and also as a Christian, how has your study of the idea of evolution affected your understanding of the doctrine of Original Sin?

In the Garden of Eden, Adam and Eve were told, "If you eat from the fruit of that tree, you shall surely die." They ate from the fruit of the tree and did not die right then, but they died spiritually, because they were kept, at that point, separate from God.

A: That is a hard one to answer in a sentence, but it is a great question. So, what is the doctrine of Original Sin? Basically, it's the idea that all humans have fallen. As described in the Garden of Eden, we were given the chance to choose between good and evil and we chose evil. Ever since then, we have been repeating that. Certainly, Original Sin is one of those doctrines of the Church that we can all confirm by personal observation—we are all fallen creatures.

Maybe your mother, Eric, is not falling into this category. I would like to excuse her if I could. Original Sin reflects our inability to live up to the moral law. But from an evolutionary perspective, it is hard to understand what this moral law is all about anyway. We humans seem to have this law in its full form, and other animals don't. But the concept of Original Sin makes no sense to a materialist.

I think this discussion of the moral law forces you into theology, into territory that science alone can't answer, and yet this is a really important question. It's another concept that has motivated me and many other people to move away from a purely naturalistic worldview, and try to ask other deeper questions that only a spiritual worldview can address.

Q: Given all that you have presented, what do you believe that God wants?

A: I hesitate to try to answer that question, because that would imply I know God's mind. My understanding of God's mind is this tiny little glimpse from time to time. I believe that God wants fellowship with us. It does make sense that all this creative effort and all the setting of parameters—and this instilling of the moral law as a means of having us appreciate both what good is, and how far short of it we are—wouldn't make a lot of sense if that was not intended to be a signpost to a good and holy God. There does seem to be one answer I can give, and that is that God is, indeed, calling out to us and hoping for a response. It took me a long time to respond.

Eric Metaxas: Look how many questions we have. You need to be more clear in your talk. I don't know what to do about this. This is terrible. We've never had this happen before. Our speakers are usually very clear. We have just a couple of long-winded questions, and that is it. So, we're not going to get to everybody. I think it is the lady's turn.

Q: This sort of relates to what he was asking about Original Sin. As a Christian and a scientist, how do you explain the issue of death? What I mean by that is that the Bible says death entered the world by sin, but if you have evolution before that, there is a lot of death before the sin.

A: Yes. Scientifically, it is clear from a vast array of evidence, the fossil record, the age of the earth, the study of DNA, and many other things that certainly organisms were living and dying before humans appeared on the scene. Does that conflict with Romans 5, which seems to be talking about death entering the world through Adam, or does it conflict with 1 Corinthians 15:21 and 22, which seems to have a similar kind of implication?

Looking at those particular verses, I think there is a serious discussion that could be had about whether those verses are referring to physical death or spiritual death. After all, in the Garden of Eden, Adam and Eve were told, "If you eat from the fruit of that tree, you shall surely die." They ate from the fruit of the tree and did not die right then, but they died spiritually, because they were kept, at that point, separate from God.

There is certainly nothing in those verses that seems to refer to the death of animals or plants. The concern is about the death of humans. If you could argue, for instance, that in God's view humans in the full "imago Dei" did not arrive on the scene until that moment, when free will and the moral law were instilled, then you don't have such a dilemma. This discussion is just one example of the way in which we should respond when someone says that evolution can't be merged together with Christian theology—we should go back to the original Scriptures and ask, "What was the intended *meaning* of those words?"

Eric Metaxas: I actually have a question. When you talk about the flagellum in the cell . . . Is that funny?

Collins: We're just not sure where you're going here.

Eric Metaxas: That is good; maybe people will listen. When people talk about intelligent design and the flagellum and irreducible complexity—some people here know what I am talking about—there is this idea that God comes in and says, "I need to do *X* or *Y* or whatever," it seems there is something sort of ham-fisted about the whole thing. It looks strange that he has to say, "No, wait a second, stop everything," and comes in and fixes something. You're coming out on the side that says that doesn't seem right, that these things like the flagellum can just arise through the process of evolution. Now, the thing seems to me—

Collins: Make your question short now. Sorry.

Eric Metaxas: So, my question is why do we feel the need to say either this was God intervening or wasn't God intervening, because if you look at what we would call *random processes*, how thinly can you slice it to where you say that God stuck his finger in here or he didn't? On some level, isn't it beyond us to be able to make that call?

A: Absolutely. I guess the reason I am unhappy with the way in which Intelligent Design has been so readily embraced by many people in the Church is that it does take a very specific view about this issue—as if that is just the way it has to be, namely, that things like the bacterial flagellum or the eye or the clotting cascade in blood could not have developed by a gradual process of evolution and had to require some supernatural intervention. That is a God-of-the-gaps approach. The gaps are being readily filled by advances in science, and basically, our human actions have put the intelligent design God in an awkward position. But my God is greater than that. My God would not have set up a process that required so much of this tweaking along the way to fix something that was so imperfect to begin with.

Eric Metaxas: Although on some global level, I think what you are saying is that he can still be the God of the gaps, if the gaps are infinitesimal?

A: Yes, in the sense that God can inhabit the process of evolution rather than going off somewhere and ignoring it. But to come in and say, "Okay, God had to invent the amino acid sequence of the thirty-two proteins that make up the bacteria flagellum, because evolution couldn't do it," no.

Eric Metaxas: And yet at some level you are saying God did—just that he didn't do it in a way that is obvious to us?

A: He preloaded it.

Eric Metaxas: Isn't it the same thing on some level?

A: No, I don't think so. Maybe it is if you let God, as God must, be outside of time. Then the distinction between preloading and inhabiting goes away.

Eric Metaxas: Okay. All right. Thank you. We have a question. You thought that was tough? We have a lawyer here.

Q: My wife says I shouldn't ask the question, but I just can't resist.

Collins: Oh, go ahead.

Q: You spoke about the fact of gravity, and I have always been very interested in this. If it were off just by a little bit, there would be fifteen changes, fifteen different parallel universes.

Collins: Or more than that.

Q: Is there a possibility that when you have an evolution, things kind of evolve for the better? Is it possible that Stephen Colbert could have evolved into Metaxas from one universe to another? Is there any possibility?

Collins: We have to decide which is more evolved and which is less evolved, and I don't think we want to go there.

Q: A quick question. Your thoughts on stem cell research?

A: In the appendix to my book, *The Language of God*, I wrote a bit about bio-ethics, including some discussion about stem cell research. Clearly, this has been an area that has been enormously controversial. For me as a scientist, I understand the controversy, although I am often troubled by the way different kinds of science get muddled together without a clear distinction. I believe that when the sperm and the egg come together, that is the creation of a human being. I don't think we should be doing that for research purposes. I don't think that seems like a respectful way to treat the dignity of a human.

On the other hand, when we consider that there are four hundred thousand or more of such frozen embryos sitting in freezers that have been produced by in vitro fertilization, something that most people do support, and that the likelihood of all of those embryos ultimately being implanted is extremely low, I think there is an argument to be made for research. I'm not going to tell you exactly what the answer would be, but I don't think it is an argument that is inappropriate to consider, whether the use of some of those for something that might help somebody with Parkinson's disease or diabetes might actually be more ethical than discarding them.

I think this issue is evolving itself in a very interesting way because of a new development in the last two years called IPS cells—induced pluripotent stem cells. This is an amazing scientific development, perhaps the most breathtaking thing that has happened in science in the last four or five years: the ability to take a skin cell and convince it, by adding just four genes, to go back in time and become what you call *pluripotent*, capable then of generating all kinds of other types of cell types, including liver and brain and muscle and heart and all of that.

You can now derive pluripotent cells from any individual. You can pluck just a single human hair and get enough cells from the root of that hair to be able to do this trick and end up with stem cells that could become almost any tissue. That seems ethically much less challenging, because you are not going through anything that you would call an *embryo*. At least, I don't think you should call it an *embryo*, because you will confuse everybody.

This technique is much more potentially valuable for therapeutic purposes, because it is your cells. It is not a transplant from somebody else that your immune system is going to reject. These are *your* cells.

And so, maybe the good news about stem cells is that the way the science has evolved now poses the opportunity so that both ethically and scientifically the things we want to do are the things, I think, we all can support.

How Good Confronts Evil:

Lessons from the Life and Death of Dietrich Bonhoeffer

ERIC METAXAS

April 9, 2010

Introduction

G ood evening and welcome to Socrates in the City. We finally got there. This is extraordinary. Yes, there are many more sentences to come, so, please hold your applause.

I have to say it is a little bit staggering to see how many of you are here tonight—especially when I happen to know in advance that the quality of the speaker is a little bit subpar.

As you may know, today marks the sixty-fifth anniversary of the death of Dietrich Bonhoeffer. So, the board of Socrates in the City decided to have a special Socrates event to commemorate that anniversary. They realized that a new biography—a staggering and shiny new biography—was coming out, and they wanted to know if they could get the author of that unbelievable tome to speak. He was very hard to get, but they were able somehow—if you believe in prayer, I think that is what it was. They just were on their faces; they were fasting and praying—and they were able to get the speaker. So, the author of that book is going to be our speaker tonight.

But, as I say, this is not really a typical Socrates in the City event. We normally have different kinds of speakers, but you wouldn't know that, if this were your first time. So, let me ask, if this is your first time at a Socrates in the City event, would you raise your hand? I am curious. Look at that. Wow. Now, be honest with me, if this is your last time at a Socrates in the City event. Yes, I know, I know. Who needs the crowds, right? It is like Coney Island indoors.

But if you're here for the first time, you probably don't know the ground rules of Socrates in the City, and we do have some strange rules. I'm guessing that those of you who are newcomers probably didn't know that you're supposed to shave your heads. But the next time you come, if you wouldn't mind . . . I hate to tell people how to live, but these old clubs have odd rules; this is a very old club. I think the head-shaving rule goes back to a lice problem or something in the early days of the club. So, yes, they require you to shave your heads, and if you wouldn't mind doing that before you arrive next time, we'd be grateful to you.

Now, those of you who have shaved your heads and who are wearing cheap synthetic wigs, which—I am eyeballing the situation—looks to be most of you, let me just say on behalf of Socrates in the City, thank you for doing that. We enjoy meeting in these clubs, and if that means shaving our heads and putting on ill-fitting, itchy polyester wigs for a couple of hours, it is all in good fun, right? So, it is worth doing. But if you are new to this thing, you didn't know that. So, thanks to you who are doing it.

Now, as I said, this a different Socrates in the City event. If you have been coming for a while—those of you wearing wigs would know this—we normally have really extraordinary speakers. By those standards today, alas, we have failed miserably. For example, some of our previous speakers—unlike tonight's speaker—were knights of the British Empire, right? We've had Sir John Polkinghorne and a few others.

So, I'm sorry, but tonight's speaker is not a knight of the British Empire. He is also not a member of the House of Lords, like some of our previous speakers. He is also not the chief rabbi of the UK. That I know of. Well, you never know.

Tonight's speaker has never been on the cover of *Time* magazine. Tonight's speaker never ran for president. We have had Socrates in the City speakers who have done all of these things and more.

Tonight's speaker is also not one of the top physicists of the twentieth century—although to be fair, the jury is still out on the twenty-first century. We don't know what he is going to do in his career.

Tonight's speaker, unlike one of our previous speakers, was not involved in Watergate . . . *directly*. So, I think we have to just face the fact that tonight's speaker is a little bit different than what we are used to.

Now, I should say this: Tonight's speaker is the first speaker we have ever had who suffers from *severe incontinence*. I believe that's why he is not here yet. He's supposed to be seated right here in front. But he is not yet here. I guess he's indisposed, as it were. They are telling me that he is fine. But he'll be here eventually. He is obviously not here yet.

So, as I say, tonight's speaker is not on par with our previous Socrates in the City speakers, and yet at the same time, I find that I have a certain affection for him. You could almost say that he's like a brother to me. In fact, and this is kind of weird, but his brother is actually my brother *also*. And it turns out that one of his parents is related to one of my parents *by marriage*. It is very strange. Yes, think about that; it works out.

Now, as I looked at the bio of tonight's speaker, I confess I had a very strange and almost spooky feeling. It made me a little bit uncomfortable, because there were some incredibly odd similarities. It was kind of like the Lincoln/Kennedy thing with the penny. You don't know about that? You should read *The National Enquirer* more often.

But there were some very strange similarities, I have to say. For example, tonight's speaker grew up in Danbury, Connecticut; I *also* grew up in Danbury, Connecticut. I thought that was kind of weird. Tonight's speaker went to Yale. I *also* went to Yale. A lot of people go to Yale, but I just thought that that was kind of weird. Tonight's speaker worked for *VeggieTales*. Now that's *really* weird, because I *also* worked for *VeggieTales*. I thought that was really incredibly strange.

But then, I read that tonight's speaker has also been published in *The New York Times* and *The Atlantic Monthly*. Now that was really truly strange, because I have *also* been published in *The New York Times* and *The Atlantic Monthly*. And then the final one—and it just gets more ridiculous—is that he has been a commentator on Fox News and CNN. When I read that, I thought, *That is unbelievable. Because I have also been on Fox News and CNN.* I mean, it just gets more and more strange. I had this feeling that tonight's speaker has been sort of shadowing me throughout my whole life. Something like the way Clare Quilty shadows Humbert Humbert in Nabokov's *Lolita*. In fact, the whole thing really did have a Nabokovian doppelgänger feel to it.

By the way, if you don't get the whole Nabokov reference, let me just say that I, as the host of Socrates in the City, know that many of you have business backgrounds. You are busy climbing the ladder of success. Maybe the last great work of literature you read was *Who Moved My Cheese?* or something like that. And I want you to know, in all honesty, that I do sincerely look down my nose at you for this. But, please, do not take that personally, because that really is the whole point of Socrates in the City—to help bring people in the financial world and business world into the rarefied world of ideas.

Socrates in the City takes its cue—you know this is what we are about—from Socrates, who famously said, "The unexamined life is not worth living," and then he blew his brains out in an alley. Unbelievable, it is just so sad. Obviously, I am kidding. But Socrates did say that, of course. We thought you know that we take that as our motto at Socrates in the City to ask the big questions and to look into the big things—the kind of stuff you aren't going to hear at the 92nd Street Y. I believe tonight they are interviewing Kirstie Alley, for example. But we wanted to get into the big, meaty questions, and that is what we are all about. Our point is to draw pseudo-sophisticated New Yorkers—that would be you—into examining the big questions.

So, as I said before, the parallels between the speaker's life and my life were really kind of freaking me out. So, that is where I got to the whole doppelgänger thing. The parallels between our lives were bizarre, but I suppose it is possible that the speaker and I could have had those similarities. So, I figured I would just let it go. But when I got to the point in his bio where it said that the speaker had *founded* Socrates in the City, I said, "No, that is just not possible." Because I know that *I* founded Socrates in the City. So, there is simply no way that he could have *also* founded it.

When I read that part of the bio, I realized that he was either nuts—a lunatic—or he was an out-and-out liar. Or he actually was the founder and host of Socrates in the City. There are only those three options. He is either a lunatic, a liar, or the founder and host. By the way, thank you for being a C. S. Lewis–literate* group of people. Explain that to your neighbors.

Now, some people would like to make tonight's speaker out to be a great moral teacher. But by making the claim in his bio to be the founder and host of Socrates in the City, he has not left that option open to us. He forces us

---

* An oblique reference to C. S. Lewis's argument that Jesus was either a lunatic, a liar, or the unique Son of God.

logically to see him as either lunatic, liar, or founder and host of Socrates in the City. I confess I think he is either a lunatic or a liar, because he can't be the host of Socrates in the City, because I know I am the host. Look at me. *I am hosting right now.*

I guess I am kind of offended that he would even claim that. So, unless he and I are the same person—and I am somehow unaware of that—then he is just lying or just plain nuts.

Now, we have never had a lunatic or a liar as the speaker of Socrates in the City before. Gerald Schroeder was a little kooky, but that was intentional. That whole Professor Irwin Corey* schtick is obviously intentional.

We also had Sir John Polkinghorne, who claimed to have been knighted by the queen of England, which sounds, on the face of it, to be insane. But we looked into it, and it actually happened. He really *was* knighted by the queen of England! So, tonight is the first time we have had someone as our speaker who was a lunatic or a liar. Please keep that in mind when he starts talking.

Is he ready? Okay, ladies and gentlemen, how about a warm Socrates in the City hand for our speaker, Eric Metaxas?

---

* Irwin Corey, the famous American stand-up comedian, a.k.a. Professor Corey, "the World's Foremost Authority," was known for his disheveled hair and "professorial" attire; Lenny Bruce called him "one of the most brilliant comedians of all time."

Talk

Thank you so much. That is certainly the longest introduction I have ever received, and I do a lot of speaking. But thank you, Eric. That's incredible.

I have to say, Eric, you are a tough act to follow. But something tells me I'm up to it.

How far can this go on? This feels like a wacky sixties or seventies sitcom, doesn't it? It really does. It's like *The Patty Duke Show*. There are all kinds of corollaries here. But I really feel like this is sort of the apotheosis of my life. To inhabit a sixties or a seventies sitcom really defines me. To the extent that I have realized that, thank you for making this fantasy real for me, for showing up here. Yes, it is a beautiful thing.

As our hermaphroditic introducer just said a few moments ago—no, he's cool with it—tonight is a special night. It is the sixty-fifth anniversary of the death of Dietrich Bonhoeffer. It also happens to be the official launch of my biography of Bonhoeffer. Now, the anniversary of his death is an important one, and we wanted to do something special to commemorate it. And having this event was all we could think of.

Writing this book was extraordinarily difficult. I would like to say a little bit about how I came to write this book.

Now, some of you are familiar with Bonhoeffer. I think if you came here tonight, you know the basics of his life. I want to tell you a little bit more about him, but Bonhoeffer is known most famously, I suppose, for having written two books. One is *The Cost of Discipleship*, and the other is *Life Together*.

These are great works. These are amazing books, and if he had done nothing else but write those, he would be deservedly quite famous. Those books have changed a lot of lives. But he is also famous, of course, for the end of his life, when he got involved in the conspiracy to kill Adolf Hitler. It's always hard to reconcile how this man of God, this theologian, could have done that. So, that's the general background of who he was, but I want to tell you a bit more about him. Unfortunately, the introduction was so long that it has severely cut into my time. Don't you hate that?

My father is Greek; hence my surname, *Metaxas*. My mother is German; hence my deep love for Siegfried and Roy.

I should begin by saying that, for me, this is a very personal book. I will say this: My father is Greek; hence my surname, *Metaxas*. My mother is German; hence my deep love for Siegfried and Roy.

But seriously, my father is Greek, and my mother is German. My mother grew up in Germany during the war, and my grandfather was killed during the war. He was one of those hundreds of thousands of reluctant German soldiers who had to go and be killed in a horribly senseless war and my mother lost her father when she was nine years old.

My grandmother used to tell me that my grandfather would listen to the BBC with his ear literally pressed against the radio speaker, because if you were caught listening to the BBC at that time, you could be sent to a concentration camp. You were not allowed to do that. But he was killed on April 4, 1944, and this book on Bonhoeffer is dedicated to him.

So, in many ways, I grew up in the shadow of World War II, and I have always puzzled about the great—really almost unprecedented—evil of the Nazis and the Holocaust and how it happened. It is something that I have thought about a lot, about the question of "What is evil and how do we deal with evil?" Bonhoeffer seems to be a perfect model for us in answering that question.

I heard about Bonhoeffer's story for the first time in 1988, and I was stunned, because I thought, *How come everybody doesn't know this story about this German pastor and theologian who got involved in the plot to kill Hitler?* The more I heard, the more I thought, *This is just haunting and extraordinary, and someday*

I'd like to make a movie about it. But I didn't become a filmmaker; I became a writer. So, I never made a movie about it. Maybe someone else will. But his story captivated me.

Now, I never intended to write a biography about anyone—I'm far too self-centered to want to spend several years thinking about someone else that way—but of course, I did end up writing *Amazing Grace*, the biography of William Wilberforce, which came out in 2007. After it came out, people kept asking me, "Who are you going to write about next?" Some people asked, "About *whom* will you next write?" Of course, *whom* is correct.

But I thought, *I don't want to write any more biographies.* I didn't even want to write the first biography. But people kept asking me, "Who will you write about next?" Finally, I thought that if I were to write about somebody, there was only one person besides William Wilberforce who captured my attention in the way that he did, and that person was Dietrich Bonhoeffer. And so, of course, I did write the book, and here we are.

So, tonight, I want to briefly tell the story of Bonhoeffer's life, and let me start with his family.

Bonhoeffer was born in 1906, into what can only be described as a spectacular family. His childhood was such a wonderful childhood that it's hard not to be jealous when you read about it. His father—and I didn't know this—was the most famous psychiatrist in Germany for the first half of the twentieth century. When the Reichstag was burned down later on in 1933, he was called upon to judge the mental state of Marinus van der Lubbe, who was the Dutch communist believed to have set the fire. So, he was a well-known and very important figure, probably something along the lines of our own Dr. Joyce Brothers. Just kidding. I meant Dr. Phil.

But seriously, he was an august figure. He was one of the most respected scientists and doctors in Europe. So, Dietrich Bonhoeffer grew up with this kind of a father, but everyone in this family was remarkable. All of his ancestors were spectacular. His mother and his brothers and sisters were spectacular. Actually, there were eight siblings, and Dietrich was the youngest of four brothers. His elder brother, Karl Friedrich, went into physics. At age twenty-three, he split the atom with Max Planck and Albert Einstein.

I've seen the atom; it's in a museum in Dresden, and it's the size of a softball. You might not know it, but atoms were much bigger in those days, much easier to split. I believe he split it with an axe. But you have got to give him credit; he is one of the first ones to split an atom. But seriously, Dietrich's brother split the atom with Planck and Einstein.

Bonhoeffer's other brother Klaus became the head of the legal department at Lufthansa. His sisters were also geniuses and married geniuses. They were all just amazing people, and Bonhoeffer grew up in that family, the youngest of four brothers.

When World War I came, his eldest brother was killed in the war. It was utterly devastating to the family. Bonhoeffer, at the age of thirteen, a year after this event, decides he wants to become a theologian. The father was, of course, a scientist, and for him, the idea of his brilliant son becoming a theologian was a little bit surprising. So, Bonhoeffer was challenged on this choice, especially by his brothers and sisters. They were all trained to think logically and to challenge things. But Bonhoeffer knew what he wanted to do, and he planned to take that kind of rigorous scientific and logical thinking into the world of theology.

In 1923, Bonhoeffer began theology studies at Tübingen, the renowned university in Germany noted for its seminary. Then, later that year, he took a trip to Rome. This was very exciting for him on a number of levels. It was there in Rome at age seventeen that for the first time, he thought very seriously about the question he would think about for the rest of his life, and that question was "What is the Church?"

I should say that Bonhoeffer was raised in the Lutheran Church, the state church of Germany. The family were not big churchgoers; Bonhoeffer's father was agnostic, but he respected the Christian faith of his wife, who was quite a serious Christian. So, the children were raised in a seriously Christian atmosphere, and the father gave that his blessing, so to speak.

So, early on, Bonhoeffer had God in his life. But when he went to Rome, he suddenly asked this question "What is the Church?" and realized that the Church is not only the Lutheran Church or the Protestant Church. It was on Palm Sunday in 1923 when it really hit him. At Saint Peter's Basilica, he saw people of every race and color celebrating the Mass. This really was an epiphany for him. He realized that this would likely be a question that he would be asking and answering for the rest of his life, and in fact, that's just what he did.

After his trip to Rome he enrolled at Berlin University. Now, it must be said that at that time to be studying theology at Berlin University was to study theology at the most prestigious place in the world. There is simply no question about that. The Berlin theological faculty was legendary. Adolf von Harnack was still teaching there, and Bonhoeffer studied with him and knew him very well. Bonhoeffer was not a theological liberal like Adolf von Harnack, but he respected him and learned from him. Bonhoeffer was an academic superstar. He earned his PhD at age twenty-one.

Anybody in this room do that? No? I didn't think so. Me either. But I should say that I've just begun working on my honorary doctorate. . . .

So, Bonhoeffer got his doctorate at age twenty-one. But in the course of answering the question "What is the Church?" on a sophisticated theological level, he also discovered that he actually wanted to work *in the church*, too. He wanted not only to be an academic theologian but also to become an ordained Lutheran minister. But in Germany in those days, you couldn't get ordained until you were twenty-five. So, at age twenty-two, he traveled to Barcelona and served there for a year as an assistant vicar in a German-speaking congregation.

Then at age twenty-four, with another year before he could be ordained, he decided to go to the United States to study for a year at Union Theological Seminary. Now, it's fair to say that Bonhoeffer did not expect to find much by way of theology at Union, and I'm afraid that in this, he was not at all disappointed. It's actually quite funny what he writes about it. I quote what he says in my book. With a PhD in theology from Berlin University, it was only natural that he would look down his nose at what "passed for theology" at a place like Union. That's his phrase.

But while at Union, he met a fellow student named Frank Fisher from Alabama, who was African-American. Frank Fisher would visit the Abyssinian Baptist Church up in Harlem, and one Sunday in the autumn of 1930, he invited Bonhoeffer to join him. What Bonhoeffer experienced there completely blew his mind. He had never seen anything like it. This was 1930, of course, and what Bonhoeffer saw was a huge congregation of African-Americans who took their faith very seriously. They were a people who weren't merely playing at religion. Many of the older people in that congregation had been born during slavery times; so they were not strangers to suffering, and their faith was quite obviously real.

Bonhoeffer had never seen anything like it. He was stunned. And so, he decided to go up there every single week afterward. He worshipped at that church during the months he was in New York and even taught a Sunday-school class there. He got very involved in the lives of the people, and it changed his life. There's little question about that.

When he returned to Germany in the summer of 1931, his friends remarked on it. Something had happened to him.

But before I go into that, let me say that something else happened to Bonhoeffer in New York, which is worth mentioning. On Easter Sunday in 1931—the only Easter that Bonhoeffer spent in America—he tried to get into one of the big mainline Protestant churches, just to see how they did Easter. But he discovered too late that since everyone goes to church on Easter, he couldn't get in. You literally needed a ticket. So, what did he do on Easter Sunday in 1931? He went instead to a synagogue to hear Rabbi Stephen Wise preach. Can you imagine? On the only Easter in his life that he spent in America, he went to a Jewish service and heard a famous rabbi.

Stephen Wise was a very big deal, a well-known and ultimately contro-versial leader in Jewish affairs in America. He was a friend of FDR, and two years later when Bonhoeffer saw what Hitler was doing to the Jews, he wrote Rabbi Stephen Wise a letter to let him know what was happening. But part of the reason I'm bringing this up tonight is that we have a special guest in our audience—the grandson of Stephen Wise, who is also named Stephen Wise. Would you raise your hand, so we can acknowledge you? Yes, there he is.

I have had the privilege of getting to know him a little bit, and I'm so glad he is here with us tonight. I should say that he has been very involved in trying to get Bonhoeffer's name on the list of Righteous Gentiles at Yad Vashem in Jerusalem. This man has been a hero in that.

But as I was saying, Bonhoeffer returned to Germany, and everyone noticed that he was somehow different. Somehow his experience at Abyssin-ian Baptist Church had changed him. His heart seems to have turned toward God in a new way.

He now took a position on the theological faculty of Berlin University and began to teach there. But from behind the lectern, he was saying things that one did not normally say in Berlin theological circles. For example, he referred to the Bible as the *Word of God*, as though it were actually alive, as though God existed and would speak through the Bible. This was not the sort of thing one heard at Berlin University at that time. Bonhoeffer also would take his students on retreats and teach them how to pray and to hear from God. He encouraged them to let God speak to them through the Scripture.

This was dramatically different from what one expected in Berlin theological circles. But Bonhoeffer was a Barthian, to some large extent, and he really did believe that there was a God behind the Scriptural text and that the whole point of studying the text was to get to the God *behind* the text. Bonhoeffer understood that God actually existed and that connecting to God was the whole point of it all.

So, Bonhoeffer was changed, and of course, Germany was changed now, too. The Nazis had had very little political power when Bonhoeffer left for New York in 1930, but when he returned, all of that had changed. He could see the trouble on the horizon, and he began to speak in his classes to his students about it. He was not afraid of saying things like "For German Christians, there can be only one savior, and that savior is Jesus Christ." That was a brave thing to say, because many Germans were, of course, beginning to look toward Hitler as their savior, as the man who would lead them out of the hell of Versailles and the ignominy of having lost the First World War. But Bonhoeffer saw that this would lead them into great trouble as a nation, and so, he began to speak out against it.

Just two days after Hitler became chancellor in early 1933, Bonhoeffer gave a famous speech on the radio in which he dissected the terrible concept of the "Führer Principle," which is really what led to Hitler's rise to power. *Führer* is the German word for "leader." Bonhoeffer explained that true authority must, by definition, be submitted to a higher authority—which is to say, God—and true leadership must be servant leadership. This was precisely the opposite of the idea embodied in the Führer Principle and in Hitler. So, just two days after Hitler became Germany's chancellor, Bonhoeffer was publicly on the record against him and his warped idea of leadership.

Somehow, Bonhoeffer saw from the very beginning what no one else seemed to see—that Hitler and the philosophy he represented could not coexist with Christianity. Hitler himself despised Christianity, but he would never say so publicly. He pretended to be a Christian because he understood that to say

Bonhoeffer saw from the very beginning what no one else seemed to see—that Hitler and the philosophy he represented could not coexist with Christianity.

what he really believed would erode his political power. He wanted to infiltrate the church with Nazi ideology and take it over from the inside, since it was the state church and since the government paid the pastors' salaries.

But Bonhoeffer understood that true Christians in Germany had to stand against the Nazified state church of Adolf Hitler. Bonhoeffer became one of the leaders in the so-called Confessing Church,* which officially broke away from the German Reich Church. He eventually was called upon to lead an illegal seminary in the Confessing Church and train up real Christians as disciples of Jesus Christ. He writes about this in his book *Life Together*— about what it means to live in a Christian community, one that takes the Sermon on the Mount very seriously. Some of the more traditional Lutherans were disturbed at what Bonhoeffer was doing. They thought that his emphasis on meditating on Scripture verses was too "Catholic," for example. Many in the theological world didn't like the idea that he put so much emphasis on prayer.

But Bonhoeffer understood that to fight evil, one must train Christians to live as Christians and learn how to pray, how to worship God and actually behave as though these things are true—not just be theoretical and theological about it. And so, Bonhoeffer was a real maverick in that sense. He was helping these young seminarians to learn how to live out their faith.

Eventually, the Gestapo shut down this illegal seminary. For a while, Bonhoeffer took it underground, and it became a bit like a floating crap game. The Gestapo didn't know where the training was happening—first it was in this farmhouse and then it was in that vicarage—and they couldn't stop it for some time. But, of course, eventually they did stop it. So, eventually, Bonhoeffer's possibilities for serving God were being winnowed down to nothing. The Nazis kept tightening the noose, and there was less and less that Bonhoeffer could really do.

---

* Also known as the Confessional Church, it was made up of a group of Evangelical Christians in opposition to the Nazi attempts to curb the German Protestant churches.

It was during this later period—on Kristallnacht in 1938*—that Bonhoeffer for the first time publicly identified the Jews who were being persecuted with the people of God in the Psalms. He saw that Hitler was persecuting the people of God. Bonhoeffer said that Christians were obliged to speak out, even if Christians disagreed with the Jews theologically. These are the people of God, and we must stand up for them.

As we know, in 1938 and 1939, there were war clouds on the horizon. Bonhoeffer knew that whenever he was called up, he wouldn't be able to pick up a gun and fight in Hitler's war. He wasn't a pacifist in our contemporary understanding of that term, although in the sixties, he was represented by the anti-Vietnam left as someone who, had he lived, would have probably been the third person in the bed with John and Yoko. But that's simply not who he was. Nevertheless, he knew that he couldn't fight in Hitler's war, and so, he was praying earnestly and asking God what to do.

He didn't want to publicly take a stand against fighting in the war, because as a leading figure in the Confessing Church, he would get everyone else in the Confessing Church in trouble. He wanted to follow his conscience, but he didn't want everyone else to have to follow his conscience. So, finally he decided that the way out of this situation was to escape to New York, perhaps to teach at Union or elsewhere. Reinhold Niebuhr pulled some strings, and Bonhoeffer got an invitation and then in early June sailed for America again.

But no sooner had he gotten off the boat than he felt he might have made a mistake. He was praying earnestly during this time, asking God to lead him. In my book I quote his diaries and letters from this period. It's extraordinary to have this window into his private thoughts as he wrestled with his future during this crucial time. In the end he really believed that God wanted him to go back, to stand with his people during this difficult time, come what may. And when he felt God calling him back to this horrible maelstrom, this place where he knew he would probably die, he went.

So, he left New York in early July, only twenty-six days after his arrival. He had no idea what he was headed for, but he knew that he must obey God.

---

* Translated literally as "Crystal Night" or "Night of Broken Glass," it refers to a series of orchestrated attacks on Jewish homes, shops, and synagogues that took place across Nazi Germany and areas of Austria on November 9 and 10, 1938.

When he arrived his Finkenwalde colleagues saw him and were shocked: "What are you doing here? We have arranged things at great difficulty so that you could escape, so that you could go back and be preserved for when all of this blows over. What in the world are you doing here?"

Well, what he was doing there was complicated and absolutely fascinating. I should say that Bonhoeffer's family had been involved in the conspiracy against Hitler for years by this time. They were already having secret conversations behind closed doors in the early thirties, and these continued through the decade. During this time Bonhoeffer had been providing moral support, helping them to feel comfortable about this conspiracy against the German head of state, when most Germans would not have been comfortable with it. But when he returned in 1939, Bonhoeffer felt that he must take another step and become actively involved.

We should also make clear that Bonhoeffer's brother-in-law, Hans von Dohnanyi, was a leading figure in the Abwehr, which was German military intelligence, and the Abwehr was the *center* of the conspiracy against Hitler. So, when Bonhoeffer returned to Germany, his brother-in-law hired him to work for the Abwehr, ostensibly to use his talents to help the Third Reich during this time of war, but in reality to join the conspiracy against Hitler. So, Bonhoeffer essentially now became a double agent. His brother-in-law's thinking was, "We can use you. You have got these ecumenical church connections around Europe. You spent this time in Barcelona and in London and all over. So, why not work for us?"

Of course, the Nazis thought Bonhoeffer was doing their bidding, but what he was really doing was going around Europe to establish contacts with his ecumenical friends so that they could get word to Churchill and Anthony Eden and the other Allies, to let them know that there were Germans inside Germany who were working against Adolf Hitler. It's an extraordinary thing. Bonhoeffer's best friend, Eberhard Bethge, said that it was at this point that Bonhoeffer went from "confession to conspiracy."

He also continued to write, of course. He was working on his magnum opus, *Ethics*, during these years. And then in late 1942, quite unexpectedly, he fell in love with the eighteen-year-old granddaughter of his dear friend and supporter Ruth von Kleist-Retzow. I am really proud to say that for the first time in this book, you get the full story of this romance. Nothing much was published about it until 1992. Bonhoeffer's fiancée's elder sister—whom my wife, Susanne, and I met a couple of years ago—published a book of the correspondence between Bonhoeffer and his fiancée, whose name was Maria von Wedemeyer. And from that I was able to really tell the story for the first time.

Maria was only eighteen; so, her mother was not really very happy with the situation. And no sooner had the mother agreed to let them make the engagement public than Bonhoeffer was arrested. This was in April of 1943. Bonhoeffer was not arrested for his role in the plot to kill Hitler, because that had not yet been uncovered. He was arrested for his involvement in what was called *Unternehmen 7*—Operation 7—so named because it involved trying to get seven German Jews out of Germany and into neutral Switzerland.

The Gestapo had been playing a cat-and-mouse game with the Abwehr. So, Bonhoeffer was taken to Tegel military prison and treated reasonably well. And he really thought that he could outfox the prosecutor and would be exonerated and be let out.

And, of course, while all this was transpiring, Bonhoeffer had great hopes that the conspirators who hadn't been arrested would succeed in killing Hitler and the whole nightmare would be over. But that's not what happened. Instead, a little over a year later—on July 20, 1944—the Valkyrie plot went awry. Stauffenberg brought a briefcase bomb into Hitler's military headquarters in East Prussia, and the bomb went off but didn't kill Hitler. So, now, for the first time in all these years, the whole conspiracy was exposed.

Thousands were arrested. Many of them were tortured. Names came out, and one of those names was Dietrich Bonhoeffer. He was suddenly known to be one of the leaders in the conspiracy to kill the Führer. So, now he was transferred to the Gestapo's high-security prison, where he was threatened with torture, although it doesn't seem that he was tortured, as his brother and his brother-in-law were.

Bonhoeffer knew that his days at this point were probably numbered. Keep in mind that this was now the end of 1944. The war was winding down. Most sane people understood that the Germans were not winning and could not win. But Hitler was not burdened with sanity; he was still convinced that the war was somehow winnable. In any case, Bonhoeffer was later transferred to the Buchenwald concentration camp.

There is very little about Bonhoeffer at this time. In the end, though, we know that he was taken to Flossenbürg concentration camp, where on the specific, explicit order of Hitler, he was executed by hanging on the morning of April 9, 1945. That is, of course, exactly sixty-five years ago today.

Now, this is where it gets particularly interesting for me, because I think the normal way we perceive this ending is to think how sad and tragic it is. The idea that he died right before the end of the war and was engaged to this beautiful young woman . . . But I don't think Bonhoeffer would have seen it quite that way. I want to underscore that everything he did, he did in obedience to the God that he knew and served. So, there was a peace in all of this that is unfathomable to someone who doesn't have the kind of faith that Bonhoeffer did.

Through history, many people have had that kind of faith, and I would venture a guess that a few people in this room do as well. You know that you can trust God, who is the author of life, and that even if he leads you to death, you can still trust him.

It is a very interesting idea. It would be comforting to us to think that Bonhoeffer went to his death that way, and I am sure that he did go to his death that way, for many reasons. Much of his writing would indicate that. In fact, he wrote a sermon in 1933 about death. In that sermon he wrote, "No one has yet believed in God and the Kingdom of God, no one has yet heard about the realm of the resurrected, and not been homesick from that hour—waiting and looking forward to being released from bodily existence."

He goes on: "How do we know that dying is so dreadful? Who knows whether in our human fear and anguish, we are only shivering and shuddering at the most glorious, heavenly blessed event in the world? Death is hell and night and cold, if it is not transformed by our faith. But that is just what is so marvelous, that we can transform death."

Bonhoeffer actually believed that. I definitely believe that. It is hard to believe that. It is a challenge to believe that, but I do believe that. Bonhoeffer went to his death as a true martyr. He went with great joy. He went with great joy.

Sixty-five years ago today, this happened at dawn. The crematorium at Flossenbürg was broken. So, Bonhoeffer shared the fate of the many, many Jews who had been killed just as he had in that very same place, in that his body was tossed on a pile and burned. That is how he left this world. But I think that for Bonhoeffer, giving his life for the Jews was an honor. The God of the Jews had called him to give his life for the Jews.

It was an honor, and I think he would have thought it a high honor to have his body disposed of in this same way—his ashes, when they were burned, would have mingled with the ashes of the Jews who had died there. Bonhoeffer really believed that obeying God unto death is the way to defeat evil, that to stand with those who have no one to stand for them—the Jews of Europe—is what God calls one to do. Even unto death.

He really believed that we are called to love self-sacrificially, to give knowing that God had created us to do that. That also means that if you are doing the thing that you realize God created you to do and calls you to do, God will be with you. So, it is not a phantasm to think that when you give him your life, he will give you back your life on the other side.

That is the story the way I have told it. And I think we have a few minutes for questions and answers.

> **It is not a phantasm to think that when you give God your life, he will give you back your life on the other side.**

Q & A

[The first questioner is the aforementioned Stephen Wise, grandson of the famous Rabbi Stephen A. Wise, whom Bonhoeffer heard speak on Easter 1931.]

Q: I just want to say that I read almost all of the citations in your book. I read your book, and it is absolutely wonderful and has a great deal that has not been said before. Everybody should read it.

A: Wow. Thank you. I hate to point out that that is not a question. No, honestly, coming from you, that means more to me than you can ever imagine. Thank you very much.

Q: Eric, I just want to say I am so proud of you for getting up here tonight in front of all these people. I know how nervous you get at just the thought of being in front of a crowd. And that did not show tonight at all.

A: That is very kind of you, and the answer is *B*. Did I get it right?

Q: The second part of the question is a question. A lot of people say Christians shouldn't be involved in politics, because Jesus wasn't involved in politics. I guess if you stretch that, you can make a case that Jesus also wasn't a spy, although do we know he wasn't sent down here by the Father to spy on Israel? That is not my question.

A: But you assure me that you have one.

Q: I do. So, Jesus wasn't a politician; he wasn't a spy. I wonder how you think Bonhoeffer would answer that criticism—that Christians are working in those areas, when that is not what Jesus did?

A: Right. People don't know this, but Jesus was an alderman in Nazareth. He served two terms with distinction.

No. I think when people say things like that, to me it reveals the paucity of their thinking. They really are not thinking. But the book on Wilberforce is all about a man whom God led to serve God and people in politics. And that is the whole point. God doesn't want everyone to put on a clerical collar. That idea is really terrible theology.

Bonhoeffer, of course, was a cleric. But you have to live in the real world. For anybody who understands the Bible and understands what it means to be a Christian, that means you have got to serve God with everything. It doesn't mean you just go off and pray. I think that Bonhoeffer is a particularly tricky example to explain, and that is why my book is so long. He is a very complicated figure, but the idea we shouldn't get involved in this or that, no.

Slavery was wrong. If politicians like Wilberforce hadn't gotten involved in politics to end slavery, we might still have slavery today. There are things today that are wrong. As long as there are human beings, there will be things that need solutions.

Now, if you worship at the idol of politics, you're worshipping a false idol. There is no question about that. I know many people who do that. They think that politics will solve the problem. You can have all the legislators in the world who think the way you do, and it is not going to change things. We need people of faith, everywhere living out their faith. But anyway, so the answer is *B*. Thank you. Next question.

Q: Obviously, Bonhoeffer and Wilberforce have a lot in common where they live their faith as he made reference to—in the political forum. Where would Wilberforce be focused today in America?

A: You know that I just spoke about Bonhoeffer, right?

Q: I am sorry.

A: And you were at like seventy-five syllables.

Q: Yes, you know what I mean. Wilberforce and Bonhoeffer obviously.

A: Wilberforce was the last book. Have another glass of wine. Go ahead, please. All right. Actually, I speak on Wilberforce a lot, and I get that question a lot, and I don't really have an answer, although if forced to give an answer, I would probably say, "In the media," because the media today is the one place where there is less salt and light than almost any other place. In other words, in politics, there are plenty of people from all across the spectrum. There are people of faith in politics today but very few people of faith in the world of media.

Q: What issue?

A: I don't know that there is a single issue. I can't say that there is one issue. To me, it is about the wider culture in general. We live in a culture largely composed of people of some religious faith, but our cultural elites are largely secular. The philosopher Peter Berger said, "America is a nation of Indians ruled by Swedes." So, yes, we are a nation that is very religious generally, as India is, but we are ruled by people who tend to be, at least in the media, very secular. It's not some conspiracy, but they just don't seem to understand people of faith. They don't get it. I really think it is important for people of faith to be involved in the media so that—at least when you turn on the TV—you're not forced to take what you can get, that you have some options. I think that there are very few options in the media today.

The folks in the media hang around with people who hang around with people who don't know anyone that is coming from a biblical worldview. They don't even know what that is. So, sometimes they scorn it, and sometimes it's just pure ignorance—and you can't completely blame them for that. But you have to teach them and help them, and I think people of faith ought to be more involved in the world of media. Anyway, that is the answer.

Q: Yes, I am sorry, but I have to focus on the trilemma that you introduced during the introduction.

A: You know, *trilemma* is the secret word tonight. You get a free book. George Fenneman, will you give him a free book? Trilemma, yes, sir, go ahead.

Q: Well, I didn't say, "Why a duck?"

A: And if you can pull us back to Bonhoeffer somehow . . .

Q: Well, I think eventually. When you said lunatic, liar, or founder of Socrates in the City, couldn't that author's profile have been corrupted over time and maybe that claim was never actually made?

A: Are you with the Jesus Seminar?

Q: This isn't an *ad hominem*.

A: The answer would be *no*. Next question.

Q: Okay. Well, did you find, since with Wilberforce you had to deal and research with the English language, was it much harder for you dealing with German and other languages having to do Bonhoeffer?

A: Yes, that is a question; thank you for that question.

And the answer is *yes*. I speak some German. I don't know any verbs, though. Only nouns and adjectives. I always need a verb guy as my wingman.

No, I don't speak enough German to have been comfortable reading in the original language, but I know enough that I can read paragraphs and sentences and things. That gave me great joy to read a lot of stuff in the original. But, yes, that was very difficult for me.

The good news—and the reason that this book exists—is because, finally, enough of Bonhoeffer has been translated into English so that I was able to write this book. As I think I say—or at least, my publicist says as often as she gets an opportunity—it is the first major bio of Bonhoeffer in forty years. And why is that? Well, because there is all this information that is now in English so that you can actually write something like this. I'm thrilled that this stuff exists. So, the answer is *B*.

Q: Eric, you didn't spend uncounted hours on this topic simply because it is history. It's fun to spend evenings amusing pseudo-intellectual New Yorkers such as myself, as you do. But my question for you is, having spent these countless hours studying Dietrich Bonhoeffer and his circumstances, is there some moment where you said, "Is there something I need to do differently about my life, in the country I live in, and the evil I face?"

A: No. But thank you for calling and sharing, and shall we take our next call, please? Welcome to Open Forum.

The answer to that, of course, is yes. But I like the first joke answer better.

For me, Bonhoeffer is a spectacular example of somebody who can teach us what it means for people to live a Christian life. He was living in a time where the evil was so clear. I have to say that we can all look to Bonhoeffer, and this is my greatest hope—that people would read Bonhoeffer, as a result of my book, and would study him, because there is, I think, no one who gives us a model for our own lives in the way that he does. He models what it is to be a person who is a serious Christian, trying to live that life out in the real world—in his case, the world of Nazis and spies.

Q: You are aware that Bonhoeffer was a theologian.

A: Actually, no, I hadn't heard that.

Q: Okay, that is what I was going to bring up. I learned a new vocabulary word today. In German, it is *anderungen wortbedeutung*, which means changing the meaning of the words.

A: Are you familiar with the German word *frage*?

Q: No. What does it mean?

A: *Frage*?

Q: Yes, what does it mean?

A: I guess the best English translation would be "question." *Was haben Sie, mein Herr, für einen frage?*

Q: It is coming. Bonhoeffer is associated with all of the enemies of Evangelicalism. His closest friends were Karl Barth; he comes to America, he goes to Union seminary, not Princeton, not Westminster, not Calvin. How do you relate to this?

A: You obviously haven't read my book.

Q: No, I haven't.

A: Shame on you. But that is a great question, and I will answer it this way. What I discovered about Bonhoeffer's theology absolutely stunned me. I find him to be, and I did not expect this going in, I found him to be as theologically orthodox as Saint Paul or Isaiah.

I think he has been hijacked by some people, most notably the theologically liberal "God is dead" movement of the fifties and sixties, who somehow absurdly thought of him as one of their own. And you don't need to know very much to pretty quickly see that that is absolute nonsense.

And to some large extent, I think my book, without trying to be polemical or without my trying to give my mere opinion, reclaims Bonhoeffer, using his own words, for contemporary Evangelicals and, of course, for lots of other Christians.

But I have to say, I was stunned by how people had over the years taken a few little things that he wrote and have misinterpreted them and have built a whole theology, a false theology, and a false image of Bonhoeffer, which really needed to have the light of truth shown on it. It really needed it. I had no idea going into this project how badly it did.

Probably, the greatest joy of having written this book is that it set to right a lot of the misconceptions about him and his theology. So, that was a great question, thank you.

Q: I really cannot wait to read this book, because it sounds as if you are clarifying a lot of things. I have been working on a play about World War Two Nazism and Adolf Hitler and a very famous priest named Alfred Delp, who was also a martyr to the Nazis. Eric, what amazes me is that in the research for this, I discovered something I had never known. I have lots of Jewish friends and have grown up surrounded by Jewish people all my life, and I have sometimes heard them having conversations that they didn't know I overheard—that the Christians killed the Jews, that this was a Christian act, and these were Christ-loving people who murdered the Jews. I was so mortified when I heard this, and then I found all sorts of little tidbits, when I did my research.

For instance, can you affirm that all Christians were required to take their crucifixes off of the wall and replace each crucifix in every home with a picture of Adolf Hitler? I wondered if you could even add others.

A: Let me just say this, in the interest of time, and I want to get to the rest of the questions, I will simply say *C*.

Basically, I go into this in depth in the book, because I became progressively scandalized the more I read about how overtly and explicitly anti-Christian the top Nazis were. Anytime anyone would dare say that Hitler was a Christian or Goebbels was a Christian, I thought, *You simply have no idea what you are talking about, because that is like saying Genghis Khan was a pacifist.* And I give pretty much chapter and verse on that in the book. The people who killed Jews were Gentiles. Some of them were churchgoing Gentiles. I really find it hard to believe that any serious Christians were involved.

Actually, I shouldn't say that, because there were a lot of deluded people who, on some technical level, were Christians or perhaps thought they were Christians. And Christians are capable of terrible things, of course, but that's another story. In the main, the Nazi leadership was just vehemently anti-Christian. Every year that passed, they became clearer about that. I have got at least a couple of chapters on that in the book.

Q: Oh, thank you so much. We all know what brand of toothpaste Britney Spears uses, but we don't know this very obvious fact.

A: I have to confess I don't know what brand she uses, but I would guess Pepsodent. Did I get it?

Q: I can see how Bonhoeffer was a pastor and a martyr and a spy. But how do you call him *prophet*?

A: I just needed it for the rhyme scheme. Prophet. Actually, it is funny you say that, because I almost titled the book something along the lines of *God's Prophet*. He was a prophet. I can't explain now, because we don't have the time, but trust me. In the book I go to great lengths to explain how I think he was a prophet in the twentieth century, and I don't say that lightly. I really think that he was. He was a Cassandra, a voice crying in the wilderness. He was one of those voices crying out that nobody listens to. They stone the prophets. We know what they do to the prophets.

Bonhoeffer could see perfectly clearly what was happening. He spoke about it; he tried to get people to hear him. They didn't hear him. On that level, he was a prophet. But he was also a prophet in the true sense—in which Cassandra was not a prophet—in that he really was hearing from God and he was trying to scream to the Church to wake up. Do you see what God is doing? We know that he failed. But ultimately, I don't think he failed.

You can't ask your question. You can't. No, no, no, I have very strict rules. I am being very generous allowing these three to speak. Go ahead.

Q: Oh, thank you.

A: We have a thing here at Socrates in the City—we are ultra-punctual. You probably don't know that I am half-German, but a lot of these people have been waiting. Some of them have to use the loo. So, we have got just another three seconds. Go ahead.

Q: Okay, three seconds. I am a seminary student at Union.

A: True.

Q: So, I'm relatively obsessed with Bonhoeffer, and I am curious. I'm sure you touch on this in your book—near the end of his life in his letters and papers from prison, he talked a lot and grappled a lot with a theology of "religionless Christianity." He saw religious jargon in the future really diminishing and a new language emerging. I'm curious as to whether you think that has happened sixty-five years later.

A: The answer is no. Again, this is the other thing. This famous out-of-context phrase that he wrote to his best friend—the genius Eberhard Bethge—the letter and the phrase ought never to have seen the light of day. To have pseudo-theologians pick over it and create theologies from it is a tragedy. It has been a tragedy for the American Church and for the international Church that they did that.

Bonhoeffer was really referring to religion as dead religion. We don't have time to go into it now, but in my book I clarify that, or I finally put it in context so people can see what he meant and what he didn't mean. In fact, Eberhard Bethge, in 1967, had a famous quote—I should memorize it—but the idea is that taking this phrase "religionless Christianity" out of context has been a horror and very destructive. Eberhard Bethge said this in 1967, and people obviously didn't listen to him. Anyway, you will have to read the book.

Q: So, you do talk about it.

A: I talk about it at length. It is very important.

Eric's Acknowledgments

If you have ever attended a Socrates in the City event, let me first thank you, the audience. But for you, these opalescent evenings strung like pearls on a decade-long necklace would have never happened. If I may be so bold: You were their oyster. It was between your gnarled shells that they came into being, and without you the talks that formed the sandy centers of these events would never have been transcribed and published for the enjoyment of so many non- and/or would-be attendees/oysters.

Nor do Socrates in the City audiences merely show up; they are a vital cog in the well-oiled machine that is Socrates in the City! The high quality of this cog is evinced in the impressive questions you will find in the Q & A parts of this book. I am extremely grateful to those of you who asked all the terrific questions, and I am no less grateful to those of you who had much less terrific questions and who also had the wisdom and restraint not to ask them. The readers of this book are in your great debt.

And a special thank-you to the Socrates in the City speakers who have blessed us with their presence and wisdom and words. Thank you for making Socrates in the City events the spectacular and pearl-like evenings they have been. And many thanks for your written and legally binding permission to repurpose your words in this attractive and much-sought-after volume. You guys are the best.

And how could I possibly forget to thank those who have served on the

Socrates in the City board? I could not. Thank you, David Young and Joel Tucciarone and Carter and Rim Hinckley and Ned and Stephanie Stiker and Stan Oakes and Jim Lane and Mark Berner. And thank you most of all, Manos and Camille Kampouris, who were at the first Socrates in the City event in 2000 and who have been a bulwark and a blessing beyond expression, not just to Socrates in the City but to me, personally. And thank you to our executive director, Justin Homkow, for making these events possible and sparkle. I know that's not a proper parallel construction, but it's from the heart; so, what the hey?

Thank you also to Brian Tart, the president of Dutton, who deemed the idea of this book laudable, and indeed laudable enough to publish this fall. *Huzzah!* And thanks to his extraordinary editorial and production team for their inestimable contributions to making this book a reality. Publishing this book in such a short period of time would not have been possible without the Herculean efforts of my dear friend Joel Tucciarone, who oversaw most of the production details and whom I thank profoundly. His help went light-years beyond what one might expect of a Socrates in the City board member, and without his myriad efforts this book simply would not exist, rendering this very acknowledgments section homeless and absurd.

Thank you, also, Victoria (Vicki) de Vries, for helping to edit into dazzling essays what were in many cases mere rambling, profanity-laced tirades without a single redeeming quality! I'm kidding, but honestly, thank you. And thank you, Kevin Milani, for first transcribing those irreverent, slurry rants so that Vicki could give them her black-coffee-and-a-cold-shower editorial treatment and make them publicly presentable. Or so we hope. Thanks, also, to Janice Weichman for her help with the bibliographies at the end of this book. We sincerely hope you, the reader, will avail yourself of the books there listed for many hours of self-examination and fun!

Have we left anyone out? Please speak loudly, because this book is about to go to print. Ah, yes, we thank most sincerely the patrons of Socrates in the City who have helped us put on these events over the last year. We especially wish to thank the Templeton Foundation for their great generosity in helping us expand the scope of what we do and, with God's help, will continue to do for many years to come. *Soli Deo gloria.*

Speaker Biographies

Sir John Polkinghorne

The 1974 Nobel laureate in physics, John Polkinghorne raised "Cambridge academic eyebrows" in 1979, when he resigned after twenty-five years from his distinguished position as a quantum physicist to become an Anglican priest.

After earning his PhD in physics from Trinity College, Cambridge, in 1955, he was appointed a lecturer in mathematical physics at the University of Edinburgh in 1956. He returned two years later to Cambridge as a lecturer. In 1968, he was promoted to the position of professor and distinguished himself by publishing two technical scientific books and numerous papers on theoretical elementary particle physics in scholarly journals. Since his training for the Anglican priesthood and ordination as a deacon in 1981, Polkinghorne has had two curateships; has served as Vicar of Blean, near Canterbury; and was appointed Fellow, Dean, and Chaplain at Trinity Hall, Cambridge. From 1988 until 1996, he served as president of Queens College, Cambridge.

Polkinghorne is a fellow of the Royal Society, a canon theologian of Liverpool Cathedral, and an official KBE (Knight Commander of the Order of the British Empire), a title that was bestowed on him in 1997. He has written five books on physics and twenty-six on science and faith, most notably *Belief in God in an Age of Science, The Faith of a Physicist,* and *Questions of Truth.* In 2002, he was the recipient of the prestigious Templeton Prize in religion. As a founder of the Society of Ordained Scientists and founding president of the International Society for Science and Religion, he has garnered both high praise and bemused skepticism.

Peter Kreeft

Dr. Peter J. Kreeft is a philosopher in wide demand as a speaker at conferences. Currently, he teaches philosophy at both Boston College and the King's College in New York. He is the author of more than sixty-three books, including *How to Win the Culture War, C. S. Lewis for the Third Millennium, Three Philosophies of Life, Handbook of Christian Apologetics, Christianity for Modern Pagans,* and *Fundamentals of the Faith.* His witty and thought-provoking writings engage readers in a wide variety of subjects from abortion to moral relativism, from angels and demons to surfing.

In 1965, Dr. Kreeft earned his PhD in philosophy from Fordham University. He also has taught as a visiting professor at more than fifteen colleges and universities across the United States.

Paul Vitz

Dr. Paul Vitz, professor emeritus of psychology at New York University, graduated with a PhD in psychology from Stanford University in 1962. He has published over one hundred articles and essays and six books, such as *Faith of the Fatherless: The Psychology of Atheism, Psychology as Religion: The Cult of Self-Worship, Modern Art and Modern Science: The Parallel Analysis of Vision,* and *Censorship: Evidence of Bias in Our Children's Textbooks.* He also has served as adjunct professor at the John Paul II Institute for Studies on Marriage and Family in Washington, DC.

His pioneering work on the cult of "selfism," which emerged in the mid-seventies, criticized "bad" psychology for fostering a culture of victimhood. Other areas of intense interest for Dr. Vitz have been children's textbooks and the connection between fatherlessness and atheism.

Richard John Neuhaus

Before his death in 2009, Father Richard John Neuhaus was president of the Institute on Religion and Public Life, a nonpartisan interreligious research and education institute "whose purpose is to advance a religiously informed public philosophy for the ordering of society." He also was founder and editor in chief of the institute's publication *First Things*.

Neuhaus, a Lutheran before becoming a Roman Catholic, possessed the remarkable ability to combine classic Protestant and Catholic thought into a coherent platform for the contemporary public square. Among his best-known books are *Freedom for Ministry, The Naked Public Square: Religion and Democracy in America, The Catholic Moment: The Paradox of the Church in the Postmodern World*, and *Believing Today: Jew and Christian in Conversation*, which he coauthored with Rabbi Leon Klenicki.

In the 1990s, he worked with Charles Colson of Prison Fellowship in organizing the group called Evangelicals and Catholics Together. As a champion of human rights and human dignity, Neuhaus served in the capacity of unofficial adviser to President George W. Bush and held presidential appointments in the Carter, Reagan, and first Bush administrations. In a national survey conducted by *U.S. News and World Report*, Neuhaus was named one of thirty-two "most influential intellectuals in America." A prolific writer, Fr. Richard John Neuhaus leaves an inspiring legacy of thought-provoking books and articles.

Jean Bethke Elshtain

Dr. Jean Bethke Elshtain is the Thomas and Dorothy Leavey Chair in the Foundations of American Freedom at Georgetown University and a senior fellow at the Berkley Center. She earned her PhD in politics from Brandeis University in 1973. For the past sixteen years, she has taught at the University of Chicago Divinity School, where she holds a permanent position as the Laura Spelman Rockefeller Professor of Social and Political Ethics.

Dr. Elshtain's writings explore the connections between politics and ethics and the relationship between male and female roles within the public and the private spheres. She has authored over a dozen books, including *Just War*

Against Terror and *Jane Addams and the Dream of American Democracy*, and over five hundred scholarly essays on a host of other contemporary issues that demand cogent thinking and a deep understanding of their political and ethical implications.

In 1996, Elshtain was inducted as a fellow of the American Academy of Arts and Sciences. She is the recipient of a Guggenheim Fellowship and holds the Maguire Chair at the Library of Congress. She is also the recipient of nine honorary degrees and a contributing editor to *The New Republic*.

Charles Colson

Charles Colson has become the voice for "compassionate conservatism." He graduated from Brown University with honors in 1953. After serving in the U.S. Marine Corps for two years, he earned his JD degree from George Washington University. In 1969, he was appointed as special counsel to President Nixon, eventually gaining a reputation as Nixon's "hatchet man."

Because of his participation in the Watergate scandal, he served seven months for "obstruction of justice" in the Nixon administration. He left prison determined to change the lives of prisoners. In 1976, he founded Prison Fellowship Ministries, which has grown into the world's largest outreach to prisoners, ex-prisoners, and their families and operates in all fifty states and over one hundred countries. He has authored and coauthored more than twenty books, most recently *The Faith*, *The Good Life*, *The Design Revolution*, *Justice That Restores*, and *How Now Shall We Live?*

N. T. Wright

In 2003, N. T. Wright was accorded the title "Bishop of Durham," and in that position, he served as the fourth-most-senior member in the hierarchy of the Church of England. He retired from the position in August 2010. Dr. Wright is currently a research professor of the New Testament and early Christianity at the University of St. Andrews, Scotland.

By way of educational background, N. T. Wright majored in classics at Exeter College, Oxford, graduating with highest honors in 1971. That same year, he enrolled at Wycliffe Hall, Oxford, to prepare for the Anglican ministry. In 1981, he completed a doctorate in philosophy. He has taught at Oxford and McGill universities and served as canon theologian of Westminster Abbey in London and was a member of the archbishop of Canterbury's Lambeth Commission on Communion. The author of more than thirty books, he goes by the more formal name *N. T. Wright* for academic texts while using his pen name *Tom Wright* for more popular works.

Alister McGrath

John Fines, author of *Teaching History*, called Alister McGrath "one of the very best scholars and teachers of the Reformation," but McGrath is also a celebrated scientist. He earned a PhD in biochemistry, specifically molecular biophysics, from Oxford University in 1977. He graduated with highest honors in theology from Oxford University in 1978 and with an Oxford doctorate of divinity in 2001.

McGrath has been at the forefront of critical engagement with contemporary culture. As a former atheist, McGrath has debated such atheists as Dawkins, Dennett, and Hitchens. His book *Dawkins' GOD*, which he coauthored with his wife, Joanna, in 2007, preceded his famous debate with Dawkins.

Dr. McGrath has written more than twenty books, including the four-volume work *A Scientific Theology*, *A Life of John Calvin*, *Glimpsing the Face of God: The Search for Meaning in the Universe*, *A Fine-Tuned Universe: The Quest for God in Science and Theology*, and *Intellectuals Don't Need God and Other Modern Myths*. Currently he is a professor of theology, ministry, and education and head of the Centre for Theology, Religion and Culture at King's College, London.

Os Guinness

Dr. Os Guinness is a well-known expert in matters of public policy and religious faith. A frequent speaker and seminar leader at business and political conferences in the United States and Europe, he is also the author and editor of more than twenty-five books, including *The American Hour, Unspeakable:*

366 — SOCRATES IN THE CITY

Facing up to the Challenge of Evil, and his most recent book, *The Case for Civility—and Why Our Future Depends on It.*

Dr. Guinness was born in China, the son of medical missionaries, but was raised and educated in England, where he earned his doctorate in the social sciences from Oxford University. He was a freelance reporter for the BBC prior to coming to the United States in 1984.

From 1986 to 1989, Dr. Guinness served as executive director of the Williamsburg Charter Foundation, a bicentennial celebration of the First Amendment, and helped to draft the "Williamsburg Charter" and coauthored the public school curriculum *Living with Our Deepest Differences.* In addition, he has distinguished himself as a guest scholar at the Woodrow Wilson International Center for Scholars and as a guest scholar and visiting fellow at the Brookings Institution. He also is known as the originator of the controversial *Evangelical Manifesto: A Declaration of Evangelical Identity and Public Commitment.*

Francis Collins

While studying for his PhD in physical chemistry at Yale University, Francis Collins became interested in molecular biology and genetics, graduated, changed fields, and went to medical school at the University of North Carolina, graduating with an MD in 1977. After residency work in internal medicine, he taught human genetics at the Yale School of Medicine, where he began developing techniques for identifying disease genes.

Collins and two other colleagues located the gene for cystic fibrosis in 1989, and then the genes for other diseases, such as Huntington's disease and the M4 type of adult acute leukemia. In 1993, he was appointed director of the National Center for Human Genome Research (whose name changed to the National Human Genome Research Institute in 2007), where he oversaw the Human Genome Project and the completed sequencing of human DNA. In 2007, he founded the BioLogos Foundation to promote dialogue between science and faith. In 2009, President Barack Obama appointed him as director of the National Institutes of Health.

In 2007, Dr. Collins was awarded the Presidential Medal of Freedom for his role in advancing genetic research and the National Medal of Science in

2008. He has written four books, the most recent being *The Language of Science and Faith: Straight Answers to Genuine Questions*, and numerous articles. Of ongoing concern to him are the ethical and legal questions related to genetics, which he continues to explore.

Selected Published Works

Sir John Polkinghorne

Questions of Truth: Fifty-one Responses to Questions About God, Science and Belief. Louisville, KY: Westminster John Knox Press, 2009.

Theology in the Context of Science. New Haven, CT: Yale University Press, 2009.

From Physicist to Priest: An Autobiography. Eugene, OR: Cascade Books, 2008.

One World: The Interaction of Science and Theology. Conshohocken, PA: Templeton Foundation Press, 2007.

Quantum Physics and Theology: An Unexpected Kinship. New Haven, CT: Yale Press, 2007.

The Way the World Is: The Christian Perspective of a Scientist. Louisville, KY: Westminster John Knox Press, 2007.

Science and Creation. Conshohocken, PA: Templeton Foundation Press, 2006.

Science and Providence. Conshohocken, PA: Templeton Foundation Press, 2005.

Exploring Reality: The Intertwining of Science and Religion. New Haven, CT: Yale University Press, 2005.

Science and the Trinity: The Christian Encounter with Reality. New Haven, CT: Yale University Press, 2004.

The God of Hope and the End of the World. New Haven, CT: Yale University Press, 2002.

The Work of Love: Creation as Kenosis. Grand Rapids, MI: Wm. B. Eerdmans Publishing Company, 2001.

Quarks, Chaos and Christianity. New York: The Crossroad Publishing Company, 2000.

Belief in God in an Age of Science. New Haven, CT: Yale University Press, 1998.

The Faith of a Physicist. Minneapolis, MN: Augsburg Fortress Press, 1996.

Peter Kreeft

Because God Is Real. San Francisco: Ignatius Press, 2008.

Socrates Meets Hume. San Francisco: Ignatius Press, 2005.

Socrates Meets Sartre: The Father of Philosophy Cross-Examines the Founder of Existentialism. San Francisco: Ignatius Press, 2005.

The Philosophy of Tolkien: The Worldview Behind "The Lord of the Rings." San Francisco: Ignatius Press, 2005.

Socrates Meets Machiavelli. San Francisco: Ignatius Press, 2003.

Socrates Meets Marx. San Francisco: Ignatius Press, 2003.

How to Win the Culture War. Downers Grove, IL: InterVarsity Press, 2002.

Refutation of Moral Relativism—Dialogues Between a Relativist and Absolutist. San Francisco: Ignatius Press, 1999.

The Snakebite Letters. San Francisco: Ignatius Press, 1998.

Angels (and Demons): What Do We Really Know About Them? San Francisco: Ignatius Press, 1995.

C. S. Lewis for the Third Millennium. San Francisco: Ignatius Press, 1994.

Shadow-Lands of C. S. Lewis: The Man Behind the Movie. San Francisco: Ignatius Press, 1994.

Christianity for Modern Pagans: Pascal's Pensees. San Francisco: Ignatius Press, 1993.

Yes or No? Straight Answers to Tough Questions About Christianity. San Francisco: Ignatius Press, 1991.

Everything You Ever Wanted to Know About Heaven . . . but Never Dreamed of Asking. San Francisco: Ignatius Press, 1990.

Making Sense out of Suffering. Ann Arbor, MI: Servant Books, 1986.

The Best Things in Life: A Contemporary Socrates Looks at Power, Pleasure, Truth and the Good Life. Downers Grove, IL: InterVarsity Press, 1984.

Between Heaven and Hell: A Dialog Somewhere Beyond Death with John F. Kennedy, C. S. Lewis, and Aldous Huxley. Downers Grove, IL: InterVarsity Press, 1982.

Paul C. Vitz

The Self: Beyond the Postmodern Crisis. Susan M. Felch, coeditor. Wilmington, DE: Intercollegiate Studies Institute, 2006.

Faith of the Fatherless: The Psychology of Atheism. Dallas, TX: Spence Publishing Company, 2000.

Psychology as Religion: The Cult of Self-Worship. 2nd ed. Grand Rapids, MI: Wm. B. Eerdmans Publishing Company, 1994.

Censorship: Evidence of Bias in Our Children's Textbooks. Cincinnati, OH: Servant Books, 1986.

Sigmund Freud's Christian Unconscious. New York: Guilford Press, 1988.

Defending the Family: A Sourcebook. Stephen M. Krason, coeditor. Steubenville, OH: Catholic Social Science Press, 1988.

Modern Art and Modern Science: The Parallel Analysis of Vision. Arnold B. Glimcher, coauthor. Westport, CT: Praeger, 1984.

Fr. Richard John Neuhaus

American Babylon: Notes of a Christian Exile. New York: Basic Books, 2009.

The Best of the Public Square: Book 3. Grand Rapids, MI: Wm. B. Eerdmans Publishing Co., 2007.

Catholic Matters: Confusion, Controversy, and the Splendor of Truth. New York: Basic Books, 2006.

As I Lay Dying: Meditations upon Returning. New York, Basic Books, 2002.

The Chosen People in an Almost Chosen Nation: Jews and Judaism in America. Editor. Grand Rapids, MI: Wm. B. Eerdmans Publishing Co., 2002.

Your Word Is Truth: A Project of Evangelicals and Catholics Together. Charles Colson, coeditor. Grand Rapids, MI: Wm. B. Eerdmans Publishing Co., 2002.

The Second One Thousand Years: Ten People Who Defined a Millennium. Editor. Grand Rapids, MI: Wm. B. Eerdmans Publishing Co., 2001.

Death on a Friday Afternoon: Meditations on the Last Words of Jesus from the Cross. New York: Basic Books, 2000.

The Eternal Pity: Reflections on Dying. Editor. Notre Dame, IN: University of Notre Dame Press, 2000.

Appointment in Rome: The Church in America Awakening. New York: The Crossroad Publishing Company, 1999.

The End of Democracy? The Celebrated First Things Debate, with Arguments Pro and Con and "The Anatomy of a Controversy." Mitchell Muncy, coeditor. Dallas, TX: Spence Publishing Company, 1997.

The Best of the Public Square. New York: Institute on Religion and Public Life, 1997.

The Naked Public Square: Religion and Democracy in America. Grand Rapids, MI: Wm. B. Eerdmans Publishing Co., 1996.

To Empower People: From State to Civil Society. Peter Berger and Michael Novak, coauthors. Washington, DC: American Enterprise Institute Press, 1996.

Doing Well and Doing Good: The Challenge to the Christian Capitalist. New York: Doubleday, 1992.

America Against Itself: Moral Vision and the Public Order. Notre Dame, IN: University of Notre Dame Press, 1992.

Freedom for Ministry: A Guide for the Perplexed Who Are Called to Serve. Grand Rapids, MI: Wm. B. Eerdmans Publishing Co., 1992.

Guaranteeing the Good Life: Medicine and the Return of Eugenics. Editor. Grand Rapids, MI: Wm. B. Eerdmans Publishing Co., 1989.

Believing Today: Jew and Christian in Conversation. Leon Klenicki, coauthor. Grand Rapids, MI: Wm. B. Eerdmans Publishing Co., 1989.

Reinhold Niebuhr Today. Grand Rapids, MI: Wm. B. Eerdmans Publishing Co., 1989.

Piety and Politics: Evangelicals and Fundamentalists Confront the World. Michael Cromartie, coeditor. Washington, DC: Ethics and Public Policy Center, 1987.

Democracy and the Renewal of Public Education. Richard Baer, coeditor. Grand Rapids, MI: Wm. B. Eerdmans Publishing Co., 1987.

Jews in Unsecular America. Grand Rapids: Wm. B. Eerdmans Publishing Co., 1987.

The Catholic Moment: The Paradox of the Church in the Postmodern World. New York: HarperCollins, 1987.

Dispensations: The Future of South Africa as South Africans See It. Grand Rapids, MI: Wm. B. Eerdmans Publishing Co., 1986.

Against the World for the World: The Hartford Appeal and the Future of American Religion. Peter Berger, coeditor. New York: HarperCollins, 1976.

Time Toward Home: The American Experiment as Revelation. New York: Seabury Press, 1975.

In Defense of People: Ecology and the Seduction of Radicalism. New York: Macmillan, 1971.

Movement and Revolution. Peter Berger, coeditor. Garden City, NY: Doubleday, 1970.

Jean Bethke Elshtain

Sovereignty: God, State, and Self. New York: Basic Books, 2008.

Just War Against Terror: The Burden of American Power in a Violent World. New York: Basic Books, 2003.

Jane Addams and the Dream of American Democracy. New York: Basic Books, 2002.

The Jane Addams Reader. Editor. New York: Basic Books, 2002.

Religion in American Public Life: Living with Our Deepest Differences. Aziza al-Hibri and Charles Haynes, coauthors. New York: W. W. Norton, 2001.

Who Are We? Critical Reflections and Hopeful Possibilities. Grand Rapids, MI: Wm. B. Eerdmans Publishing Co., 2000.

New Wine in Old Bottles: International Politics and Ethical Discourse. Notre Dame, IN: University of Notre Dame Press, 1998.

Real Politics: Political Theory and Everyday Life. Baltimore, MD: The Johns Hopkins University Press, 1997.

Augustine and the Limits of Politics. Notre Dame, IN: University of Notre Dame Press, 1996.

Promises to Keep: Decline and Renewal of Marriage in America. David Blankenhorn, coeditor. Lanham, MD: Rowman and Littlefield, 1996.

Democracy on Trial. New York: Basic Books, 1995.

Politics and the Human Body: Assault on Dignity. J. Timothy Cloyd, coeditor. Nashville: Vanderbilt University Press, 1995.

Just War Theory. Editor. Oxford, UK: Basil Blackwell, 1990.

Power Trips and Other Journeys. Madison, WI: University of Wisconsin Press, 1990.

Women and War. New York: Basic Books, 1987.

Meditations on Modern Political Thought. Westport, CT: Praeger, 1986.

The Family in Political Thought. Editor. Amherst, MA: University of Massachusetts Press, 1982.

Public Man, Private Woman: Women in Social and Political Thought. Princeton, NJ: Princeton University Press, 1981.

Charles Colson

The Faith: What Christians Believe, Why They Believe It, and Why It Matters. Grand Rapids, MI: Zondervan, 2008.

The Good Life. Carol Stream, IL: Tyndale House Publishers, 2005.

Lies That Go Unchallenged in Popular Culture. Carol Stream, IL: Tyndale House Publishers, 2005.

The Design Revolution: Answering the Toughest Questions About Intelligent Design. William A. Dembski, coauthor. Downers Grove, IL: InterVarsity Press, 2004.

Justice That Restores. Carol Stream, IL: Tyndale House Publishers, 2001.

How Now Shall We Live? Nancy Pearcey, coauthor. Carol Stream, IL: Tyndale House Publishers, 1999.

Burden of Truth: Defending the Truth in an Age of Unbelief. Carol Stream, IL: Tyndale House Publishers, 1998.

Being the Body. Nashville: Thomas Nelson, 1996.

Loving God. Grand Rapids, MI: Zondervan, 1996.

Evangelicals and Catholics Together: Toward a Common Mission. Richard John Neuhaus, coeditor. Nashville: Thomas Nelson, 1995.

A Dance with Deception: Revealing the Truth Behind the Headlines. Waco, TX: Word Publishing, 1993.

The Body: Being Light in Darkness. Waco, TX: Word Books, 1993.

Why America Doesn't Work. Jack Eckerd, coeditor. Waco, TX: Word Publishing, 1991.

Against the Night: Living in the New Dark Ages. Ann Arbor, MI: Servant Publications, 1989.

God and Government. Grand Rapids, MI: Zondervan, 1989.

Kingdoms in Conflict. New York: William Morrow & Co., 1987.

Life Sentence. Grand Rapids, MI: Fleming H. Revell, 1979.

Born Again. Ada, OK: Chosen Books, 1976.

N. T. "Tom" Wright

Surprised by Meaning: Science, Faith, and How We Make Sense of Things. Louisville, KY: Westminster John Knox Press, 2011.

Virtue Reborn. London: SPCK, 2010.

Justification: God's Plan and Paul's Vision. London: SPCK, 2009.

Jesus, the Final Days: What Really Happened. London: SPCK, 2008.

Surprised by Hope: Rethinking Heaven, the Resurrection, and the Mission of the Church. New York: HarperCollins Publishers, 2008.

Acts for Everyone, Part 1: Chapters 1–12. London: SPCK, 2008.

Acts for Everyone, Part 2: Chapters 13–28. London: SPCK, 2008.

Simply Christian: Why Christianity Makes Sense. New York: HarperCollins, 2006.

Judas and the Gospel of Jesus: Have We Missed the Truth About Christianity? London: SPCK, 2006.

Evil and the Justice of God. London: SPCK, 2006.

The Resurrection of Jesus: John Dominic Crossan and N. T. Wright in Dialogue. Minneapolis, MN: Augsburg Fortress Press, 2005.

Paul: Fresh Perspective. Minneapolis, MN: Augsburg Fortress Press, 2005.

The Last Word: Beyond the Bible Wars to a New Understanding of the Authority of Scripture. San Francisco: Harper, 2005.

Matthew for Everyone, Part 1: Chapters 1–15. 2nd ed. Louisville, KY: Westminster John Knox Press, 2004.

Matthew for Everyone, Part 2: Chapters 16–28. 2nd ed. Louisville, KY: Westminster John Knox Press, 2004.

The Resurrection of the Son of God. Minneapolis, MN: Augsburg Fortress Press, 2003.

The Challenge of Jesus: Rediscovering Who Jesus Was and Is. Downers Grove, IL: InterVarsity Press, 1999.

Following Jesus: Biblical Reflections on Discipleship. Grand Rapids, MI: Wm. B. Eerdmans Publishing Co., 1997.

Alister McGrath

Darwinism and the Divine. Malden, MA: John Wiley & Sons, 2011.

Flight of the Outcasts, vol. 2 of *The Aedyn Chronicles*. Grand Rapids, MI: Zondervan, 2011.

Why God Won't Go Away: Is the New Atheism Running on Empty? Nashville: Thomas Nelson, 2011.

Chosen Ones, vol. 1 of *The Aedyn Chronicles*. Grand Rapids, MI: Zondervan, 2010.

Mere Theology: Christian Faith and the Discipleship of the Mind. London: SPCK, 2010.

A Fine-Tuned Universe: The Quest for God in Science and Theology. Louisville, KY: Westminster John Knox Press, 2009.

Heresy: A History of Defending the Truth. New York: HarperCollins, 2009.

Science and Religion: A New Introduction. Malden, MA: Wiley-Blackwell, 2009.

The Christian Vision of God. Minneapolis, MN: Augsberg Fortress Press, 2008.

The Open Secret: A New Vision for Natural Theology. Malden, MA: John Wiley & Sons, 2008.

Christianity's Dangerous Idea: The Protestant Revolution from the Sixteenth to the Twenty-first Century. New York: HarperCollins, 2007.

The Dawkins Delusion? Joanna Collicutt McGrath, coauthor. Downers Grove, IL: InterVarsity Press, 2007.

Resurrection. Minneapolis, MN: Augsburg Fortress Press, 2007.

Theology: The Basic Readings. Malden, MA: Wiley-Blackwell Publishers, 2007.

Redemption. Minneapolis, MN: Augsburg Fortress Press, 2006.

Dawkins' God: Genes, Memes, and the Meaning of Life. Malden, MA: Blackwell Publishing, 2005.

Incarnation. Minneapolis, MN: Augsburg Fortress Press, 2005.

Creation. Minneapolis, MN: Augsburg Fortress Press, 2004.

The Twilight of Atheism: The Rise and Fall of Disbelief in the Modern World. New York: Doubleday, 2004.

A Brief History of Heaven. Malden, MA: Blackwell Publishing, 2003.

Glimpsing the Face of God: The Search for Meaning in the Universe. Grand Rapids, MI: Wm. B. Eerdmans Publishing Co., 2002.

Knowing Christ. New York: Doubleday, 2002.

The Reenchantment of Nature: The Denial of Religion and the Ecological Crisis. New York: Doubleday, 2002.

In the Beginning: The Story of the King James Bible and How It Changed a Nation, a Language, and a Culture. New York: Doubleday, 2001.

The Journey: A Pilgrim in the Lands of the Spirit. New York: Doubleday, 2000.

T. F. Torrance: An Intellectual Biography. New York: T&T Clark International, 1999.

A Passion for Truth: The Intellectual Coherence of Evangelicalism. Downers Grove, IL: InterVarsity Press, 1998.

Historical Theology: An Introduction to the History of Christian Thought. Malden, MA: Blackwell Publishers, 1998.

I Believe: Exploring the Apostles' Creed. Downers Grove, IL: InterVarsity Press, 1998.

The Christian Theology Reader. Malden, MA: Blackwell Publishers, 1996.

The Blackwell Encyclopedia of Modern Christian Thought. Malden, MA: Blackwell Publishers, 1995.

A Life of John Calvin. Malden, MA: Wiley-Blackwell, 1993.

Christian Theology: An Introduction. Malden, MA: Blackwell Publishers, 1993.

Intellectuals Don't Need God and Other Modern Myths. Grand Rapids, MI: Zondervan Publishing House, 1993.

Bridge-Building: Effective Christian Apologetics. Downers Grove, IL: InterVarsity Press, 1992.

Understanding the Trinity. Grand Rapids, MI: Zondervan Publishing House, 1990.

Iustitia Dei: A History of the Christian Doctrine of Justification. Cambridge, MA: Cambridge University Press, 1986.

Os Guinness

The Last Christian on Earth: Uncover the Enemy's Plot to Undermine the Church. Ventura, CA: Regal, 2010.

Socrates Meets Kant. San Francisco: Ignatius Press, 2009.

The Case for Civility—and Why Our Future Depends on It. New York: HarperCollins, 2008.

Unspeakable: Facing up to the Challenge of Evil. New York: HarperCollins, 2005.

The Call: Finding and Fulfilling the Purpose of Your Life. Nashville, TN: Thomas Nelson, 2003.

Rising to the Call. Nashville: Thomas Nelson, 2003.

Time for Truth: Living Free in a World of Lies, Hype, and Spin. Grand Rapids, MI: Baker Books, 2002.

The Great Experiment: Faith and Freedom in America. Colorado Springs, CO: Navpress Publishing Group, 2001.

Long Journey Home: A Guide to Your Search for the Meaning of Life. Colorado Springs, CO: WaterBrook Press, 2001.

Steering Through Chaos: Vice and Virtue in an Age of Moral Confusion. Colorado Springs, CO: NavPress Publishing Group, 2000.

Character Counts: Leadership Qualities in Washington, Wilberforce, Lincoln, and Solzhenitsyn. Grand Rapids, MI: Baker Books, 1999.

God in the Dark: The Assurance of Faith Beyond a Shadow of Doubt. Wheaton, IL: Crossway Books, 1996.

The Dust of Death: A Critique of the Establishment and the Counter Culture and the Proposal for a Third Way. Downers Grove, IL: InterVarsity Press, 1973.

Francis S. Collins

The Language of Science and Faith: Straight Answers to Genuine Questions. Downers Grove, IL: InterVarsity Press, 2011.

Belief: Readings on the Reason for Faith. New York: HarperCollins, 2010.

The Language of Life: DNA and the Revolution in Personalized Medicine. New York: HarperCollins, 2010.

The Language of God: A Scientist Presents Evidence for Belief. New York: Free Press, 2006.

Eric Metaxas

Bonhoeffer: Pastor, Martyr, Prophet, Spy. Nashville, TN: Thomas Nelson, 2010.

Everything You Always Wanted to Know About God: The Jesus Edition. Ventura, CA: Regal Books, 2010.

It's Time to Sleep, My Love. New York: Feiwel and Friends, 2008.

Amazing Grace: Wilberforce and the Heroic Campaign to End Slavery. New York: HarperCollins, 2007.

Everything Else You Always Wanted to Know About God (but Were Afraid to Ask). Colorado Springs, CO: Waterbrook Press, 2007.

Everything You Always Wanted to Know About God (but Were Afraid to Ask). Colorado Springs, CO: Waterbrook Press, 2005.

Peach Boy: A Japanese Folktale. Edina, MN: ABDO Publishers, 2005.

God Made You Special (VeggieTales). Grand Rapids, MI: Zondervan Publishing House, 2002.

Squanto and the Miracle of Thanksgiving. Nashville, TN: Thomas Nelson, 1999.

The Bible ABC. Nashville, TN: Tommy Nelson, 1998.

Don't You Believe It!—An Actual Parody. New York: St. Martin's Griffin, 1996.

Uncle Mugsy and the Terrible Twins of Christmas. New York: Madison Square Press, 1995.

The Birthday ABC. New York: Simon & Schuster, 1995.

About the General Editor

Eric Metaxas is the author of two acclaimed *New York Times* bestselling biographies: *Bonhoeffer: Pastor, Martyr, Prophet, Spy* and *Amazing Grace: William Wilberforce and the Heroic Campaign to End Slavery*. Called a "biography of uncommon power," *Bonhoeffer* was named 2010 ECPS Book of the Year and appeared on numerous 2010 "Best of the Year" lists. In 2011, Metaxas was the recipient of the Becket Fund's Canterbury Medal for Religious Freedom.

Metaxas grew up in Danbury, Connecticut, and graduated from Yale University, where he edited *The Yale Record*, the nation's oldest college humor magazine. His humor writing has been published in *The Atlantic Monthly* and *The New York Times*. Woody Allen has called these pieces "quite funny," and the musician Moby has said, "[Eric Metaxas is] one of the funniest people I know." Metaxas is the host and founder of Socrates in the City, the acclaimed New York speakers' series.

Metaxas has written over thirty award-winning children's books, including *It's Time to Sleep, My Love*, and *Squanto and the Miracle of Thanksgiving*. Eric has also written books and videos for VeggieTales and provides the voice of the narrator on the VeggieTales video *Esther*.

He has appeared as a cultural commentator on CNN, the Fox News Channel, and the History Channel and has been featured on many radio programs, ranging from NPR to Focus on the Family.

Eric's popular apologetics trilogy, *Everything You Always Wanted to Know*

About God (but Were Afraid to Ask), has been praised by Ann B. Davis, who played Alice on *The Brady Bunch* ("I am absolutely smitten with this book!"), pastor Tim Keller ("The difficulty is not to gush"), and Dick Cavett ("Metaxas deserves a prize").

Eric lives in Manhattan, New York, with his wife and daughter.